GOD'S TOUCH

GOD'S TOUCH

Faith, Wholeness,
and the Healing Miracles of Jesus

Bruce G. Epperly

Foreword by John B. Cobb Jr.

Westminster John Knox Press
Louisville, Kentucky

Book design by Sharon Adams
Cover design by Terry Dugan Design

First edition
Published by Westminster John Knox Press
Louisville, Kentucky

This book is printed on acid-free paper that meets the American National Standards Institute Z39.48 standard.♾

PRINTED IN THE UNITED STATES OF AMERICA

01 02 03 04 05 06 07 08 09 10—10 9 8 7 6 5 4 3 2 1

Library of Congress Cataloging-in-Publication Data

Epperly, Bruce Gordon.
    God's touch: faith, wholeness, and the healing miracles of
Jesus/Bruce G. Epperly; foreword by John B. Cobb Jr.—1st ed.
        p. cm.
    Includes index.
    ISBN 0-664-22281-1 (pbk.)
    1. Spiritual healing. 2. Jesus Christ—Miracles.
3. Healing—Religious aspects—Christianity. 4. Holistic
medicine—Religious aspects—Christianity. I. Title.

BT732.5 .E66 2001
234′.131—dc21   00-063402

Contents

A Word of Thanks

*I*n the ecology of life, we experience God's healing and transforming touch in many ways. This book was composed during an unexpected time of personal transition during which I was called to give up the comfort of a familiar position in order to embrace the possibilities of new creation and surprising adventure. A number of persons supported me by their affirmations, prayers, and comments as this book grew from thought to written word.

Within my own communion of saints, I would like to begin with my my wife and soul mate, the Rev. Kate Epperly, D.Min., who has been my constant companion, support, partner in parenting, and wisdom giver for more than twenty years. Her critical insights, loving partnership, and commitment to healing are found on every page. In addition, I would like to thank Professor John Cobb, who embodies the spirit of creative transformation and supports his former students in their own professional adventures; Ms. Mary Jane Pagan, whose healing practice mediates the touch of God; Mrs. Maxine Gould, my mother-in-law, for her unconditional support; the Rev. Patricia Adams Farmer, whose appreciation of my work calls me to an even greater commitment to excellence; and Professor Howard Clinebell, for his support and pioneering commitment to holistic health and pastoral care.

G. Nick Street, my editor at Westminster John Knox, provided a number of insightful and creative suggestions as well as support of this project. I am also thankful to the Louisville Institute and Lilly Foundation, whose support enabled me to give my full attention to completing this book during a time of external transformation and challenge.

I am grateful for the love and the values that I received from my parents. Little did I know when I watched the pioneer television healers Kathryn Kuhlman and Oral Roberts as I sat beside my mother forty years ago that my vocation would be called to be a partner in the revival of the healings of Jesus for mainstream and liberal Christians. My father's patient endurance of a paralyzing stroke is a daily inspiration to me. My brother Bill's courageous response to mental illness is also an inspiration in my quest to articulate the possibility of healing even for those who may never be cured. Finally, I am grateful to the supportive and affirmative love of my son Matthew, who embodies the spirit of holistic adventure that is at the heart of this book.

Foreword

*D*ualisms have now become unpopular. For that, we can be grateful. Rejecting dualisms opens the door to creative new departures. Unfortunately, while the door is more open than it has been for a long time, few walk through it. Most reject the dualisms in theory and continue to act on them in practice.

Nowhere is this truer than in Christian reflection and action with respect to healing. In theory we reject the dualism of soul and body, of psyche and soma. We believe that the two are intimately interconnected. But in practice, the church continues to avoid dealing with the body. If one is emotionally disturbed, at least some pastors feel they are trained to help. If one has a physical ailment, the church recommends the hospital.

Sometimes the aid given by a pastor to one who is emotionally disturbed is hardly distinguishable from the aid given by a secular psychotherapist. But some pastors do see God at work in the healing of the psyche and understand themselves to be working with God in this process. If, however, they judge that the problem is physical in origin, they are unlikely to enter seriously into the process of healing. They expect a medical doctor to prescribe drugs or perform an operation. The dualism of psyche and soma is alive and well in these practical responses.

Another dualism functions in the background of typical Christian thinking. It is the dualism of the natural and the supernatural. This dualism achieved special sharpness in the eighteenth century. At that time nature was understood as functioning in a mechanical way, obeying rigid laws. Christians understood these laws to be imposed by God. The nature ruled in this way included human bodies.

Given this understanding of nature, two positions were possible with respect to the actions of God. Some held that having imposed laws on nature, God acted in no other way. The laws were perfect, and to violate them would be an imperfection. Healing the sick, then, depended entirely on gaining knowledge of these laws and using this knowledge to the advantage of the patients.

Others, however, believed that God had power over the divinely instituted laws that ruled nature. God could act in ways contrary to the laws. Such acts were supernatural, and the resultant miracles were to be sharply distinguished from natural events. This applies to bodily healings. Most of them are effected by natural causes as these are understood by physicians. But some are caused directly by God. When we pray for healing, we are asking God to override natural laws and act in this direct way.

Liberal Christians, on the whole, have been skeptical of this kind of supernaturalism. The claims of faith healers often seem offensive as well as incredible. If God acts at all in such supernatural ways, it is hard to understand why so many faithful and devout people receive no answers to their prayers for healing. The explanation that their faith is insufficient only adds guilt to their burden of physical sickness. It seems to liberal Christians better to leave the physical world to natural laws, and healing to physicians.

Bruce Epperly is free from both of these dualisms and understands deeply the implications of that freedom. He does not think of God as a supernatural being who interrupts the course of nature from time to time in arbitrary ways. And he rejects the sharp separation of things of the body from things of the soul. He gives rich expression to ways of thinking that are at once more Biblical and more contemporary. In doing so, he offers helpful guidance to the church as it renews its interest in healing.

Instead of thinking of God as the transcendent lawgiver who either leaves the world alone or intervenes from time to time, let us think of God as the Spirit of life and growth and healing that pervades the world. Instead of thinking of the spheres of body and soul as separate, let us think of all human events as involving both somatic and psychic elements. Let us think of the soma as made up extensively of living cells, each of which has a life of its own. Let us think of the psyche as a more complex pattern of living events, a flow of human experiences. Let us think of God as acting in all of these cells and all of these events, working for their healthy functioning.

In this vision, God plays a role in all events and controls none. To understand any event fully is to include God in the explanation. But no event can be explained simply by supposing that God caused it to be as it is. Most of the explanation of all events is always to be found in their total context and background. In that specific situation God always acts graciously. Sometimes that gracious action makes a decisive difference between health and sickness. Sometimes renewed health is not possible.

In this vision our choices and attitudes also make a great difference. A positive, receptive attitude affects the functioning of all the cells in the body. Expectation of improvement helps us to improve, as the now well-known placebo effect makes clear. Still placebos are less effective in most instances than drugs that have active ingredients relevant to the disease. A healthy attitude does not replace other healing forces.

God works in us to heal our attitudes. Improved attitudes open us to more effective working of God both in the psyche and in the soma. These changes can alter body chemistry. But equally, changes in body chemistry effected by drugs can alter our attitudes and open us to God's healing work within us.

If reality is like this, what is the role of the church? First, we need to help people understand realistically how God works in them and how they can work with God. Many beliefs about God block God's healing work rather than enhance it. For example, the church's teaching about God often induces feelings of guilt and anxiety, which make for somatic and psychic sickness. Second, we need to contribute realistically to the healing of all who are sick, whether that sickness is primarily psychic or somatic.

Most of the time our realistic contribution may seem modest. Obviously we will encourage those with serious problems to seek specialized psychiatric and medical help. We will be careful not to create unrealistic expectations. But we will also be careful not to minimize the effectiveness of love, understanding, therapeutic touch, and intercessory prayer. All that we do we will offer to God to use for the divine work of healing.

The church should recover the field of healing for the sake of the world. Far more people are aware of their need for healing than of their need for the forgiveness of sins. Of course, these are related, and involvement in healing can lead in some instances to awareness of the need for forgiveness. But healing is an important goal in and of itself. It does not have to be a means to something else.

Although it would be a mistake for the church to enter this field in order to build up its institutional strength, serious participation in healing is likely to attract many who are not interested in what the church now offers. Although healing is an end it itself, it is so related to the whole of the church's message that it can be a way into the fuller gospel. A church that gives itself to others in this way may gain new life for itself.

There is another respect in which entering the ministry of healing can help the church as a whole. The view of nature as a machine, inherited from the eighteenth century, is still pervasive in society and permeates the church as well. It has led to God seeming largely irrelevant, if not unreal, to many people, even to active members of the church. The practice of healing in the church will lead to a very different sense of the human body and, indeed, of nature as a whole, one that is far more open to the work of God. That new sensibility will carry over to worship and instruction and to personal devotional life as well.

Epperly shows us what should be apparent to all from reading the Gospels, that the ministry of healing was central to Jesus. To take up this ministry is to be true to him. Further, Epperly shows in surprising detail how much we can learn about healing from reading the biblical stories with greater care.

Progressives may fear that to take up the ministry of healing will distract the church from its prophetic mission of confronting the injustices in society, as well as the degradation of the environment that threatens the human future. Epperly shows us that if we follow Jesus, that will not happen. The sickness of individuals is bound up with the sickness of society and of the Earth itself. To work toward true healing of individuals leads us to seek changes in the wider world. We cannot have healed individuals in a sick world.

But here, as elsewhere, our interconnectedness is such that influence goes both ways. The sickness of individuals contributes to the sickness of society. Healed individuals by their health tend to heal the society. Furthermore, healed individuals are able to work for social justice with a sustained effectiveness not possible for the sick. The importance of concern for structural change is no reason to neglect the needs of individuals and small communities.

Paul reminds us that we do not all have the same gifts. Some who have the gift of preaching may not have the gift of healing. Some who have the gift of teaching may not be good preachers or effective in healing. Some who have the gift of healing may not be good preachers or teachers. Of course, this is a matter of degree, but this degree is important. There have been a few truly great healers even in the recent context when faith healing has been seen somewhat askance. A church that encourages healing may discover more highly gifted healers among its members.

To speak of gifts may be misleading. It may imply that gifts simply exist and need to be discovered. But we all know that the gift of preaching, to take one example, requires cultivation. There are some people who, it seems, cannot become effective preachers however hard they try, and there are others who seem to excel almost spontaneously and effortlessly. But seminaries typically require all students to take courses in preaching, believing that whatever gifts students bring, there is need for honing them.

We may expect a similar situation with respect to the gift of healing. The disciplines that strengthen that gift will be very different from those that improve preaching. They may be more closely related to spiritual practices than to study. That does not reduce their importance or the likelihood that when the church takes this ministry seriously there will be opportunities to hone natural gifts.

As the church moves into this field, it will be important to remind ourselves of the diversity of gifts. To undertake a ministry of healing should not lead those without this gift to feel inferior. There are other ministries of the church. Every Christian has a distinct calling. By the same token, the importance of other gifts should not lead to belittling this one.

Epperly is not alone in calling us to return to the following of Jesus in his ministry of healing. But it is safe to say that no one speaks more clearly and convincingly than he of why this is important and of why it should be understood. This book is an important contribution to a small but growing literature about a great opportunity. May it make its significant contribution to the movement within the church that is already responding to this challenge!

John B. Cobb Jr.

Chapter One

The Touch of God

*T*oday, religion, science, and medicine are in the midst of a profound spiritual transformation. Scientific and religious dogmatism is crumbling before a new and lively vision of reality. This cultural and religious transformation involves not only the growing scientific interest in the benefits of religious commitment for persons' health and the widespread use of alternative and complementary medical approaches from the East and West, but also the transformation of persons who have found unexpected healing and wholeness as a result of their own commitment to spiritual change. Clearly, the modern worldview, upon which scientific and political materialism, one-dimensional theological liberalism, and conservative fundamentalism have stood throughout our lifetimes, no longer meets the spiritual and medical needs of the twenty-first century. Beyond the horizons of the crumbling modern worldview lies an uncharted land whose signposts are holograms and quarks, studies on the power of prayer and spiritual healing, near-death experiences and energy medicine, and the revival of ancient healing practices in partnership with modern technology. The quest for healing of body, mind, and spirit is changing the face of medicine and spirituality, and it is changing the lives of ordinary persons. At the edges of their own personal frontiers, persons in crisis are discovering the power of the healing Christ.

After her divorce Anne felt helpless and adrift. As she unwillingly began her new life as a single parent, she blamed her husband for his insensitivity and narcissism, but she also blamed herself for the failure of her marriage. Guilt-ridden, she constantly asked herself, "Would my husband have left me, if only I had been a better wife and mother?" A failure in her own eyes and a sinner in the eyes of a childhood god she feared but could not love, she saw little hope for personal change and empowerment. Perceiving herself to be the victim of events beyond her control, her main goal was merely to get through the day and make it from paycheck to paycheck. She dreaded waking up each morning to a life of loneliness, hopelessness, boredom, and fatigue. She could barely muster enough energy to care for her nine-year-old daughter and five-year-old son.

A few months after her divorce was finalized, Anne noticed a lump in her breast. The initial biopsy found it to be cancerous. At that moment, her first response was to cry out, "God, are you punishing me for my failure as a wife and mother? Haven't you hurt me enough by breaking my heart and robbing me of my future?" Though it was found that the cancer had not spread to her lymph nodes and required only minor surgery, Anne kept the diagnosis to herself and quietly prepared to die. In her mind, the word *cancer* had only *one* meaning—pain and death—and she could do nothing but passively await the inevitable outcome.

Although Anne was only an occasional churchgoer, the week after the surgery she chose to attend her local church. As she looks back on that Sunday morning, Anne recalls, "Although I didn't trust God at the time, I wanted to make a bargain with him. Keep me alive until my children grow up, and I'll be the best mother I can be! Even though I believed that God had better things to do than to listen to my desperate prayers, I also believed that I might find temporary comfort in the chapel or, at least, discover someone other than myself to blame for my personal misery."

That Sunday morning, the scripture lesson was on Jesus' encounter with the man at the pool of Bethzatha (John 5:1–15). Jesus' words to the paralyzed man challenged the victim mentality Anne had cherished for most of her life. She confesses that when she heard the words of scripture, "Do you want to be healed?" she felt as if a voice was speaking from deep within her spirit. "At that moment, I knew God was speaking directly to me. All my life, I had resisted change. I had blamed other persons for my personal failures. I had a greater investment in failure than in success and in sickness than in health. I realized that deep down I really didn't want to be healed, because being healed meant standing on my own two feet and taking responsibility for the rest of my life. It meant choosing to become a partner with others and no longer depending upon them to shape my destiny."

While at first Anne felt guilty about the negativity that had characterized much of her life, as she listened more closely to the sermon and pondered the minister's words over the next few weeks, she realized that Jesus did not condemn the paralyzed man for his past failures or even blame him for his current passivity. The Healer challenged him to stand on his own two feet and start his life over again. From deep within her spirit, Anne heard a voice, "You can begin again," and then mumbled to herself, "I can begin again! I can stand on my own feet. Maybe God is on my side after all! Maybe God has always been on my side, and I just didn't know it!"

For Anne, the healing process wasn't easy. She knew it would take more than surgery or a momentary spiritual insight to heal her spirit. She would have to overcome years of negativity and isolation. She would also have to overcome her habitual sense of victimization. She would need a transformed mind to let go of her past negative mental and behavior patterns. And she would need to explore new images of a god who was neither punitive, authoritarian, nor specifically masculine in nature—a god with the face of a healer rather than a judge. While she sought the most appropriate and noninvasive medical treatments for her cancer, she also committed herself to a spiritual quest. At the advice of her minister, she began to practice a form of meditation called "centering prayer" and use visualization and guided meditation techniques to image her body as a healthy and beloved friend. She also visualized herself as active and empowered in her relationships with her ex-husband, parents, and current employer. She imaged the cancer surrounded by a healing light that restored order to the chaos of the cancer cells. Much to her surprise, Anne gradually became the person she visualized herself to be. Though introverted by nature, Anne chose to join a cancer support group and began to share her pain with her friends and family. In sharing her personal story and listening to the challenges that the other women were facing, Anne found her own voice and a growing sense of her own personal power. She entered spiritual direction with a pastor who specialized in mind-body wholeness and who taught her to see God's healing presence in even the most apparently God-forsaken situations.

Today Anne is free of cancer, but more importantly she is free of the passivity, resentment, and victim mentality that had imprisoned her for so many years. She has even forgiven her ex-husband, and together they now care for their secure and happy children. Now each day, regardless of its potential problems, she awakens with the affirmation, "This is the day that God has made, I will rejoice and be glad in it!" Today Anne proclaims, "Jesus spoke to me that day, and the healing of my spirit began just as the scars from my surgery were healing. I know Christ is alive. He touched me and I became a new creation! I knew I would be healed even if the cancer came back." Like countless others, Anne experienced the surprising touch of God that would change her life forever. God touched her quietly from the inside, inviting her to become a companion in personal transformation; *and* God also touched her gently from the outside through the care of physicians, nurses, and friends.

When he was diagnosed with a herniated spinal disk, David sought the best medical care possible. But, even after a regimen of physical therapy, he could still barely walk or sit without experiencing tremendous pain. The medications he received eased the physical pain but also left him often feeling mentally confused and virtually unable to continue his work as an executive at a major Washington, D.C., accounting firm. Invasive surgery and prolonged recovery lay before him. Fearing the consequences of back surgery, he visited a holistic health clinic and began acupuncture treatments and herbal remedies. While his pain diminished, he had misgivings about the philosophy behind the care that he received. As an active evangelical United Methodist layperson, his conflict was theological in nature: he wondered why his own prayers and those of his friends appeared to make no difference in his overall physical well-being. But, he also worried that his use of acupuncture and other energy treatments might compromise his faith as a Christian. Although he saw no conflict in seeing a secular physician and utilizing a body-based medical approach that gave no consideration to his spiritual life, being treated by an eclectic Buddhist acupuncturist raised serious doctrinal and spiritual concerns for him. "Can I be faithful to Jesus Christ and also use Asian medical remedies?" David asked his pastor in bewilderment. He worried that he might regain physical health but lose touch with what was most precious to him—his personal relationship with Jesus. In the spirit of the current slogan he asked himself "what would Jesus do" about Chinese medicine, herbs, and energy work?

After weeks of personal turmoil, he sought the advice of a spiritual guide who integrated an appreciation for complementary medicine with his deep Christian faith. David found an inner peace that mirrored his growing physical well-being when he discovered that God is present in every healing technique. David found God in the healing touch of the acupuncture needle, but also in the counsel of a spiritual friend who awakened him to the gracefulness of a God whose healing love centers on everyone and whose healing power unites both East and West.

At the turn of the twentieth century, the question of Jesus' healing touch unsettled and transformed the Japanese Christian

Mikao Usui. A scholar and minister, Usui became the principal and chaplain at a Christian boys' school in Kyoto. Following one of the school's worship services, a group of senior boys asked him if he believed in the Bible. When Usui asserted his belief in the inspiration of scripture, his students challenged him to perform a healing just as Jesus had done. When Usui further hesitated and then responded in the negative, his students challenged his lack of faith and asserted that if he did not truly believe in the power of God, how could they take his spiritual advice seriously?

This dramatic moment led to a profound spiritual and geographical journey for Usui. First, Usui journeyed to the United States in hope of discovering the secrets of Jesus' healing ministry. At the American seminary where he sought guidance, the possibility of healing in the modern world was seen as irrelevant and unimportant for the faith of twentieth-century persons. The rationalist, one-dimensional theology of Protestant liberalism Usui encountered at the seminary even questioned the veracity of the New Testament healing stories. Disappointed, Usui returned to Japan in search of insight within the Buddhist tradition of his parents. Although the monks admitted that Gautama the Buddha had on several occasions healed the sick, today's Buddhism, they asserted, focused solely on spiritual well-being and left physical concerns to the medical doctors. Undaunted, Usui continued to study ancient Buddhist scriptures in their original Indian language, Sanskrit. In his scripture studies, Usui discovered a number of ancient Tibetan Buddhist healing symbols but found no methodology for their application. Still hopeful of finding the path toward healing, he decided to follow the spirit of Christ and Buddha by seeking out a secluded place for intensive prayer and meditation. On the twenty-first day of his spiritual retreat, Usui had a mystical experience that not only confirmed the healing power of the ancient symbols he had been studying but also gave him a technique for their use in physical and spiritual healing. From that point on, Usui joined Christlike compassion and Buddhist wisdom in bringing wholeness to the sick of mind, body, and spirit through the practice of reiki, a hands-on technique for mediating divine healing energy.[1]

Today Usui's followers embody the touch of God as their own touch becomes a channel for God's universal healing energy. As divine energy flows through their healing hands, it brings balance and energy to healer and patient alike. Reiki practitioners believe that within each cell is a healing light ready to beam brightly when it is touched by the loving intention of oneself or another. In the touching of East and West through the practice of reiki, the unboundedness of God's love is made manifest to persons of all religious traditions.

The stories of Anne, David, and Mikao Usui are not unique in today's transformed spiritual, cultural, and medical environment. Everyday persons are discovering the powerful synthesis of spirituality and complementary medicine in the renewing and revitalizing of their lives. Jesus is being rediscovered by Christians and non-Christians alike not only as a great spiritual and ethical figure but also as a living source of the healing of body, mind, and spirit in the present age. This emerging healing movement is diverse and global in nature. Ironically, its greatest proponents are often found outside the institutional church. Because of this fact, the journey of many Christians to Eastern or new age spiritualities often creates a chasm between their Sunday morning religious experience and the more lively spirituality that has transformed their daily lives. More than a few Christians have left the church entirely, citing as their main reason Christianity's inability to respond holistically and practically to their deepest needs for spiritual growth and personal healing.

In the quest to understand the significance of the discovery of Jesus as a powerful healer for the twenty-first century and

---

1. For a more detailed description of Usui's healing journey and the practice of reiki, consult Helen J. Haberly, *Reiki: Hawayo Takata's Story,* Garrett Park, Md.: Archedigm, 1990.

to embody his healing power for our time, the Christian church has often been—to quote Martin Luther King Jr.— "a taillight rather than a headlight." This short-sighted and often ignorant attitude of many religious leaders is reflected in an apocryphal story about a nurse supervisor who became disturbed when a number of her nurses began to utilize a form of healing touch in their patient care. After a number of days of observing the nurses in her ward using healing touch as well as medication to treat their patients, she sought to put an end to their healing experiment by posting a sign that stated, "There will be no healing in this hospital!" The same could be said for those ministers and church leaders whose ignorance and mistrust of the dynamic and transformative spirit of Christ, as well as the holistic spiritual healing modalities available to us today, leads to a similar edict, "There will be no healing in this church!" But, in spite of their fear of change and unwillingness to embrace the surprising healing spirit of God, the touch of God is nevertheless transforming persons within and outside the church. Recognized or not, Christ the healer is alive and active in our world!

In his reflections on the impact of Jesus' compassionate approach to healing on the formation of Western medicine, physician J. W. Provonsha proclaims that "the spiritual 'Father of Medicine' was not Hippocrates of the island of Cos, but Jesus of the town of Nazareth."[2] Innovative biblical scholar Marcus Borg confirms this judgment: "Behind this picture of Jesus as a healer and exorcist, I affirm an historical core. . . . I see the claim that Jesus performed paranormal healings and exorcisms as history remembered. Indeed, more healing stories are told about Jesus than any other figure in the Jewish tradition. He must have been a remarkable healer."[3] While other

---

2. J. W. Provonsha, "The Healing Christ," *Current Medical Digest* (Dec. 1959), 3.

3. Marcus Borg and N. T. Wright, *The Meaning of Jesus: Two Visions* (San Francisco: HarperSanFrancisco, 1999), 66.

religious figures, including Buddha, Elijah and Elisha, Aesculapius, and the shamans of ancient and modern religions embodied a concern for healing and wholeness, no other figure incarnates the passion for the healing of mind, body, and spirit as did Jesus of Nazareth.

According to the Gospel of Matthew, Jesus' own sense of call as God's Messiah, or chosen one, was intimately related to his ministry of spiritual and physical healing. When John the Baptist's disciples ask Jesus if he is the one their teacher expected, Jesus responded: "Go and tell John what you hear and see: the blind receive their sight, the lame walk, the lepers are cleansed, the deaf hear, the dead are raised, and the poor have good news brought to them" (Matt. 11:4–5). The gospel accounts of Jesus' life weave together a profound concern for holistic healing that includes the transformation of body, mind, spirit, economics, ethnic and gender relationships, and power structures as the manifestation of God's love for the world. While the Greek philosophers of his time often counseled an escape from the imprisonment of physical existence, Jesus' ministry centered on the experience wholeness in *this* world of embodiment, as well as in the future realm of the spirit. In his deeply insightful work on Christian healing, Episcopal priest and theologian Morton Kelsey reminds us that "forty-one instances of physical and mental healing are recorded in the four gospels" and "nearly one-fifth of the entire gospels is devoted to Jesus' healing and the discussions occasioned by it."[4] To the Galilean healer who came that persons might have abundant life (John 10:10), no healing was too ordinary or too difficult for God's concern.

In his incarnation of God's love for the world, Jesus transformed many of his religious tradition's understandings of spirituality; but foremost he transformed Judaism's understanding of health and illness, and the powers of life and death

---

4. Morton Kelsey, *Psychology, Medicine, and Christian Healing* (New York: Harper & Row, 1988), 42–43.

working through them. Many of his first-century contemporaries—like many persons today—identified illness with divine punishment for immoral behavior. In contrast, Jesus clearly placed the divine Parent fully on the side of healing. Although Jesus recognized that our actions and thought patterns may be manifested in the health of body, mind, spirit, and relationships, Jesus also maintained that God is not the source of disease and persons are not completely responsible for their health or illness. The God whose love found its embodiment in Jesus opposes anything that hinders abundant life and wholeness, whether it be blindness, leprosy, AIDS, cancer, mental illness, or negative thinking. Jesus' life and healing ministry witness to the fact that God wants us to experience joy, well-being, and health in every aspect of our lives. The God who creates our bodies as the temple of God wants us to experience wholeness in all its complex and dynamic dimensions.

In contrast to first- and twenty-first-century Gnostics, Jesus proclaimed that the physical world is not an illusion or an impediment to spiritual transformation but is an icon, or window through which divine beauty is revealed in our lives and relationships. God's healing touch is revealed in the normal functioning of the immune and cardiovascular systems, in the processes of healthy digestion and elimination, in the gentle and imperceptible healing of physical and emotional wounds, as well as through the dramatic and unexpected spiritual, physical and emotional transformations that often accompany prayer, meditation, medical intervention, or healing touch. For those who follow the great healer Jesus, God's creative, healing intention is alive wherever wholeness is promoted and restored, even when the name of Jesus is not explicitly invoked.

Jesus proclaimed that the healing spirit of God would continue beyond his earthly life: "The one who believes in me will also do the works that I do and, in fact, will do greater works than these. . . . I will do whatever you ask in my name, so that the Father may be glorified in the Son. If in my name you ask me for anything, I will do it" (John 14:12–14). Jesus' commission to his disciples affirms that "they will lay their hands on the sick, and they *will* recover" (Mark 16:18, italics mine). The touch of God incarnate in Jesus' life is still at work in every transformative and reconciling moment, and we are the channels of this healing touch today!

Despite Jesus' emphasis on the presence of God's healing touch in all things, the Christian church gradually turned its attention from the care of the whole person in this lifetime to the destiny of the disembodied soul in the next life. Even today many evangelical and conservative churches still understand their primary mission in terms of preparing persons for eternal life.[5] Despite their affirmation of the importance of *this* world in God's plan of salvation, few mainstream or liberal Protestants and Roman Catholics take the healing ministry of Jesus seriously, and even fewer consider the possibility that God's transformative work would include the healing of body, mind, and spirit as well as the transformation of unjust and disempowering social and political structures.

The reasons for mainstream and liberal Christianity's neglect of Jesus' healing ministry are fourfold. First, many sensitive and educated Christians have been rightly scandalized by the techniques, claims, and theological viewpoints of conservative and Pentecostal Christian faith healers. Television healers and tent-meeting evangelists describe healing as God's supernatural intervention in the lives of the chosen. Out of nowhere, the divine thunderbolt strikes diseased persons and restores them to health. To the most cynical of observers, it is amusing that this divine intervention comes most readily following a generous gift in the offering plate or by VISA or MasterCard over the phone. At the same time, many of the same evangelists who assert that God supernaturally "zaps" people with divine healing also claim that God "strikes down" others with AIDS, cancer, or Alzheimer's either to teach them

---

5. The shift from holistic spirituality to preparation for eternal life is described in Kelsey's *Psychology, Medicine, and Christian Healing,* 157–86.

a lesson, strengthen their faith, or punish them for their individual or social misdeeds. Mainstream Christians rightly ask: "What parent would strike down a child with cancer or a young father with Lou Gehrig's disease just to increase their faith or amend their behavior?"

At the same time, other mainline Christians are infuriated by popular beliefs that claim that if you only have enough faith, your child or you will be healthy, wealthy, and wise. This "name it and claim it" theology has left in its wake not only those who have claimed and apparently received supernatural healings but also many whose faith has been destroyed or guilt has increased when the hoped-for healing did not occur. As one woman tearfully asked me after the death of her child, "How much faith was enough to save her? How many prayers were needed to heal my daughter? I had my whole church and everyone I knew praying for her. Wasn't that good enough for God to restore her health?" While these "name it and claim it" ideologies assert that they are glorifying God, they ultimately place the burden of health and illness entirely on us. The fault cannot be ascribed to God or the preacher but most terribly to the very victim who is already weighed down by guilt, grief, and pain.

Second, many mainstream and liberal Christians are equally perplexed and scandalized by the wild and unsubstantiated claims of certain new age healers, whose work combines everything under the sun from acupuncture to affirmations, herbs to healing touch, crystals to karma cards, I Ching to iridology.[6] From the rationalistic perspective of many mainline Christians, the claims of such healers defy any consistency either of worldview or metaphysics. While many people have benefited from the new age synthesis of ancient and modern healing techniques, others have found themselves caught in a downward spi-

---

6. For those who desire a more extensive study of the new age movement, I suggest my own book, *Crystal and Cross: Christians and the New Age in Creative Dialogue* (Mystic, Conn.:Twenty-Third Publications, 1996), and Ted Peters, *The Cosmic Self* (San Francisco: HarperSanFrancisco, 1991).

ral of guilt and self-accusation when, despite all their efforts, the cancer remains aggressive or their negative thinking persists. While the affirmation that "you create your own reality" empowers some persons, others drown in the tragic realities they have apparently created for themselves and their families.

I met Susan at a reception following a wedding I had performed. With an edge in her voice, she approached me, "That was a beautiful wedding, pastor. But I can't stand religion anymore. The whole idea of God frightens me." As we sipped cocktails, I found myself to be her captive audience as she related the story of her childhood in a religiously conservative household. As part of her childhood catechism, she was told that each child is born with a white heart and that with every sin a black spot darkens the heart. If your heart gets dark enough, she was told, you will go to hell. As an adult in search of a guilt-free faith, Susan sought the wisdom of new age healers. While she was initially ecstatic by their message of the power of the mind to transform every aspect of a person's life, she soon experienced the dark side of mental omnipotence. She was told that she was entirely responsible for her chronic fatigue syndrome. If she only lived by positive affirmations, she would enjoy perfect health. When her young child experienced chronic ear infections, one new age healer even blamed her for her child's health problems. Burdened by the guilt of her imperfections and helpless to change her external circumstances, Susan abandoned religion entirely. Susan was initially amused when I told her that she should fire the vindictive God of her childhood and return her omnipotent mind to her new age teachers for a refund. As we parted company, Susan warned me that she would be calling me. She was interested in hearing about a way to change her life that would not plunge her further into guilt. She yearned for a god who was really on her side.

In their quest for self-actualization and perfect health, other new agers succumb to self-centered lives, lacking compassion and patience for the karma of their fellow travelers along the journeys of their many past lives. In any event, by whatever name we use to describe it, the power source or teacher—the immortal spirit, the new age therapist, the impersonal karmic force, or the supernatural God—remains unscathed by failure: if you're sick, after all, it must somehow be your own fault! Deal with it yourself! Some new agers even shun the sick for fear that their negativity might contaminate their own fragile spiritual journeys.

Sadly, many mainstream and liberal Christians identify the healing power of God and the surprising synchronicities of faith with these extreme and often unfounded views of spiritual healing. They fail to see alternative manifestations of God's healing presence in their lives and their churches. They have been imprisoned by what they do *not* believe about healing rather than the positive and life-affirming healing possibilities in their midst. They have forgotten that faith lives by affirmation and not negation.

Third, others have rejected the healing Christ because of the immature, archaic, and destructive images of God as heartless, arbitrary, judgmental, vindictive, and emotionally distant. These unexamined theological images, often inherited from dysfunctional church or parochial school teachers obsessed with hierarchical authority and anxious about the temptations of embodiment, live on in feelings of guilt and unworthiness and projections of a divine killjoy who is out to get us for the slightest infraction. With a god like this, who needs human enemies! Jesus' image of God as loving parent, joyfully seeking abundant life and welcoming the outcast, has been lost amid the mire of these toxic theological images.

But perhaps the most decisive factor in mainstream and liberal Christianity's neglect of Jesus' first-century healing ministry and ongoing healing presence in the world has been the influence of the modern worldview, inspired by pivotal figures such as Isaac Newton, René Descartes, Immanuel Kant, and Charles Darwin. At the heart of the modern worldview is the interplay of a number of philosophical beliefs, including the separation of mind and body; the separation of organisms, be they atomic or human, from their environment; the banishing of divine action to either supernatural intervention from outside the universe (the traditional deus ex machina, or god of the gaps) or to the irrelevance of a first creative principle (the divine clockmaker, who gets things started and then goes on an eternal holiday, except perhaps when summoned by prayer or global crisis); the closed system world of deterministic cause and effect; the tendency to reduce the activity of mind or spirit solely to physical interactions; the definition of causal relationships in terms of the immediate environment (thus rendering intercessory prayer or extrasensory perception an absurdity). Such a worldview leaves no place for the gentle, subtle touch of God that radiates within and without to heal the diseases of mind, body, and spirit and the transformation of the mind that brings wholeness to diseased persons. To these one-dimensional thinkers, the healing stories of Jesus are either myths from a bygone era or vestiges of ancient superstition. Within the confines of their compartmentalized and mechanistic worldview, they assert that Jesus' healings could not have involved a heightening of the divine presence but merely reveal the alleviation of psychosomatic dysfunctions or changes in self-understanding, social position, or spiritual concern. Public prayers in church or at the bedside, from this rationalistic perspective, merely provide comfort, care, and community support. They cannot influence the course of an illness, except by autosuggestion, nor can they open the door to the surprises of divine creativity.

Fortunately, the experiences of many scientists and persons of faith are challenging the sole supremacy of this materialistic, dualistic, and individualistic worldview. The spiritually oriented images of the new physics and its world of fractals, intimate relational webs, all-encompassing holograms, and nonlocal and distant causal relationships provides a new and refreshing image of everyday reality and mystical experience. Along with the insights of mystics and physicists, these emerging integrative images of health, healing, and medicine are symptomatic of a profound spiritual movement that promises to transform church and hospital alike.

The first-century healings of Jesus are coming alive to many twenty-first-century persons both inside and outside the church as a result of four intellectual, cultural, and religious factors: the rise of the new physics; the emerging global religious and medical culture; the growing scientific awareness of the power of prayer and the positive benefits of spirituality and religious commitment; and the pioneering work of healers within the Christian church. I believe the synchronous emergence of these factors reflects God's call to transformation in our time!

At the heart of the new physics is the vision of dynamic relationship.[7] The universe exists as a cosmic dance in which each being arises in relationship with its neighbor. Vitality and responsiveness characterize not only our human experiences but also the experience of the simplest energy events. In the dance of relationships, every moment of experience—human and nonhuman—is the result of its response to countless environmental factors. The process of creation and re-creation constantly occurs within a synthesis of complex relationships. No person, cell, or molecule exists in isolation but has a dynamic relationship with everything in the universe. In this web of interrelationships, there are no hard boundaries between body and mind, person and environment, flesh and spirit, or medicine and spirituality. No event can be attributed to just one cause. For example, while the incidence of lung cancer is intimately related to smoking, the fact that some smokers contract cancer and others do not results from the interaction of a number of subtle and often neglected factors such as genetic characteristics, quality of relationships with spouses and children and friends, positive or negative attitude toward life, and spiritual commitments. The dynamic relationality of the new

---

7. For a further discussion of the metaphysical side of the "new physics," see Fritjof Capra, *The Tao of Physics* (New York: Bantam Books, 1977), and Ken Wilber, editor, *Quantum Questions: Mystical Writings of the World's Great Physicists* (Boulder, Colo.: Shambala, 1984).

physics suggests that although overall health results from the interplay of many factors such as diet, exercise, relationships, spirituality, and the subtle movements of God, it is also conditioned by other factors such as economics, workplace environment and job satisfaction, and level of education.

The world of the new physics, like its metaphysical companion process theology and philosophy, suggests that even God must operate within a dynamic and relational matrix. Within the ever-turning dance of relationships, the action of God as an omnipresent but not omnipotent force affects to some degree everything that exists, and everything that exists also shapes the nature of God. In the spirit of Jesus' own vision of God, this infinitely caring love extends even to the "least of these," that is, the very cells of our bodies. Although this deeply compassionate God seeks health and goodness in all things, God's power does not hold absolute sway over every event. Thus, for example, God is not responsible for the birth of a child with blindness (John 9:1–12), but must work in partnership with us to bring about the greatest possible healing and well-being for that child and all others who suffer from disease and neglect. As we reflect on the healing stories of the Gospels, we will see that the healings of Jesus are seldom unilateral acts of divine power but exist in partnership with human faith and openness to the constant surprises of God's grace. Jesus' unique wisdom rests in the testimony that the greatest power is found in the love that receives as well as gives.

Today, vital religious experience is grounded not only in the embrace of the insights of the new physics but also in the profound insights of non-Western religious and medical traditions. The supremacy of Western medicine has been challenged, but also enriched, by its encounter with Chinese acupuncture, East-West reiki, mystical therapeutic touch, Indian ayurvedic medicine, and Native American healing techniques. In that same spirit, Christian faith has been enriched by its encounter and openness to Hindu and Buddhist meditation and breath prayer, physical yoga postures, and the growing understanding of the relationship between Chinese *chi* energy and the dynamic and pneumatic power of the Holy Spirit. Christians are learning to let go of the identification of Christianity solely with Western medicine and Western philosophy. Just as early Christianity sought to synthesize Greek and Hebrew under-standings of the world, human nature, and spiritual existence, today's Christians are challenged to explore the relationship of the subtle movements of the Tao to the Creator of the universe and the compassionate Healer Jesus to the Buddhist bod-hisattva. In real life, this means that if Christians are able to affirm that "wherever truth and healing are present, Christ is present," then they must also balance their commitment to Christ as "the way, the truth, and the life" with the reflections of Christ's presence in other religious traditions, even includ-ing the often maligned new age movement of North America. As they explore the edges of complementary medicine, many Christians are discovering that the Chinese understanding of *chi*, or dynamic energy, for example, is more conducive to understanding Jesus' healing ministry than Descartes' mind–body dualism or the Greek understanding of the disembodied soul.

Just as Christians have expanded their horizons in dialogue with science, physicians and nurses today are beginning to take into account the significance of religious commitment and spiritual discipline for overall well-being as well for the prevention of and response to illness. While once labeled as irrelevant, if not eccentric and childish, by psychiatrists and other physicians, various religious practices and commitments are now being identified with lower blood pressure, relief from arthritis, healthy lifestyle patterns, greater self-esteem and increased ability to cope with chronic illness and grief, and decreased chances of contracting certain life-threatening dis-eases. Whether the health benefits of religion can be attributed to positive thinking, the placebo effect, simple autosuggestion, ritualized activities in times of transition, the social dynamics of community, or a combination of all of these factors, contemporary science leaves us with little doubt that religion can make a positive difference in a person's overall well-being. The ancient practice of meditation has been found by physicians such as Herbert Benson at Harvard Medical School not only to quiet the mind and bring experiences of peace and emotional well-being but also to lower blood pressure, decrease stress, and enhance immune system functioning. Other studies suggest that prayer changes things. While more theological reflection and scientific research needs to be done in the exploration of the power of prayer, a growing body of evidence indicates that prayer enhances the well-being of persons recovering from heart bypass surgery and other ailments. While we cannot rule out the placebo effect or the impact of other unknown pray-ers on the human control groups (those persons not formally objects of prayer), studies on the impact of distant prayer on mice and fungi (both of whom seem immune to the placebo effect and are seldom the objects of human intercessory prayer!) indicate that focused spiritual healing techniques can enhance the healing recovery from wounds and accelerate the growth of fungi and other plants. Science has only recently discovered what persons of faith have known from the first movements of human history: when persons pray, unexpected and surprising transformation occurs. As these results emerge, the church is called to be a laboratory for prayer, in which intercessory prayer, laying on of hands, support groups, meditation, and forgiveness radiate forth as a vital response to human need in its many forms.[8] The church is called to incarnate the healing ministry of Jesus in light of contemporary science and medicine.

---

8. For more detailed discussions on the relationship between spirituality, medicine, and health, see Larry Dossey, *Healing Words: The Power of Prayer and the Practice of Medicine* (San Francisco: HarperSanFrancisco, 1994); Bruce Epperly, *Spirituality and Health, Health and Spirituality* (Mystic, Conn.: Twenty-Third Publications, 1997); Dale Matthews, *The Faith Factor: Proof of the Healing Power of Prayer* (New York: Viking, 1998).

Long before physicians discovered that prayer is good medicine, a small pioneering group of Christian healers from mainstream and liberal churches also recognized that the spirit of Jesus the healer is alive and active, even when it is not noticed. These healers lived and ministered in the belief that the divine quest for abundant life is still vitally at work in the world. Like Mikao Usui, they recognized that if the gospel stories were true, then God is still at work in our world to heal body, mind, and spirit. They discovered that a robust theology and practice of healing called them to appreciate God's healing intentions in all of its forms, whether in medicine, psychology, and non-Christian religions.

Agnes Sanford and Morton Kelsey pioneered a holistic vision of health and healing that inspired not only their fellow Episcopalians but also seekers after healing within and beyond the church. According to Agnes Sanford, the healing light of Christ is not bound by space or time, for "Jesus Christ is with us and heals today."[9] Not far from human life or untouched by human pain, but in the midst of our daily lives, "God is within us and without us. He is the source of all life; and of unimaginable depths of inter-stellar space. But he is also the indwelling life of our own little selves. And just as the whole world full of electricity will not light a house unless the house itself is prepared to receive that electricity, so the infinite and eternal God cannot help us unless we are prepared to receive that light within ourselves."[10] These miraculous releases of healing energy are built into the nature of the universe. For those who quietly open themselves to God's healing power through compassionate prayer and imagination, the whole world is full of miracles. In the spirit of quantum physics, Sanford proclaims that "the body is not hard, solid matter, but is made of specks of energy . . . the body is full of light" that

---

9. Agnes Sanford, *The Healing Light* (St. Paul, Minn.: Macalester Park Publishing, 1972), 13.

10. Ibid., 19.

lives by the healing light of God.[11] Healing is facilitated by our awareness and alignment with this ever-present healing light.

In this same spirit, Episcopal priest Morton Kelsey, whose work is grounded in the psychological vision of Carl Jung, proclaims that healing involves a synergy of conscious and unconscious factors. In awakening to our deepest self, the divine within, we find the wholeness that brings spiritual healing even when a cure is not possible.[12] According to Kelsey, there is a spiritual world beneath the world of the senses. When the power of the spiritual world breaks into human experience, then signs, wonders, and healings become everyday realities.

With their interest in extrasensory perception and the wisdom of the higher self, Methodists Ambrose Worrall, an aeronautical engineer, and his wife Olga pioneered a healing ministry in Baltimore for forty years and built a bridge between Christianity, parapsychology, and today's new age movement. In the spirit of modern science, the Worralls maintained that ordinary and dramatic healings do not violate the laws of nature but reveal the deeper divine laws that stand at the basis of our everyday reality. As a child, Olga confounded her family and friends with her experiences of clairvoyance and visions of energy fields or auras and her desire to heal the sick. In a similar fashion, Ambrose Worrall astounded his Methodist Sunday school teacher by asking why Christians could not still perform the miracles of the New Testament. When his teacher replied that the days of healing ended with the early church, the young Worrall asked himself, "Did not Jesus set an example to us—to do as he did? Why should God stop such healing after sending his Son to give us an example of his healing love?"[13] Like Kelsey and Sanford, the Worralls saw the world as permeated by divine energy that can be called upon at any moment: "We are surrounded by healing power,

---

11. Ibid., 31.
12. Kelsey, *Psychology, Medicine, and Christian Healing.*
13. Agnes and Olga Worrall, *The Gift of Healing* (Columbus, Ohio: Ariel Press, 1985), 33.

just as we are surrounded by magnetic fields, electricity, air, ether, and all the other forces that we do not see but which we are able to measure and study in various ways."[14] Like Kelsey and Sanford, the Worralls embraced modern Western medicine but also utilized prayer and meditation, imagination and visualization, spiritual intuition, dreams and visions, and the laying on of hands as means of bringing wholeness to persons in spiritual and physical need. In their reclaiming of Jesus' ministry for the twentieth century and beyond, these spiritual adventurers explored the territory that lies beyond and yet permeates everyday, ordinary life and consciousness, the mysterious and healing presence of the divine and the unexpected, ambient world of the spirit. Their journeys beckon each one of us to seek that wider horizon of experience where the adventures of science, medicine, and spirituality meet.

I believe that the healing Christ is alive and at work in our lives today. Not bound to a particular time, place, or religious movement, or confined to the worldviews of ancients or moderns, the healing Christ still brings direction to the lost, welcome to the outcast, and wholeness to those broken in mind, body, and spirit. As the omnipresent embodiment and intensification of God's aim at wholeness and creative transformation, the living Christ—embodied in the life and healings of Jesus of Nazareth—is as much a part of the world of C-T scans, MRI's, acupuncture, therapeutic touch, and meditation as the first-century Jesus was a part of the world of demon possession, religious taboos, exorcisms, and laying on of hands. Not bound by a particular healing methodology, the healings of Jesus invite us to open ourselves to the healing touch of God found in all things, whether in the laboratory, the operating room, the reiki or acupuncture table, or the chapel.

Today we are challenged to read the scriptural accounts of Jesus' healing ministry from a new perspective. As revelations of God's constant and all-encompassing aim at wholeness of

14. Ibid., 173.

mind, body, and spirit, the healings of Jesus and the biblical witness to them are as alive and empowering today as they were at the dawning of the first millennium. When we read them with open hearts and awakened minds, they still transform our lives. As we awaken to their timeless truth and discover that their story is also our own story, these ancient accounts invite us to experience the always contemporary, healing touch of God.

As you read my interpretations of the healing stories of Jesus, I invite you to become part of a healing journey. I believe that these stories are as transformative today as they were two thousand years ago. We can still embrace these stories—which are not bound by fundamentalism, rationalism, ancient metaphysics, or the Western worldview—as our own and find our own healing as we become the characters of these stories. We can encounter the living Christ whose healing touch shines through these stories and through our own healing journeys.

My own interpretation of these stories is grounded in the lively practice of healing ministry as a Christian theologian, minister, Bible teacher, spiritual guide, and researcher in spirituality and health. It is also grounded in the ongoing and open-ended personal and communal dialogue that brings together biblical scholarship, contemporary psychology, the new physics, complementary medicine, Eastern and Western philosophy, new age spirituality, and the recent studies on the power of prayer and the significance of spirituality and religious commitment in health and illness. Reading these biblical stories in light of God's presence in today's multifaceted healing movements rescues them from a spirit-suffocating fundamentalism and a spirit-deadening liberalism. While it is important to take seriously the insights of contemporary mainline biblical scholars such as N. T. Wright and Luke Timothy Johnson, as well as more innovative biblical scholars such as Marcus Borg, John Pilch, and John Dominic Crossan, we must also let the stories speak for themselves in the healing of our own lives and the lives of persons in spiritual, emotional, and physical crisis.

The healing stories inspire and reflect my own commitment to live and share the healing ministry of Jesus in my own prayer life, pastoral ministry, spiritual direction, and use of healing arts such as visualization, meditation, affirmations, reiki, and laying on of hands within liturgical and pastoral care settings. These stories continue to inspire moments of personal healing in my own life and the lives of others. Their power is grounded both in the life of the first-century Jesus, who brought healing to the sick and welcome to the outcast, and in the living Christ, whose transforming presence within our lives and relationships still inspires and brings forth wholeness.

In the spirit of the healing Christ, I invite you to enter each healing account imaginatively and spiritually as well as intellectually. Each chapter, including this one, weaves together theological reflection, biblical inspiration, and practical action and concludes with an experiment in healing and wholeness. These exercises in transformation can become a part of your own personal spiritual formation or can enhance the well-being of you and others as part of a healing and wholeness group.

It is my prayer that you will not only find yourself in these stories but, more importantly, encounter the healing Christ who awakens the dead, heals the sick, forgives the guilt-ridden, welcomes the stranger, and embraces all those who seek transformation and healing in our time.

An Experiment In Healing
And Wholeness

Healing begins with the most basic experience of life—the simple act of breathing. God's Spirit blows through all things, giving them life and inspiration. When we open ourselves to this holy breath, we experience balance, energy, clarity, and focus in our lives. Simply breathing in and out, with an awareness of our many thoughts, as well as the One who breathes through us, centers us and delivers us from habitual thought patterns. In the simple act of breathing, we may discover that beneath the shallowness of our usual patterns of breathing and spirituality is the deeper, more centered breath of the Holy Spirit.

In this experiment in healing and wholeness, simply do what comes naturally. Accept the abundant grace that comes with each breath. While sitting comfortably with your eyes closed, take time to do the following:

1. Begin with a prayer for openness to God's Spirit breathing through your life.
2. Gently inhale and exhale, opening to divine energy with each inhalation, letting go of stress and fatigue with each exhalation.
3. When your mind wanders, as it no doubt will, simply notice the thought or emotion, and then gently bring it back to the Spirit breathing through your life.
4. Close your time of quiet breathing with a prayer of thanksgiving.

Similar to the Buddhist practice of mindfulness meditation, this gentle breath prayer awakens us to the deep peace that undergirds and quiets the chattering mind.

One of my spiritual mentors, Alan Armstrong Hunter, taught me and my wife the following variation on this breath prayer nearly twenty-five years ago when we were in seminary and graduate school at Claremont, California. With each new breath, Alan Hunter reminded us simply to say, "I breathe the Spirit deeply in." With each gentle exhaling, we were advised to express the words, "I blow it out gratefully again." In your own embodiment of this breath prayer, you may also choose to exhale with words that describe your current emotional state, such as "I blow it angrily out again" or "I blow it anxiously out again" or "I blow it peacefully out again." With each breath, we affirm the vital energy of God's Spirit that fills us with peace even as it relieves the daily stresses of life. As we awaken to God's healing breath within our own gentle breathing, the energy that created the universe flows through us, transforming our lives and reviving our spirits.

Now there was a woman who had been suffering from hemorrhages for twelve years. She had endured much under many physicians, and had spent all she had; and she was no better, but rather grew worse. She had heard about Jesus, and came up behind him in the crowd and touched his cloak, for she said, "If I but touch his clothes, I will be made well." Immediately her hemorrhage stopped; she felt in her body that she was healed of her disease. Immediately aware that power had gone forth from him, Jesus turned about in the crowd and said, "Who touched my clothes?" And his disciples said to him, "You see the crowd pressing on you; how can you say, 'Who touched me?'" He looked all around to see who had done it. But the woman, knowing what had happened to her, came in fear and trembling, fell down before him, and told him the whole truth. He said to her, "Daughter, your faith has made you well; go in peace, and be healed of your disease."

(Mark 5:25–34; also Matt. 9:18–26, Luke 8:40–48)

Chapter Two

Your Faith Has Made You Well!

As North Americans live longer, the chances are likely
that we will die *with,* but not necessarily *of,* certain
chronic illnesses. With the advent of creative medical
and clinical interventions, even the dying process can
extend from months to years in duration. Still, the days
are long and difficult for those who live with chronic illness. While once their bodies were friends and illness
was merely a temporary inconvenience in the normal
passage of life, now pain and debilitation have become
routine and habitual. In the midst of constant pain and
inconvenience, there is a yearning to turn back the clock
to the good old days before illness struck. Daily prayers
are filled with petitions for a pain-free day or a cessation
of the humiliation and dependence that chronic illness
often brings.

Chronic illness is the dominant type of illness in the
modern world, shaping the daily lives and future hopes
of over 30 million Americans. Words like cancer, stroke,
heart disease, arthritis, multiple sclerosis, Alzheimer's
disease, HIV, and Crohn's disease remind us that the
experience of disease can often be more terrifying than
death itself. Greater longevity can bring adventures of
geography and spiritual growth, but it can also bring
emotional and spiritual challenges in the face of prolonged suffering and anticipatory grief. The prospect of

living longer brings the fear of debilitation and dependence to many Americans. Fearing the worst-case scenario, elders purchase long-term nursing home care insurance in order to have a financial legacy to leave their children and grandchildren. Medical advances in neonatal care save lives, but they also bring about lifelong challenges for those who survive spina bifida and other birth defects.

In light of this, I suspect that many of us can imaginatively relate to the story of the woman healed of the hemorrhage. While the gospel accounts do not reveal her exact diagnosis, most commentators suggest that her ailment may have been gynecological in nature. For twelve years, she had endured the indignity, discomfort, anxiety, and depression that often accompany chronic gynecological illness. While once she might have asked, "*When* will I get well?" now she hopelessly asks, "*Will I ever* get well?" Twelve years! Four thousand, three hundred eighty days! One hundred five thousand, one hundred twenty hours! Six million, three hundred seven thousand, two hundred minutes, most of which were lived out in both desperate hope of recovery and debilitating resignation born out of the tedium of unremitting pain and disease.

No doubt, like many persons today, she went from physician to physician, and medication to medication, always on the lookout for a miracle cure, a healing talisman, or a magical potion that would restore her former state of well-being. As the scripture notes, "she had endured much under many physicians, and had spent all she had; but was no better, but rather she grew worse." Like many persons today, the exact nature of her illness and the appropriate response were a matter of controversy and disagreement even among her many physicians.

There is nothing abstract about chronic illness, especially when it involves ourselves or a member of our family. For some persons, illness becomes the primary reality of life and the primary focus of their attention, both in its unremitting pain and in their vigilant quest for a cure. Even in the brief moments of respite, the reality of their vulnerability and the eventual recurrence of pain always lies just beneath the surface of conscious attention.

For Sally, a 75-year-old, retired high school teacher, just getting up in the morning is a major ordeal. She wakes up stiff each morning, the pain in her joints often so great that she can barely lift herself out of bed. Some days, it takes virtually all of her energy to fix breakfast or turn the steering wheel of her car. Other days, especially when the weather changes or the barometer falls, she just stays in bed with game shows and reruns of television detective shows as her only companions. Even moving to Florida from her beloved Washington, D.C., made little difference in the arthritis that has handicapped this once-avid golfer, gardener, and knitter. She has taken virtually every test in the world and has tried virtually every pharmaceutical remedy. She pores over medical journals and health magazines at the hospital and on the internet and scrutinizes advertisements in the local new age paper in search of the smallest shred of hope. She even peruses articles on amazing cures touted by the supermarket tabloids. To her chagrin and disappointment, the amazing claims are not so amazing after all, and the side effects from many of the wonder drugs are just as debilitating as the arthritis she endures every day.

In despair over the ineffectiveness of modern medicine to bring her relief, Sally has reconsidered the folk remedies and alternative treatments she arrogantly scoffed at a decade ago. Now she explores the wealth of alternative and complementary forms of medicine with the same hope that once marked her visits to physicians, even though her insurance provides only a modest reimbursement for the acupuncture, magnet therapy, colonics, herbal remedies, and reiki treatments she has tried. She listens expectantly to the testimonies of acquaintances who have found relief through folk remedies. While each of these alternative treatments has provided some relief from her pain, eventually the pain, debilitation, and attending hopelessness return.

In pursuit of a cure, Sally has even changed her diet. Vegetables and rice have replaced her favorite filet mignon and cheeseburgers. Herbal teas now substitute for her favorite blend of Starbuck's coffee and chocolate milk shakes. She has noticed a slight improvement in her overall well-being, but as her savings are depleted by her efforts, she wonders if anything will really work. Sally jokes, not without a bit of irony, that she has by now spent over a year of her life with doctors, spiritual healers, and acupuncturists. She wonders if it has all been worth it! In words that echo the psalmist's laments, she cries out on her bad days, "How long must I endure this pain, O God? How long?"

When Sally reads the stories of Jesus, she especially identifies with the woman with the hemorrhage. She knows a great deal about enduring the pain of medical care! She only wishes that her faith could make her well! She hopes daily for an infusion of divine power, even as she wonders if the healing stories of Jesus can make a difference in the lives of persons today or if they are merely a vestige of an earlier, more naïve and superstitious time. She wishes that her pastor would preach on Jesus' healings and that her Presbyterian church would consider initiating a healing service. In her devotional time, Sally often asks, "Do such healings happen today? Why can't I touch the hem of Jesus' garment? Is there any garment to touch at all? Why can't I be healed?"

For Everett, a 90-year-old, retired American Baptist minister, "going home" is his greatest hope—home to the modest three-bedroom house in a suburb of San Francisco, home to be with Jesus, home to be reunited with his recently deceased wife of 46 years. For 87 years, he looked younger and worked harder and, frankly, outlived most of the "class of 1910." Although he complained about the aches and pains and hearing loss of his advancing years , he often joked that "somedays I feel 90 and other days I feel 60!" At least, that's how he felt until the day of the stroke—a severe cardiovascular incident that left him entirely paralyzed on the left side, unable to move himself without assistance, having to endure the indignity of diapers and the loss of bowel and bladder control, having to live with emotions that he can no longer control. Once an avid reader, now he seldom reads anything except notes from friends and faxes from his son on the east coast. Mild-mannered all his life, now he throws occasional tantrums and turns his wheelchair defiantly toward the wall when the regimen of nursing-home life becomes too frustrating. Even reading the Bible requires too much attention and focus for him to manage. His speech now is so slurred that only a few of his closest friends and caregivers even try to understand. Most of his friends have have given up altogether and merely nod their heads helplessly at his futile attempts at communication.

In words that seem a mixed blessing to Everett and his family, his doctor now pronounces his heart and pulmonary system to be in great shape for a man his age. He could go on for years now! But would he really want to? While he is seldom able to articulate his deepest feelings, no doubt Everett occasionally wishes that he had died on that fateful day in October 1997. Each day is much like the previous one—diapers to be changed, a few hours in the uncomfortable wheelchair, a few hours of watching television that he can barely comprehend due to his hearing loss, a visit from friends from his church and his son, three meals that he can eat only with great effort, and an afternoon ice cream cone to keep his weight up. In his own words, Everett confesses his feelings of helplessness, "All I can do is wait to die!" While some persons die too soon, for others, such as Everett, the inexorable forces of life go on day after day long after life has lost its zest and meaning. Though the subtleties of theological reflection no longer come easily to him, I am sure that Everett also wonders if God hears his prayers anymore. Is his paralysis a burden that God has given him—one last test before he is finally called home to God, his wife and family—or a punishment for some previous misdeed or failure in his ministry? If it is the latter, there seems to be but little redemptive value in the hopelessness he feels each day.

Chronic illness is not, however, restricted to the elderly. Chronic illnesses and physical challenges such as epilepsy, spina bifida, Crohn's disease, and diabetes affect even the young, who must anticipate a lifetime of struggling with an illness they neither deserve nor asked for. Janet, a third-year medical student diagnosed with Crohn's disease, wonders if she can withstand the rigors of the psychiatric residency program which begins in the coming year. While most of the time her disease is under control, her memories of diarrhea, intestinal blockages, and surgery remind her that she can never take her health for granted. Unlike friends who act as if their youth is a guarantee of immortality and indestructibility, Janet and other youthful sufferers of chronic illness must deal with the challenges of their disease with each step and each day. Crossing the street, going to the bathroom, or cooking a meal can become of test of patience and stamina for persons with chronic diseases. What would be an occasional inconvenience for others has become for them normal and expected. While their disease may challenge them to personal and spiritual growth and thus become an unexpected blessing, it permeates every aspect of life, reminding them constantly of the fragility of their lives. While their disease may inspire their career choices, as it did in the case of Janet, occasionally still they ask themselves, "Why me? What test is God giving me? If only I were a little weaker, perhaps God wouldn't challenge me so!"

The woman with the flow of blood experienced the many dimensions of chronic illness. In the Judaism of her time, disease had moral and social as well as physiological components. Perhaps, deeper than the physical pain this woman endured was the spiritual pain that her illness inflicted upon her. The nature of her disease—involving the flow of blood—constantly rendered her ritually unclean. She could no longer attend synagogue and join in the corporate worship of her religious community. Further, as an unclean person, she was also taboo; that is, by even the most casual contact with others, she could render them ritually unclean. As the words of her scriptures pronounced, every bed she slept in or chair she sat upon would be rendered unclean, and everyone who touched her chair or bed, even accidently, would also be rendered unclean until they participated in the appropriate rituals of purification (Lev. 16:19–30). If she were married, she could no longer share the same bed with or have sexual relations with her husband without contaminating him. No doubt even old friends avoided her. Though they pitied her, they could not risk sharing her pain too intimately for fear that they too might become infected and unclean.

Yet, beyond even these indignities, her religious tradition's understanding of the connection between health and righteousness *and* disease and sin no doubt made her the object of the moral judgments of others and possibly even herself. There must be a reason why she is sick. The powerful words of Leviticus 26 gave one explanation: her illness was divine punishment for her personal unrighteousness. No doubt she—like many persons today—asked herself, "What have I done wrong to deserve this pain and humiliation? How can I get right with God and thus experience health once more?" While her first-century Jewish religion would not have shared the emphasis on the positive power of the mind characteristic of today's new age and human potential spiritualities, she might have, in her own way, asked herself the new age question, "Did I create the reality of my illness? If so, do I have the power to escape this prison of negativity?"

In her experience as a social and religious outcast, this woman embodied the experience of countless chronically ill persons who not only have felt physically isolated by their disease but also have experienced the shunning and moral judgment that others place upon them. Just think of the diatribes of preachers who identify AIDS with divine punishment for the "abomination" of homosexuality. The living, flesh-and-blood humans, whose primary aim in life is to love and be loved, are lost in the rhetoric of hate and fear.

That day, the woman with the hemorrhage needed more than a physical cure; she needed a healing that not only would change her physical well-being, but would transform her social and religious status, her spiritual and emotional life, her relationship with God, and her own self-image. Every aspect of her life would need transformation if she were truly to be made whole.

We can imagine the ambivalence that this woman felt when she heard that Jesus was coming to her town. Perhaps, when she heard the news, she was tempted to stay at home, bolt the doors, and wait until the healer had passed by. After all, her hopes had been shattered so often before. Did she really want to risk one more disappointment? Was Jesus any different from all the other physicians and healers she had encountered? Would he blame her for her illness, as so many other "good" people had done before? Would he preach a sermon to her on patience with adversity or the need to find healing through repentance? Was she emotionally strong enough that day to expect a miracle, even as she also prepared herself for one more failure?

In spite of her anxiety, doubt, and fear, the woman ventured forth from the safety of her home, risking once again the possibility of pain and disappointment. Her illness had taught her the meaning of courage and faith. Indeed, the courage and faith that guided her that day were grounded, not in the absence of fear and doubt, but in her willingness to do whatever was necessary in order to find healing, in spite of all the forces that encouraged her to endure her illness passively. So, on that day, this unnamed woman ventured forth with fear and trembling and ambivalence and anxiety. But she also ventured forth with courage and hope and the willingness to risk everything for one more chance to be healed.

In words that have echoed through the ages, inspiring healing and personal transformation, Jesus proclaimed to the woman, "Daughter, your faith has made you well; go in peace and be healed of your disease." Without her faith and her willingness to take a chance on God, this woman would never have been healed. As she came up to Jesus, her mind was centered on him above all else. Over and over again, she repeated the words of her personal mantra: "If I but touch his clothes, I will be healed," as a means of focusing her spiritual energy and dispelling any doubt or fear that might paralyze her. In that moment, Jesus the healer became her "ultimate concern," the center around which her whole life revolved. For a moment, all the other centers of her life—her past feelings of failure and disappointment, her physical pain, her sense of moral and spiritually inadequacy—retreated into the background. Jesus the healer alone became the center of her universe and the hope of her salvation and wholeness. All her previous feelings of indignity, doubt, and fear found their meaning in touching the healer who holds all things together in love. For a brief and life-transforming moment, she experienced the forces unleashed by the faith that reformer Martin Luther described as "a lively, reckless confidence in the grace of God." She touched God and in response received God's healing touch.

Today we hear much about the faith factor in health and illness. Hundreds of studies clearly indicate what the prescientific followers of Jesus experienced firsthand: trust in God and religious commitment promote physical, spiritual, and emotional well-being and can even dramatically transform our lives. Long before the current interest in spirituality and medicine, Jesus affirmed, "If you had faith the size of a mustard seed, you could say to this mulberry tree, 'be uprooted and planted in the sea,' and it would obey you" (Luke 17:6). Echoing Jesus' words, physicians and researchers now point out the importance of the placebo effect in health and illness. The theory of the placebo effect states that our belief systems can literally and quite dramatically manifest themselves in our physical well-being. For example, our trust in the efficacy of a medication not only activates the power of the placebo (a medically inert substance often used in pharmaceutical trials) but also enhances the benefits of chemical, homeopathic, and herbal medications. Routinely, in pharmaceutical trials the effects of placebos are as high as 30–40 percent, compared to the 80 percent effectiveness necessary to place a drug on the market. I have found that the effects of taking a pain reliever manifest themselves psychologically and physiologically long before they have become medically efficacious. No doubt, in our time, when certain herbal remedies such as Saint-John's-wort, ginseng, and golden seal, as well as alternative interventions such as magnets, are not yet regulated by the Food and Drug Administration and thus may be "uneven" in quality, these remedies still *work* even though the pill may contain only a minor amount of the advertised ingredient. Our faith can truly make us whole!

On the other hand, the power of negative thinking—what physicians and researchers describe as the nocebo effect—to elicit certain negative health symptoms, even though there is no chemical basis for their occurrence, has also been demonstrated in both pharmaceutic trials and everyday experience. Many of us come down with the symptoms of a cold or the flu within a few minutes of encountering a cold- or flu-ridden person or watching a pharmaceutical commercial on television! In clinical trials, persons often experience the suggested negative side effects of so-called medications—diarrhea, headache, nausea—even though they have ingested only a "sugar pill."

We can never underestimate the power of the mind or mental suggestion to cure or kill. Accordingly, the words that physicians, nurses, ministers, and friends use in relationship to those who are sick are morally and spiritually significant. Andrew Weil and others have spoken of the destructive impact of some of the language physicians use with the patients they treat.[1] When a physician says, "There is nothing more we can do," or describes the trajectory of an illness in absolutely negative terms, he or she is only further contributing to the phys-

---

1. Andrew Weil, *Spontaneous Healing* (New York: Alfred A. Knopf, 1995), 59–67.

ical and spiritual deterioration of the patient. Indeed, absolutely negative and hopeless prognoses may often be medically inaccurate, not only because each person uniquely manifests his or her illness, but also because there is always a slim chance of a spontaneous remission, not to mention the surprising release of healing energy that occurs through spiritual rituals such as prayer and the laying on of hands. Only a person of great faith and ego strength can transform her doctor's edict that persons like her have only a 10 percent survival rate to the affirmation, "I am not a statistic. I am a person. I can be one of the 10 percent who survive!"

Faith can move mental, physical, emotional, and spiritual mountains. Without the woman's willingness to reach out for healing, even though it meant violating social taboos related to gender and illness by touching Jesus, she would not have been healed. But the healing she received was not entirely in her own hands. Her faith shaped, but did not entirely create, her health reality. Jostled by the crowd, Jesus identified that "a power had gone forth from him" that could not be reduced to the impact of this woman's faith.

As is typical of the Gospels, this account does not give us a technical description or a philosophical treatise on the power that healed this unnamed woman. Nor can we assume that the diseases described in scripture can be identified with current ailments. Nevertheless, these diseases and their potential cures radically shaped the lives and relationships of those who experienced them. In similar crucial biblical contexts, the actual cause of certain events pushes the limits of the imagination: we receive no technical description of the virgin birth, the resurrection of Jesus, or the methodology to access divine healing. Indeed, the most pivotal moments of divine manifestation in scripture and in our personal lives defy any formulae we would employ to replicate them. While Christian fundamentalists seek clarity in understanding divine revelation and new agers formulate healing technologies, there is a virtue in the vagueness of these biblical accounts: their vague polyvalency invites us to open ourselves to the mysterious and uncontrollable presence of God *and* challenges us not to limit God's healing presence or the process of healing to *one* particular place, time, or methodology.

Healing of body, mind, and spirit may occur unexpectedly and in virtually any context *and* by virtually any modality, be it laying on of hands, prayer, surgery and medications, herbal remedies, or non-Western medicine. Dramatic and undramatic healings may occur in our lives, as the story of the paralyzed man whose friends brought him to Jesus suggests, even when we are doing absolutely nothing to secure the healing we need (Luke 5:17–26). In contrast to those who limit God's healing to a particular type of medicine or form of prayer, I believe that wherever there is healing, God is present, by whatever name or technique the healing is invoked.

In today's multireligious and multicultural context, we have acquired many words to describe the power that went forth from Jesus. The New Testament uses the word *dunamis,* a root of the modern word *dynamic,* to describe this overwhelming and life-transforming power of God. Traditional Chinese medicine and contemporary forms of healing such as acupuncture, acupressure, reiki, and therapeutic touch all speak of *chi* or *ki* as the universal energy giving life and vitality to all things.[2] Ayurvedic medicine of India uses the term *prana* to describe the life force in all things. From these traditions, we have learned that health and illness relate to the flow and balance of universal energy within our individual lives.

Although biblical writers lacked a sophisticated philosophical or medical understanding of this healing energy, the Hebraic and Christian tradition speaks of the *breath* and

---

2. For a clear and informative discussion of Chinese energy medicine and the philosophy of *chi,* see Bill Moyers, *Healing and the Mind* (New York: Main Street Books, 1995), and David Eisenberg, *Encounters with Qi* (New York: W. W. Norton, 1995).

pneuma of life as a manifestation of the lively Spirit of God
in the world of embodiment and inspiration. To be spiritually aligned with this life-giving breath is to have abundant
life, while to turn from the energy of God is to open oneself
to the spiritual, emotional, and physical imbalances that are
often manifest in illness. Jesus' own description of the rela-
tion of God and humankind in terms of the intimacy of the
vine and its branches suggests that our spiritual connection
with God manifests itself in the quality of every aspect of
our lives.

> Abide in me as I abide in you. Just as the branch cannot
> bear fruit by itself unless it abides in the vine, neither can
> you unless you abide in me. I am the vine, you are the
> branches. Those who abide in me and I in them bear much
> fruit, because apart from me you can do nothing. Whoever
> does not abide in me is thrown away like a branch and with-
> ers; such branches are gathered, thrown in the fire, and
> burned. If you abide in me, and my words in you, ask for
> whatever you wish and it will be done for you. (John
> 15·4–7)

God's spirit, the immanent power of God for wholeness and
salvation, was the ground of Jesus' healing ministry and is still
the source of healing in our time. The breath of God, touching
each one of us, is the dynamic source of life, empowerment,
creativity, and adventure. Unbridled and unbounded, this
divine spirit, whose presence is described by words such as
pneuma, chi, and *prana,* was the inspiring—the inbreathing
force—of Jesus' own ministry of personal, relational, spiritual,
and physical transformation. Invoking God's word to Isaiah,
Jesus proclaims, "The spirit of the Lord is upon me, because
he has anointed me to bring good news to the poor. He has
sent me to proclaim release to the captives and recovery of
sight to the blind, to let the oppressed go free, to proclaim the
year of the Lord's favor" (Luke 4:18–19).

The spirit of God calls us to trust that God's dynamic healing
energy is working within our own lives, calling us to abundance

even in the midst of chronic illness, personal struggle, and apparent failure. In the words of Agnes Sanford, healing is "simply channeling the flow of energy from God's being through man's being."[3] Using the example of electricity, Sanford adds that God's healing power is like the electricity that lights our homes. When we turn on the switch or plug in the lamp, the dynamic "healing light" of God is made manifest.

When I give a reiki healing treatment, I experience a healing energy flowing through the palms of my hands toward the recipient of the treatment. Although I have opened myself to this healing energy through the traditional reiki healing attunements and ongoing commitment to my spiritual life, this divine energy is not primarily the result of my own exertions. It wells up gracefully within me and beyond me, activated by my willingness to participate in the divine-human partnership. In this same spirit, our prayers and touch are factors in opening to God's omniactive and many-faceted healing energy. From this perspective, our faith or lack thereof can be a matter of life and death, spiritually and physically. In the gospel story, this woman's faith was necessary for the healing to occur, but her faith alone could not secure the healing. Her touch was itself a gift of God's energy working tenderly within her hopes and dreams.

This healing story points to a dimension of healing far more subtle than the proclamations of Christian and new age healers who place total responsibility for health and illness in the hands of the one who is in need or those who pray for her. "Just name it and claim it," shouts the evangelist. "Soak your problem with prayer, and you will be released of your burden," avers the faith healer. "Since you create your own reality, just change your mind, and the results will immediately follow," advises the new age spiritual healer. While such changes in

---

3. Agnes Sanford, *The Healing Light* (St. Paul, Minn. Macalester Park Publishing, 1972), 13.

attitude and spiritual focus make a difference and can bring about surprising personal healings, the dark side of these approaches is evident in the feelings of guilt, disappointment, and alienation from God that often emerge when the expected healing does not occur.

A young woman came to me in tears. A medical student and part-time researcher, Susan had struggled for years with migraine headaches that left her unable to study or go to class when they struck. "I've been praying for a healing," she confessed, "but I feel like a failure in God's eyes. My minister told me that if I only had enough faith, my migraines would disappear; but still nothing happens. He told me that my need for medication was a sign of how little faith I had in God. But every time my work load gets too heavy, I have another headache." The stress of her medical studies and her fear of a recurrence of her migraines were only increased by her pastor's spiritual advice. Whenever the migraines returned, she felt not only the pain and debilitation of the headaches but also the anxiety and stress of her spiritual failure.

In responding to her need, I suggested that she begin a practice of centering prayer, or Christian meditation, that involves the nonjudgmental focus on a particular prayer word, such as "peace," "God," "light," or "love" for fifteen to twenty minutes twice a day as a tool for spiritual growth. I reminded her that meditation and contemplative prayer not only enable us to experience God's presence in our lives but also have been found by medical researchers to produce striking physiological effects—the decrease of stress, the lowering of blood pressure, and the enhancement of the immune system's function. I also suggested that when she began to experience a migraine coming, she should immediately open herself to God's healing light and focus imaginatively on the divine light flowing through her body and opening the blood vessels in her head and neck. Further, I told her that she should not hesitate to take any appropriate, prescribed medication to alleviate her symptoms.

In my counsel to her, I did not guarantee that following my advice would cure her migraines, but I invited her to awaken to the healing and empowering force of God within her life just as she was, regardless of the outcome. I assured her that neither her illness nor her recovery was entirely in her own hands, but involved the interplay of her efforts, God's presence, anxiety-producing factors, and her own physical condition. I further assured her that the use of appropriate medication for pain relief was not a sign of her faithlessness, but rather reflected an openness to the God who heals through medication as well as meditation *and* pharmaceuticals as well as faith. Even if she did not experience a lessening of symptoms, she could still claim with the apostle Paul that God's grace is sufficient for her. In her creative synthesis of faith in God, personal spiritual discipline, and appropriate medication, she experienced freedom from the domination of her illness.

After a few months, during which we met regularly for meditation and conversation, Susan related that while she still had occasional migraines, the symptoms were much less severe and that she no longer lived in fear of the next headache. At my advice and in consultation with her physician, she began a course in acupuncture and biofeedback, which along with her daily discipline of prayer, meditation, and stress-reduction techniques, virtually eliminated her migraines. Susan's faith has led her to focus on preventing rather than merely responding to the migraines. Her faith, that is, her willingness to trust God's presence in her medications and spiritual practices had made her well, but her healing also involved the guidance of a spiritually open pastor, the graceful touch of God, and movements of grace within her body.

Tragically, there is much toxic or life-destroying theology that contaminates the experience of sickness and healing. Too often, both naïvely pious and conservative Christians and imaginative new agers blame the victim for her failure to get well. As we reflect on the creative image of healing for our time, we must avoid the extremes of *impotence* and *omnipotence* in our understanding of the interface of divine power and human responsibility. On the one hand, many persons attribute illness and health entirely to the hand of God. In their minds, the touch of God both cures and kills, for there must always be a divine reason for the events of life and death. Yet, if God is fully responsible for health, God must also be fully responsible for the tragedies of life—the auto accident that kills two promising teenagers, the cancer that strikes a young father, the blood tranfusion that brings HIV to a young child, the Alzheimer's that destroys the spirit.

We must also challenge the belief that God is unaware or unconcerned with our needs. Terms like *divine perfection* and *changelessness* often imply that if God were to experience the pain of the world, then God's divinity would be jeopardized. Such views hold that God's knowledge is somehow unchanging and complete and ultimately indifferent to our own joys and sorrows. For others, human freedom is protected by the image of a God who creates the world order and then, like an absentee landord, withdraws to let the world go on its way without intervention or guidance. In leaving us alone, this God also leaves us without any spiritual support in facing the challenges of life. In either case, we can expect neither help nor sympathy from a God who seems too distant and disinterested to bear our pain and suffering.

Still others exalt human power. "We create our own realities," they proclaim. "You are 100 percent responsible for every event in your life!" "If you have enough faith, you will be healed!" While these affirmations may free some of us from the prison of helplessness and liberate others to take responsibility for their lives, too often the burden of responsibility is so great and the reality that we believe we "create" so painful that we are tempted to abandon all responsibilty for the tragedies of life. Today many persons suffer from new age guilt. While I agree with the new age manual *A Course in Miracles* that we "are not the victims of the world we see," I also assert that we are not wholly responsible for our lives.

Between narcissistic omnipotence and debilitating helplessness lies a dynamic and holistic vision of faith and spirituality that affirms a dynamic and intricate ecology of life. In this vision, the power of God, faith, and a multitude of environmental, cultural, and familial factors are interwoven in the creation of each moment's experience. From this perspective, reality is seen as ever-changing, interconnected, and complex in nature. Although certain factors may appear to be compelling in determining our health and illness—(lifelong use of tobacco, unprotected sex, unhealthy eating habits, genetic inheritance)—no *one* factor is all-determining. Within this constantly shifting and evolving life ecology, health and illness, much like wealth and poverty, are the products of many factors.

From this perspective, we can discern the interplay of divine and human power in every healing encounter. While the mechanics of healing will always remain somewhat mysterious, I believe we can assert a divine-human partnership or synergy in every transformative event. The faith of the woman with the hemorrhage was essential for her healing. Her focus on Jesus' loving power placed the burdens of her illness in the background. No longer dominated by her illness, she began to see herself and the world differently. She saw her illness through the compassionate eyes of Jesus. Her faith empowered her to *touch God* in a way that enabled the energy of divine love to *touch* her life in a new way.

When Jesus asks his disciples, "Who touched me?" the touch he is describing is multidimensional and transformative in nature. Touch can be, as we know all too well, manipulative, objectifying, and dehumanizing—the kind of touch that blocks the healing touch of God. Yet gentle, healing, and welcomed touch can also be transforming and liberating. Without physical touch, the body wastes away, and without spiritual touch, the spirit withers. Focusing solely on Jesus as the source of her healing, this woman *touched* with her whole heart—she touched in the way that true lovers touch one another, as a parent caresses a child, as the helpless drowning man reaches up for rescue. And, in the midst of the crowd, God was *touched,* and the energy of divine healing flowed into her from within and without, dramatically transforming her life.

While we cannot fully understand it, some moments reveal God's character and power more than others, just as some moments reveal who we really are more fully than other moments. Although God is omnipresent and thus revealed in all things, God is also personal and chooses to reveal the divine power in innumerable personal ways. Whether it be the intensification of divine presence in the incarnation and healing ministry of Jesus, in intense moments of inspiration and spiritual ecstasy in our own lives, or in the ardent hope for healing and the actual healing of this woman's illness, God is truly present and truly received in the interplay of events to bring forth a dramatic and exceptional change. As many faith traditions assert, such high-intensity releases of divine energy, often described as "miracles," are not contrary to nature. Rather, they reveal a deeper force at work within the processes of life—the love manifest in the divine circle "whose center is everywhere but whose circumference is nowhere." When we touch God with all of our being, with faith as well as doubt, we may experience another kind of touch, a deeper touch, *the touch of God, which comes from within and from without*—a healing touch that "makes all things new."

These exceptional moments of divine energy and inspiration may occur gradually or dramatically, but in each case, they reflect a heightening of God's presence in partnership with greater human openness. While it is always God's will that we have abundant life, this experience of abundant life may not be fully realized for many reasons, both environmental and personal. Still, each disease manifests a unique configuration of causes that shapes our lives at any given moment, and this configuration can be changed. Within the constant atomic and cellular transformations that are constantly occuring at every level of our bodies, the divine energy may burst forth within our lives, and healing can occur at any moment.

The physical cure we seek for ourselves or others may not come to pass. But even when we may not be physically cured of our illness, *we are still healed when our touch joins the touch of God.* Within the many factors impinging our lives in each moment, God may have something more important and more expansive than physical healing awaiting us.

On that day when she touched Jesus, this woman experienced a miracle—a release of divine power that addressed her deepest needs. Her chronic illness was cured, but just as important as the physical cure she received, she experienced a healing that encompassed every aspect of her spiritual life, relationships, memories and emotions, and place in society. She was now truly well; she could now go forth in peace and wholeness. The same transformation can and does happen today for all who reach out to receive and give the touch of God. This transformation can touch your own life too!

An Experiment in Healing and Wholeness

Today, many persons are discovering the power of meditative prayer to transform their physical and spiritual lives. Centered in God's presence, we not only experience greater creativity and insight into God's direction for our lives, we also experience a reduction in the stresses of life. Among Christians, the practice of centering prayer has provided ordinary persons with an effective method of experiencing God's still, small voice amid their busy schedules.

The practice of centering prayer is exceedingly simple. The hard part is simply taking time each day to be still. Centering prayer weaves together the experience of focus, distraction, letting go, and refocusing in the following manner:

1. While sitting in a comfortable position, close your eyes and say a brief prayer such as the Lord's Prayer or an extemporaneous prayer.
2. Begin to repeat your prayer word, that is, a meaningful word such as "love," "peace," "joy," "light," "Christ."
3. When your mind wanders, simply bring it back to the prayer word without judgment or self-criticism.
4. After fifteen to twenty minutes, conclude gently with a moment of prayer and relaxation.

Today, persons are also transforming their understanding of Bible study. In the spirit of Ignatius of Loyola, the founder of the Society of Jesus (the Jesuits), who discovered God's presence while he was recovering from a war injury, many persons are integrating scripture study with imaginative visualizations. These biblical visualizations invite the reader to become part of the gospel story as he or she imagines the scene, encounters Jesus, and becomes a character in the drama of divine transformation.

As you seek to embody the healing touch of God, take a moment to reread the passage at the beginning of this chapter. Imagine yourself as the woman suffering from the chronic disease. (You may choose any gender to represent her life experience.) What is the disease that is troubling you? How has it changed your life? What limitations has it placed on you? Imagine what it feels like to be socially unclean. Imagine what it feels like to be constantly disappointed in your quest for healing.

You have just heard that an amazing healer is coming to your town. You feel a certain ambivalence: you want him to heal you, but you are afraid of failure and disappointment. You worry that he may even judge you for your illness. Experience your ambivalence as you choose to find Jesus.

As you reach the center of town, a crowd has gathered. What is the crowd like? Does anyone notice you? In the midst of the crowd, you see the healer, Jesus. What does he look like? What is he doing? As you begin to walk toward Jesus, you chant the words, "If I but touch his clothes, I will be made well." Let the words flow from your lips as you edge your way through the crowd, heedless of the dirty looks you may be receiving.

At last, you are standing next to Jesus. You reach out to touch him. What is it like to touch the healer? But, as you touch him, something unexpected happens. A power flows from his garment into your body. What does the power feel like? Experience that power in whatever way is appropriate (as a healing light, an odd tingling, a sharp jolt). See this power engulfing your chronic illness, permeating it, transforming it, cleansing it, and releasing it. How are you feeling now?

Though the crowd surrounds and jostles you, the only one you see is Jesus. Now he turns to you and asks, "Who touched me?" You come before him on bended knee. In that moment, he simply says, "Your faith has made you well; go in peace, be healed of your disease." How do you feel when you hear these words spoken specifically to you? What is it like to know that Jesus is addressing you personally?

You get up slowly and head for home. You know that your life will never be the same. You are healed. You are at peace. Whether or not your own chronic illness immediately disappears or continues as part of your life, you now have God's healing and peace. Take a moment to say a prayer of thanksgiving for the dynamic power of God that flows through your life.

Many persons find that journaling their imaginative meditations is transformative. As they write down their experience, new dimensions emerge and new insights occur. Further, the process of journaling serves to create a map of one's own spiritual journey and enables a person to appropriate consciously God's gentle and dramatic movements in her or his life. After experiencing this or another guided meditation, you may choose to write down your thoughts and experiences as a means of discerning God's call in your life today.

Now in Jerusalem by the Sheep Gate there is a pool, called in Hebrew Beth-zatha, which has five porticoes. In these lay many invalids—blind, lame, and paralyzed. One man was there who had been ill for thirty-eight years. When Jesus saw him lying there and knew that he had been there a long time, he said to him, "Do you want to be made well?" The sick man answered him, "Sir, I have no one to put me into the pool when the water is stirred up; and while I am making my way, someone else steps down ahead of me." Jesus said to him, "Stand up, take your mat and walk." At once the man was made well, and he took up his mat and began to walk. Now the day was a sabbath. So the Jewish leaders said to the man who had been cured, "It is the sabbath; it is not lawful for you to carry about your mat." Buthe answered them, "The man who made me well said to me, 'Take up your mat and walk.'" They asked him, "Who is the man who said to you, 'Take it up and walk'?" Now the man who had been healed did not know who it was, for Jesus had disappeared in the crowd that was there. Later Jesus found him in the temple and said to him, "See, you have been made well! Do not sin any more, so that nothing worse happens to you."

(John 5:2–14)

Chapter Three

Do You Want to Be Healed?

A number of years ago, our family took a journey through the British Isles. In the spirit of the Beatles' album, our journey was a "magical, mystery tour" as we explored the sacred places of the Celts, Druids, and early Christians. We pondered the intricate architecture of Stonehenge and walked among the stones at nearby Avebury. We hiked to the top of the Tor of Glastonbury, known in the Arthurian legends as the magical isle of Avalon. We explored the pathways and gardens of Findhorn, one of the birthplaces of the new age movement, where nature deities were said to communicate their ecological and horticultural wisdom to its founder Eileen Caddy.[1] We hiked the verdant paths and prayed in the Chapel of the Isle of Iona, where Columba first planted Christianity in Scotland. A few years later, we took a spiritual pilgrimage to the energy points of Sedona, Arizona, a mecca of new age spirituality, and to Canyon de Chelly, an historic center for Native American spirituality. Throughout history and in every culture, humankind

---

1. For an extensive discussion of new age spirituality, see Bruce Epperly, *Crystal and Cross: Christians and the New Age in Creative Dialogue* (Mystic, Conn. Twenty-third Publications, 1996), and Ted Peters, *The Cosmic Self* (San Francisco: HarperSanFrancisco, 1991).

has experienced certain places as mysterious and miraculous. Places such as Lourdes, Fatima, and Medjugorje are magnets for spiritual pilgrims and persons in search of spiritual and physical healing. In such "thin places," as Celts described them, the boundary between the divine and human is particularly transparent. Healing energies and spiritual guidance are transmitted to spiritual seekers. Even the secularist, whose worldview has little room for divinity, may note the "set-apartness" of churches by her or his reverent behavior and marvel at the architectural beauty of the Sistine Chapel in Rome or the cathedral of Notre Dame in Paris.

In that holiest of cities, Jerusalem, one such "thin place" was to be found at the pool of Bethzatha. It was a place where broken and desperate humanity could be "touched by an angel." According to the legend of the place, every so often the divine hand would move and its touch would ripple the waters. For those who were vigilant, the rippling waters were an invitation to healing, *if* they could seize the moment and lower themselves into the pool or be placed there by close friends or helpers. Thousands, no doubt, came in search of a cure, and, no doubt, thousands left uncured and disappointed, perceiving that they had arrived too late to receive the blessing of the place. Still, pilgrims came day after day, their need so great that they would wait patiently for the hour of their deliverance, no matter how long it might take. Others may well have taken up residence under the arches. With nowhere else to go, they hoped against hope for the rare moment when the waters would ripple and they might find a cure. While today we might recognize the place as an anomalous center of geothermal activity, from which healing minerals and salts are released from the bowels of the earth, to the faithful pilgrims and their families God was at work, providing a means of healing to those who had the requisite faith and perseverance.

For thirty-eight years, this unnamed man lived in the shadow of the pool, awaiting a cure that never came. While the scriptures do not give us the exact nature of his illness, the overall description of his encounter with Jesus implies that his illness involved a paralysis of body, mind, emotions, and spirit. For thirty-eight years, his only companions had been those who were blind, lame, and paralyzed and their caregivers and families. No doubt, the juxtaposition of his companions' cries of pain and hopelessness and their expectations that a cure was just a moment away permeated the man's psyche and dominated his thinking.

Once upon a time, he had friends who kept him company and sought to help him get to the pool when moments of healing occurred. But keeping vigil with the sick is hard work, and few can devote their lives to the full-time care of others. Today many of us work hard to adjust our already busy daily schedules just to visit a friend in the hospital or a parent in a nursing home. Perhaps this man may have driven his friends away by the passivity and the victim mentality that dominated his thinking. Perhaps they still came for a few minutes each day, taking time out from their jobs and responsibilities, knowing they would hear the same litany of woe and helplessness that they had heard the day before.

Contemporary medical research suggests that all illness has a psychosomatic component and that the burdens of physical illness can overwhelm even the most hopeful spirit in the same way that negative attitudes can manifest themselves in physical fatigue. But on this day the man was alone, and his hopes of a cure had nearly vanished, along with his friends and family. His experience of social isolation was as devastating as the physical paralysis. Perhaps he recognized that he was likely to live out his life waiting for something to happen, alternately hoping that somehow God would intervene supernaturally and despairing that nothing would ever alter his life of passive misery.

But that day, an unexpected stranger entered this invalid's life. While most persons who walked by averted their eyes and closed their ears to the pleas of the sufferers, this stranger stopped right where the man was lying, fixed his eyes upon him, and asked the startling question that would transform his life: "Do you want to be made well?" What a ridiculous question to ask a man who has been paralyzed for thirty-eight years! How insensitive can the healthy Jesus be toward the pain and suffering of the man who lies before him? Doesn't everyone want to be healed? Doesn't everyone want new life? We all desire spiritual transformation, don't we? But perhaps for the paralyzed man, and *for ourselves,* the answer is really not that clear-cut. How would we answer if Jesus came to us today, revealed to us our deepest hurt, and then asked, "do you want to be healed?"

Strangely enough, the paralyzed man did not respond in the affirmative. Perhaps he did not know of Jesus' healing power, and out of a sense of personal offense at the audacity of such an obvious and insensitive question, he chose not to share his deepest hopes. Nevertheless, he eventually replied, and his response to Jesus was quite self-revealing: "Sir, I have no one to put me into the pool when the water is stirred up; and while I am making my way, someone else steps down ahead of me." You can almost hear the anguish and hopelessness in his voice. For thirty-eight years at the pool, this man has yearned for a healing. No doubt, on many occasions he dragged himself toward the pool, exhausting his last ounce of spiritual and physical stamina, but he never made it to the pool in time. He had never experienced the angelic touch, nor had he ever fully reached out to be healed.

There were good reasons, the man asserted, why he had not been healed. "First, no one cares enough about me to stand beside me throughout the day and carry me to the pool at the right time. I am all alone and have no resources to assist my healing. Why aren't people more charitable and patient with the infirm and paralyzed? Why doesn't somebody help me?" Second, the other infirm persons who daily gather around the pool are also unconcerned about his plight. "Someone gets ahead of me. By the time I get there, the moment of healing has passed. Don't they realize how long I've been here? Don't they realize that it's my turn to be healed now? Don't they care about persons other than themselves?" The paralyzed man believed that his healing lay entirely in the hands of others, and not in his own attitudes and behaviors. He lived in the world of the "if only": if only I had friends . . . . if only someone put me at the head of the line . . . if only someone else could solve my problems . . . if only other persons were less self-interested . . . then I would be healed!

Fatigued by years of waiting, the man claimed no personal responsibility for his own illness. Just as he blamed others for the persistence of his illness, he depended entirely on others for his cure. Clearly his paralysis was spiritual and emotional as well as physical in nature. While some persons today claim omnipotent power of the mind to determine their fate, this man clearly saw himself as an impotent victim of powers beyond himself. At that moment, he was so caught up in his own personal drama that he did not realize that the Healer was standing right before him. He was so hyponotized by the lore of this healing place that he assumed that there was only *one* way he could be healed. He never asked himself what might happen if he jumped into the pool anyway, regardless of whether he was first or second or tenth in line. Like the Pharisees who will soon confront him with his infraction of the sabbath laws, this man's own spiritual myopia may have prevented him from recognizing the possibility of *other* healing moments and *other* healing modalities. While the pool at Bethzatha and places like Findhorn, Lourdes, Sedona, and Iona may be uniquely powerful places for the revelation of divine inspiration and healing power, this same power is also distributed in the most common and unlikely places. Every place and every moment can become a "thin" place, an epiphany, opening us to the life-transforming presence of God. Divine healing can be mediated by chemotherapy, surgery, and medication; it can also be mediated by healing touch, acupuncture, and prayer.

Although Jesus had compassion on this man, his compassion did not blind him to the man's responsibility for his cure. Jesus was neither a co-dependent caregiver, compulsively called to solve everyone's problems, nor an overaccommodating enabler, whose kindness would only further disempower the paralyzed man. Jesus simply asked, "Do you want to be made well?" and then commanded this man, in spite of all his excuses, to "stand up, take your mat and walk!" If you want to be healed, you need to take responsibility for your life. You need to take the risk of failure if you are going to walk again. You need to face the pain of your passivity and your role in your illness, if you are to be made well. If health and illness result from many factors, including spiritual and emotional as well as environmental and physical forces, then our commitment to stand on our own feet and to claim the resources God has given us can heighten the forces of recovery and healing at work in our lives. Our own commitment to healing, like the faith of the woman with the hemorrhage and the man at the pool at Bethzatha, can make the difference between life and death *and* health and illness.

Now we do not know the mechanics of the healing at the pool of Bethzatha. John's Gospel simply states, "Jesus said to him, 'Stand up, take up your mat and walk.' At once the man was made well, and he took up his mat and began to walk" (John 5:8–9). But, like the healing of the woman with the hemorrhage, Jesus' healing at the pool has two components: the divine command and the human response. This time, however, the command came before the interplay of faith and action. The grace of God precedes our conscious acceptance of it. Even as the man at the pool was fixating on his paralysis and enumerating the reasons why he could not stand on his own two feet, Jesus was calling him to the wholeness born of responsibility and empowerment. As Jesus' loving commitment to this man's healing embraced him, this man momentarily forgot his paralysis and his own spiritual passivity. In a split second, he stood up spiritually, risking disappointment and failure *and* freeing himself from the burdens of thirty-eight years of illness; then, from the inside out, he stood up physically and began to walk.

Without Jesus' empowering words, the man would have remained paralyzed. But apart from his effort to stand up on his own, the healing power would never have flowed through him. Sometimes you have to really want to be healed, and you have to commit yourself to transformation with all your heart, in order for God's power to manifest itself in your life. For those who embrace the divine-human synergy, miraculous releases of power may occur in body, mind, spirit, and relationships.

At fifty, Bob was presented with a second chance to change his life. For nearly two decades, Bob's whole life centered around his work. Sixty- and seventy-hour weeks were the norm for this ambitious attorney. Constantly on the go, his diet was fast food, deli sanwiches, pizza, and coffee. With little time to exercise, his weight ballooned to more than 250 pounds. Although he had been married for two decades, he spent very little time with his wife and children. Their holidays were regularly interrupted by crises at the office. Unless he was productive, Bob felt useless. Despite Bob's hectic schedule, life went along smoothly until he felt the pains of angina. He denied the pain and the shortness of breath until his wife demanded that he see a doctor. Bob was shocked when his doctor told him that he was a heart attack waiting to happen. If he continued his lifestyle, he would either be dead or need a heart bypass within a year. In response to the news, Bob immersed himself more completely in his work. He continued to eat fast foods and avoid aerobic exercise until his wife confronted him: "Do you want to die or be healthy? Make up your mind. I don't want to be a widow in the next few years."

At that moment, Bob knew that the paths of life and death stood before him. He knew that he could no longer live by denial of his physical or spiritual condition. He knew he would have to change his life. But did he really want to? Did he really want to make the changes necessary for a healthy life? As he talked with his physician and his pastor, Bob realized that changing his diet and exercising more often were only the tip of the iceberg. He needed to change his whole way of looking at the world. He needed to discover what really mattered to him.

With the help of his physician and his pastor, Bob drew up a life plan that included a low-fat and low-calorie diet, regular exercise, and centering prayer for spiritual growth and stress reduction. He also realized that he would need to develop new habits if he was to regain his health. Although it took every ounce of courage and self-discipline, Bob tackled his greatest addiction: his compulsion to work long hours and see himself as indispensible to the law firm he managed. Though it was a struggle, Bob began to spend more evenings at home and at his children's extracurricular events. He learned to delegate responsibilities to his junior partners. He took most Saturdays and Sundays off and even left his cell phone at home when he was not on call.

Today Bob is fifty pounds lighter and angina-free. He has discovered the joy of family life and community service. He and his wife are now as close to one another as they were in the first days of their marriage. Bob is changed person. He chose to be well, despite all his misgivings and compulsions.

Sometimes we must stand up in the midst of our fears. Standing up for health and well-being may mean risking failure and ridicule. Standing up for spiritual and emotional health may mean upsetting the status quo in our own family and in our own life. It may mean letting go of our previous ambitions and values. Health, like the grace of God, may be—as theologian Dietrich Bonhoeffer proclaimed—free, but it is never cheap. Creative transformation is always accompanied by destruction and sacrifice. As we seek our own healings, we must open ourselves to God's examination of our own motivations: Do we really want to get well? How much are we willing to sacrifice in order to have a new life?

Despite the pain and debilitation that often accompany illness, for many persons, sickness has its own personal advantages. As medical intuitive Carolyn Myss suggests, many persons define themselves by their wounds and expect the whole world to adjust to their real or imagined disabilities. According to Myss, this attitude can be described as "woundology." Yet fixation on our woundedness has a tremendous cost: " When we define ourselves by our wounds, we burden and lose our physical and spiritual energy and open ourselves to the risk of illness."[2]

Early in life, many children learn the advantages of physical illness. In the darkness of the night when fears overwhelm the child, she may cry out to her parents. But more often than not, she receives little parental "mirroring" for her fears and anxiety. However, as soon as she invokes the possibility of an upset stomach, she finds that her parents rush to her side. Later on in life, we realize that a sore throat can mean a holiday from school, and a cold can liberate us from an unwelcome examination.

When we are ill, especially with obvious symptoms, we can claim the sympathy of others. We don't have to make serious decisions or take responsibility for our lives. We can manipulate others into doing what we want, and we can sit idly on the sidelines and let others take care of us. As long as we are ill, we believe that there will be someone who will take care of us. But there is a cost to the conscious and unconscious benefits of illness. Our world may shrink to the size of the illness itself. A sore throat may mean a holiday from school, but it also means passively looking out the window as the neighborhood children play games after school. Many persons are so unconsciously committed to their illness that they give themselves no opportunity to experience the joy of well-being. Further, our failure to take responsibility for our participation in illness or the opportunity to grow amid illness also diminishes our own personal stature. The personal stature born of courageous self-transformation cannot occur apart from the active

2. Carolyn Myss, *Why People Don't Heal and How They Can* (New York: Harmony Books, 1997), 6.

recognition that, regardless of what life gives us, we still have the freedom to choose how we interpret our lives. As psychiatrist Viktor Frankl asserts, even in the most dehumanizing situations, such as the Nazi death camps, prisoners still can find freedom when they recognize that sickness, torture, and imprisonment do not rob them of the freedom to choose to be human and to commit themselves to an unknown future.[3]

As he listened to the man's excuses, Jesus simply challenged him to look at his life and his lifelong personal choices: How much do you really want to be well, especially when health will mean greater responsibility and more demands on your life? In that moment, the paralyzed man chose to let go of his passivity and his excuses. He chose to be an actor rather than a victim. For a fleeting moment, he chose to become responsible for his future. As he walked, at first haltingly and then with growing confidence, he entered the brave new world of employment, responsibility, and self-affirmation.

But the day was the sabbath, and to perform even as simple an action as carrying his mat violated the law of his religion. Once the object of pity and charity, now he became the object of anger and righteous indignation. In *People of the Lie* psychiatrist Scott Peck asserts that many persons not only fear but also unconsciously undermine the healing and growth of others, especially members of their own family.[4] Life transforming health and vitality are often threatening to the status quo within a dysfunctional family, church, or other institution. Old roles and dependencies are no longer in effect. After years of rigorous observance in a family or social unit, dysfunctional patterns take on the aura of unchanging religious law. When a member of a family or a good friend experiences an emotional, physical, or spiritual healing, she is no longer a helpless inferior in need of support or special treatment; she has now

---

3. Victor Frankl, *Man's Search for Meaning* (New York: Washington Square Press, 1963).

4. M. Scott Peck, *People of the Lie* (New York: Simon & Schuster, 1983).

become an equal, able to stand on her own two feet. Her new-found health of body, mind, or spirit may challenge the "emperor's new clothes" of family dysfunctionality, for some families are tragically bound together by the negative attention paid to their "sick" members. A family, for example, may choose unconsciously to provide inadequate medication or mental health care for its schizophrenic child in order to have a buffer between emotionally distant parents, a dependent but loyal child, or a companion for the parents' old age.

In focusing on one member's dysfunctionality, other family members do not have to face the meaninglessness, depression, or neuroses that characterize their own lives. When the child stands up on his feet and begins to journey toward spiritual, physical, or emotional well-being, the parents may uncon-sciously sabotage the child's healing process by undercutting the therapeutic process or withdrawing funds for medication or psychotherapy. Indeed, in some families, a parent's own mental stability is bought at the price of his or her own child's mental illness. Since all healing is relational and eco-logical, the movement toward well-being in one person can positively transform a whole family unit or congregation, bringing well-being to everyone, or it can be confronted with resistance and denial.[5] Jesus' own contemporaries feared what might happen if God's healing presence broke through the strict rules of social and religious behavior. Their sense of their own personal wellness, ritual holiness, and spiritual superior-ity required others to be spiritual inferiors and social outcasts.

The threatening nature of health and well-being is obvious in social issues, as well as in personal and family relationships. As a nation, we must ask ourselves, "Do we really want liberty and justice for all? Do we really want to rebuild the inner cities and provide adequate education and training for the poor?" If

5. For a discussion of health and illness in family life and congregational set-tings, see Edwin Friedman, *Generation to Generation* (New York: Guilford Press, 1985).

racism is, as some have described it, "America's original sin," infecting every aspect of our society, how badly do we really want to address the racial inequalities that undergird the power and financial well-being of the white majority? While every person, regardless of her or his birth or ethnicity, is responsible for standing up for transformation, how much are we willing to sacrifice for the well-being of those whose shouldering of the heavy burden of discrimination may require a helping hand for them to stand up? It takes a tremendous amount of courage to support the uncertain growth of those who have long been sick or underprivileged, even as we let go of our long-held privileges of class or health status. But when transformation of the "sick" individual or group occurs in a dysfunctional family or church group, or an unjust social structure, there is also the possibility that the whole system may be healed!

Self-responsibility is hard won and easily lost. When the religious leaders challenged the man for carrying his mat on the sabbath, his answer was factual, but only partly true. Rather than affirming his recent miracle or challenging their narrow and life-denying religiosity, the man once again made an excuse for his new life situation. In fact, he blamed Jesus for his violation of the law! "The man who made me well said to me, 'Take up your mat and walk.'" He omitted the fact that *he* was now the one carrying his mat. Perhaps he has not yet realized the extent of his new found self-responsibility. Old patterns of thought are difficult to break. For thirty-eight years, his personality had constellated around his victim mentality. His perspective would require a constant commitment to choose the course of his life and unceasing willingness to take responsibility for the consequences of his decisions. This transformation was still was in its infancy. His words to the religious leaders echo the ancient legend of Adam and Eve. When God confronts Adam and Eve with their choice to eat the fruit of the forbidden tree, Adam blames Eve, while Eve blames the snake. That day, the healed man blamed Jesus for his violating of the law, even though the bedroll was in his own hands!

While Jesus could easily have publicly defended his role in the the man's healing and taken responsibility for the cure, John simply notes that "Jesus had disappeared in the crowd." The point of the healing was spiritual as well as physical: to empower this man to stand on his own two feet and take responsibility for his destiny. While the divine presence would continue to be at work in his life, he now had to commit himself to a spiritually responsible life, regardless of the personal or social cost. In partnership with God, he had to become his own authority on his spiritual and physical life from now on. Authentic spiritual growth is not about excessive dependence on God or slavish obedience to religiously grounded rules; spiritual growth nurtures freedom, creativity, and interdependence with God and our companions.

Later that day, we catch another glimpse of the nature of this man's ailment and the necessity for a whole hearted commitment to the healing process if he is to remain well. Jesus finds the man in the temple and challenges him to claim his role in healing and sickness, "See, you have been made well! Do not sin anymore so that nothing worse happens to you." At first, these words appear to echo the linear, cause-and-effect calculation of rewards and punishments articulated in Leviticus. But in light of Jesus' denial of such simplistic understandings of the relationship of health and illness (John 9:1–3) and his affirmation that God seeks abundant life for all persons (John 10:10), his words of warning take on a deeper meaning. Clearly this man had to fight for his health each step of the way. And so must we! The healed man was given the antidote to his spiritual and physical paralysis: Stand up. . . . Choose life. . . . Be responsible for your decisions. . . . Don't play the victim. He knew what he needed to do to remain healthy, but Jesus reminded him that within moments of his healing, he had already returned to the attitude of passive victimization that had led to his prolonged illness. Like a member of a twelve-step group, this man could maintain his healing only by committing himself daily to a life of integrity and self-responsibility in partnership with a higher power. The spiritual and physical momentum resulting from his healing could be insured only if he was constantly vigilant toward the internal and external forces that had kept him passive, dependent, and sick. With all of his being, he had to say yes to life over and over again. He had to choose to be responsible in the smallest as well as the largest areas of his life. He had to choose to say no to the voices of those whose behaviors would keep him dependent and passive. He had to be "transformed by the constant renewing of his mind" rather than being conformed to old habits of health, behavior, and social custom. His healing was not merely a miraculous moment but an evolving creative process of relationships with himself, God, and others.

In his book *The Prophetic Imagination,* Old Testament scholar Walter Brueggemann asserts that one of the defining characteristics of the Hebraic tradition of prophecy was the presention of an alternative reality to the evil and injustice of the present age.[6] Cut free from the prison of the status quo, we can imagine and then embody creative alternatives to our current lifestyle and value system. For a moment the paralyzed man shared in this prophetic imagination, when, in spite of the heaviness of habit and social custom, he saw himself standing up and then stood up on his own! He imagined himself as empowered and self-determining in mind, body, and spirit. He visualized an alternative future and novel possibility, and in partnership with Jesus he embodied that alternative. Healing is always to some degree counter-cultural, for healing means seeing our lives differently, awakening to new talents, saying no to limiting visions of ourselves, whether they come from the church or temple, the physician, the prognosis for our illness, or from caregiving persons whose own stability depends upon our weakness and dependence.

---

6. Walter Brueggemann, *The Prophetic Imagination* (Philadelphia: Fortress, 1978).

In this healing encounter by the pool at Bethzatha, we see a God very different from those images of a God who sanctions the status quo or supports legalistic structures of faith. Instead, God is the source of unrest, prophetic imagination, transformation, and adventure in our individual lives and relationships. God constantly agitates the comfortable and comforts the agitated! In every moment of life, God is presenting us with an image of who we can be in that particular moment and that particular setting. God reminds us of our deepest personal dreams. This divine inspiration may come as an insight, a feeling of dissatisfaction with our present life, or a synchronous encounter. But it never allows us to "stay seated"; it always bids us to "stand up and walk." Following God's moment-by-moment guidance may mean listening to our imagination and awakening to the dreams of a new world. It may also mean challenging unjust social structures or national priorities that perpetuate poverty and illness. For Desmond Tutu and Nelson Mandela in South Africa, it meant both agitation for freedom, justice, and change, and reconcilation with the very persons who had oppressed them. For others, it may mean imagining alternative behaviors within a dysfunctional family. When we follow God's guidance, *our wounds are transformed into wonders!*

In this man's life, God did a new thing, and this same God is constantly doing a new thing in our lives. God urges us moment by moment and day by day to claim our personal healing and to stand on our own two feet as we journey toward the exciting future God is planning for us.

An Experiment in Healing and Wholeness

In the spirit of the prophetic imagination, we will once again enter into the scriptural narrative via guided meditation. As you begin your meditation, take a few minutes to be still and listen for God's presence in your life. After reading the passage, place yourself in the sandals of the paralyzed man.

Look around you at the scene at the pool of Bethzatha. Notice your companions, listen to their conversations, observe the passersby. Look at the healing pool in the distance. For a moment, ponder your situation as a person who has been the victim of a life-diminishing paralysis.

Now reflect on your own life situation: Why are you here? Where are you feeling paralyzed today? In what ways does this passivity dominate your life? How have you been limited by these tendencies in your life?

As you ruminate on your own experience of paralysis, a figure stands before you and engages your attention. You recognize the figure as Jesus the healer. What thoughts and emotions arise from your encounter with the Healer?

As you gaze at one another, Jesus asks one very simple question: "Do you want to be healed?" What is your response? What you say to Jesus? Do you have any excuses for your present situation in life? Are there any benefits of your current situation? Do you really want to be healed of your ailment?

In the silence, Jesus commands you, "Stand up and walk." See yourself slowly raising your body and awkwardly taking one step after another. What is it like to stand up and move around for the first time in many years?

What do you need to do in order to stand up and go forth in your own life? What is it like to feel the burden of passivity and paralysis lifted from your life? With the burden of your own particular paralysis lifted, where will you go and what will you do right now? Now see yourself walking and then running with the ecstasy of liberation.

In your own imagination, see yourself actively engaged in some new and creative behavior. As you explore this new-found freedom, take a moment to thank God for urging you to take responsibility for your life.

Recently, my wife Kate gave me a T-shirt that states, "Sweat your prayers." In light of today's emphasis on walking, I invite you to explore the many dimensions of walking prayer. Many persons enjoy slow, meditative walks in which they seek to be mindful of their breathing or the very process of walking itself. Still others focus on the beauty of the environment as they stroll through the woods or along the shore.

In my own morning spiritual disciplines, I often practice an aerobic walking prayer. While I have used a number of approaches, the following is one of the easiest. As I begin my walk, I simply notice the quality of my breathing and attempt to breathe deeply at a regular rate. After a few minutes, I change the focus of my breath. With each breath, I imagine healing light entering my body, permeating my mind and brain, neck and shoulders, heart and circulatory system, stomach, legs, and feet. As I exhale, I let go of any tension or stress I may be experiencing at the moment. When my mind wanders, I return to my focus on healing light without judgment or self-criticism. As I conclude my walk, I experience the healing light of God surrounding my body with energy and protection as I put on "the whole armor of God."

As he walked along, he saw a man blind from birth. His disciples asked him, "Rabbi, who sinned, this man or his parents, that he was born blind?" Jesus answered, "Neither this man nor his parents sinned; he was born blind so that God's works might be revealed in him. We must work the works of him who sent me while it is day; night is coming when no one can work. As long as I am in the world, I am the light of the world." When he said this, he spat on the ground and made mud with the saliva and spread the mud on the man's eyes, saying to him, "Go wash in the pool of Siloam" (which means Sent). Then he went and washed and came back able to see.

(John 9:1–7; see also John 9:8–41)

Chapter Four

Beyond Impotence
and Omnipotence

"*W*ho sinned, this man or his parents, that he was born blind?" This question reflects the quest to understand the reason for personal suffering, as well as to discern our own responsibility in sickness and in health. Long before the problem of evil became an issue for philosophical speculation, it was an issue of personal meaning. All theological reflection begins with the experience of pain and the quest for healing. My experience dealing with human agony in the hospital room and in the pastor's study constantly reminds me that even the staunchest atheist seeks to find a meaning to the suffering he and his family experience.

Historically there have been many attempts to explain the suffering that persons face. "Who sinned?" is catalyst for one possible answer. Today, with the growing impact of Asian religions and the new age movement on American life, many persons see suffering as grounded wholly in one's own personal responsibility and the penance for deeds in a past life. The Eastern and contemporary new age doctrines of karma proclaim that a person reaps in this lifetime what he or she has sown in a previous lifetime. According to this belief system, every event is conditioned by our attitudes, decisions, and actions from an earlier time. New age healer Louise Hay proclaims that "we are 100 percent responsible for all of our experiences. . . . We create our experiences, our reality, and

everyone in it." Like many other new age thinkers, Hay
believes that we create our current realities by our attitudes
and thoughts. By our thought patterns we draw certain persons
and events into our lives. While many earlier Christian
thinkers asserted that good and evil fall equally from the hand
of an omnipotent God, many of today's new age thinkers see
good and evil as the result of the omnipotent power of the
human mind. For them, "my will" has replaced "God's will"
as the ultimate reason for good or ill fortune.[1]

If they were asked who sinned, these new age thinkers
would clearly reply, "This man did! His sin is his punishment
for the spiritual blindness or ignorance of an earlier lifetime
and is now his opportunity for spiritual transformation." This
image of an omnipotent mind, whose thoughts create its own
reality, is evident in Louise Hay's observation that

> we are all on an endless journey through eternity. We come
> to this planet to learn particular lessons that are necessary
> for our spiritual evolution. We choose our sex, our color,
> our country; and then we look around for the perfect set of
> parents who will "mirror" our patterns. Our visits to this
> planet are like going to school.[2]

But for many of us this spiritual institution of higher education
seems like a prison in which we experience the results of
actions we can neither remember nor garner spiritual benefit
from. Sadly, in this lifetime few of us ever learn the spiritual
lessons that the events of our lives intend to teach us, because
the suffering is too great and our consciousness too limited. At
a conscious level, the toddler diagnosed with leukemia finds
no spiritual explanation for her pain, nor do the children fated
for mental retardation because of the rampant malnutrition in

---

1. For a more detailed discussion of new age understandings of suffering, see
Bruce Epperly, *Crystal and Cross: Christianity and the New Age in Creative Dialogue* (Mystic, Conn. Twenty-Third Publications, 1996).

2. Louise Hay, *You Can Heal Your Life* (Santa Monica, Calif. Hay House,
1984), 36.

certain developing nations find any metaphysical and spiritual truth within their disability. Can any past life insights be given to the refugees fleeing "ethnic cleansing" in Kosovo?

Confronted with the profound personal responsibility entailed by the linear, cause-and-effect understanding of good and evil stressed by certain new age spiritual leaders, many persons are plunged into the depths of guilt over the world they have created. Their sense of failure and spiritual guilt seldom promotes healing. While Hay and others see their philosophy of mental omnipotence as an inspiration to personal change, since those who have the power to create their cancer or depression also have the power to free themselves from its chains, the burden of such personal omnipotence is too great for many persons. Their guilt and depression only further depress their immune systems and block them from the wellsprings of healing that God has placed within all of us. The tendency within the new age movement, not only to blame the victim for her or his illness, but also avoid those persons whose struggles and negativity might contaminate one's own spiritual journey, can isolate a person just when he or she most needs a supportive community. Caught in tragedies of their own making and unable by force of will or spiritual practice to effect any significant change in their lives, persons who once believed they created their own reality now cry out with the apostle Paul, "For I do not do what I want, but I do the very thing I hate. . . . I can will what is right, but I cannot do it. For I do not do the good I want, but the evil I do not want is what I do. . . . Wretched man that I am! Who will rescue me from this body of death?" (Rom. 7:16, 18–19, 24)

Depressed and guilt-ridden, a young woman sought spiritual counsel from me. Diagnosed with cancer, she had begun seeing a new age healer in addition to her physician. At first, she experienced greater well-being of body and spirit as a result of the interplay of her healing affirmations, touch therapy, and chemotherapy. But when her cancer remission plateaued, the new age healer asked her, "Why are you choosing to hold on to your cancer? What lesson do you still need to learn? Why can't you learn to let go of your anger and love yourself and others more?" As meaningful as this spiritual diagnosis was to the new age healer, it was a virtual death sentence to this insecure young woman, who had already been trying her best to find healing of body, mind, and spirit.

When she realized that neither she nor God was fully responsible for her illness, she discovered a new sense of freedom and empowerment that enabled her to live with her uncertain prognosis. The message of grace and forgiveness enabled her to recognize that she was a beloved daughter of God just as she was, and that God's love for her did not depend on her success in effecting a cure by positive affirmations. With new vigor and a light spirit, she plunged into a treatment regimen that included chemotherapy, pastoral counseling, self-acceptance, and meditation. Today she is healthy in body, mind, and spirit.

While the biblical tradition as well as contemporary medical research affirm that our thoughts and behaviors can cure or kill us—this, after all, is the truth behind the placebo effect as well as the many lifestyle-related diseases of our time—health and illness cannot be fully understood in a strictly linear, one-cause-and-one-effect fashion. Indeed, the recognition that health and illness result from a variety of causes, some of which were beyond her control or God's intention, was the first step in this young woman's healing journey.

Many conservative Christians see new age spirituality and its emphasis on the role of karma, mental omnipotence, and past lives as demonic examples of pride and self-worship. When a new age healer's practices actually benefit a patient, these Christians assume it must be the result of some type of demonic intervention. Even when these spiritual treatments are successful in transforming the patient's life, these conservative thinkers still contend that these non-Christian healing affirmations and therapeutic techniques are merely a form of self-hypnosis or wishful thinking, since they do not include the explicit invocation of Christ's name. From their perspective, authentic healing comes only through God's biblically authorized vehicles: the laying on of hands within a liturgical or charismatic service, the prayers of believers in Jesus' name, the encounter with scripture, and, ironically, the techniques of secular Western medicine. In their minds Western medicine is the only appropriate technological reflection of Christian spirituality, since it comes from the West, on the one hand, and does not suggest a competing theological worldview, on the other hand!

Yet the counsel of many of these same conservative Christians also contributes to the contrasting feelings of spiritual omnipotence and devasting guilt and helplessness. Despite their affirmation of the power of God, many Christians have also been tempted to blame the victim by inadvertantly placing total responsibility for illness on the one who is sick. Their understanding of illness differs little from that of Jesus' contemporaries, who asserted that this man's blindness had only two possible causes: his parents' sinfulness and the sinful behavior the man himself in utero. Many of Jesus' contemporaries smugly asserted that the righteous are always rewarded by success and long life, while the evil are always punished with poverty and illness. According to this philosophy, people ultimately get what they deserve in life at the hand of a God whose justice is directly and umambiguously revealed in the most minute details of everyday life.

> If you follow my statutes and keep my commandments and observe them faithfully, I will give you rains in their season, and the land shall yield its produce, and the trees of the field. . . . You shall eat your bread to the full and live securely in your land. . . . I will look with favor upon you and make you fruitful and multiply you. (Lev. 26:3–4, 5b,9)

On the other hand, those who turn from God's clearly articulated rules face divine punishment in the form of poverty, oppression, and illness.

> But, if you will not obey me, and do not observe all these
> commandments, . . . I will bring terror on you; consump-
> tion and fever that waste the eyes and cause life to pine
> away. . . . I will set my face against you, and you shall be
> struck down by your enemies. (Lev. 26:14, 16–17)

While we live in an orderly universe in which our behaviors
and thoughts have consequences—for example, a lifetime of
smoking may lead to emphysema or lung cancer, unsafe sex to
the occurrence of AIDS and other sexually transmitted diseases, alcoholism to cirrhosis of the liver, obesity to hyperten-
sion and stroke, and negative thinking to stress and
failure—health and illness both come to the wise and the fool-
ish, the moral and the immoral. In real life, there is no exact
correlation between morality and health!

While these clearly articulated understandings of the "faith
factor" provide easy solutions to life's problems, they can
lead to disastrous spiritual outcomes. The anguish of persons
with AIDS and their families has been heightened by self-
righteous Christians who identify the outbreak of AIDS with
divine punishment for homosexuality. Such punitive theological perspectives forget that AIDS also affects the children of
intravenous drug users, spouses who unknowingly have inter-
course with their HIV-infected partners, and hemophiliacs
who receive HIV-infected blood transfusions. Further, they
forget the lessons of history. The great cholera epidemic of
1849, for example, was also identified with divine judgment
on America's immoral behavior. Who today would make a
moral connection between divine punishment and cholera,
polio, or smallpox? But persons in the past saw widespread
incidence of these afflictions as a result of the personal and
social sins of America.

These theological interpretations not only inflict pain upon
innocent persons and persons simply trying to make it through
another day. Also, these theological viewpoints are often a
projections of our own fears, biases, and personal brokenness.
People forget that while Jesus called all persons to the highest

standards of moral and spiritual commitment, he also welcomed the outcast, the unlovable, and the sinner as spiritual
friends, and he chose to become unclean so that these stigma-
tized moral and ethical outcasts might find healing. God's care
for those who are lost and broken is unconditional. As the spiritual model for modern medical practice at its best, Jesus
treated persons with compassion, regardless of the reasons for
their ailment.

Today, many parents feel tremendous guilt over their child's
illness of mind, body, or spirit. When a child is diagnosed in
late teens with schizophrenia, his or her parents often feel as if
they are to blame. In their anguish at seeing their child in
despair, they ask themselves, "Was there some genetic proclivity toward mental illness we did not know about? Why
didn't we notice the problem earlier? Could our child raising
or our prenatal care have caused this illness?"

In the scripture reading, as the Pharisees became more frus-
trated with the man's replies, they appeared to blame his parents entirely for his condition: "You were born entirely in
sins," they exclaim to the man and his parents (John 9:34). In
everyday life, we cannot rule out the impact of parental attitudes, lifestyles, or genetic inheritance on certain illnesses.
After all, secondhand smoke can damage the lungs of a child;
excessive use of tobacco or alcohol during pregnancy can lead
to birth defects; and some mental illness may be inherited
from one generation to another. But excessive self-blame does
not produce the reformation of character or personal strength
necessary to respond creatively to the pain or disability the
child now experiences. Nor, in most cases, is a parent fully
responsible for a child's health and illness. Health and illness
are typically the result of many factors, intricately woven
together in the ecology of life.

Too often the guilt of parents and friends has been multi-
plied by well-meaning, but pious and simplistic Christians,
who counsel, "If you only prayed more or sacrificed your
pride or gave up your career and stayed home, your daughter

would get well," or "If you only trusted God more fully, your son would have recovered!" While such counsels are meant to glorify God and turn persons toward a God-fearing spirituality, they ironically end up placing the responsibility for the healing, as well as the sickness, of our loved ones entirely in our hands. From this perspective, God's intervention depends entirely on *our* faith, rather than our faith depending on *God's* love. Trust in our own spiritual omnipotence and guilt over our misused freedom leaves little room for the gentle movements of the Healer who seeks abundant life for us and our children. No longer a friend, this cosmic "hanging judge" becomes our greatest enemy and threat. Aloof and dispassionate, this god is merely a bystander, unable or unwilling to provide the healing antidote for our own feelings of guilt, helplessness, or shame.

Even in our so-called sophisticated and scientific age, examples of life-denying theology abound. For example, a young boy sneaks furtive glances at the models in his older brother's *Playboy* and obsesses on the swimsuit edition of *Sports Illustrated*. When weeks later he experiences headaches and blurred vision and requires glasses to correct his eyesight, he wonders if God is punishing him for his adolescent sexual fantasies. A woman in her forties, once a lively participant in the "summer of love" of the 1960s and now an evangelical Christian, is tormented by guilt when she receives the diagnosis of ovarian cancer. She asks her pastor, "Is God punishing me for my sexual behavior in the sixties? It's just not fair, because if I die, it will be my children and husband who suffer as well as myself! What kind of God would threaten my life today for sexual experimentation when I was a teenager?"

Tragically, the interplay of divine punishment and human power leaves a toxic theological residue even among marginal believers: their unexamined "pop" theology leaves many persons thinking they are so bad that God has no choice but to punish them in this life and the next or that God is so vindictive that he takes offense at the slightest affront to his majesty.

Both God and the one who is suffering become the participants in a dysfunctional relationship. Divine and human omnipotence issue in a web of cause and effect that imprisons both God and humankind. In such a predicament, we cry out with the apostle Paul, "Who will rescue me from this body of death? . . . Who will rescue me from the reality I have created? . . . Who will rescue me from the vengeance and pettiness of this dysfunctional God?"

Other persons explain illness by asserting that illness and health are *entirely* a matter of God's will. "God kills, and God makes alive!" they smugly assert. As some followers of John Calvin's theology suggest, the fate of each person is the result of God's eternal plan. Like the Force of the *Star Wars* saga, God moves inexorably through all things, including the deadly proliferation of cancer cells and the healing remission if it comes.

Recently, when a car crash that killed two teenagers, one of whom was a good friend of my son, on an icy road in Michigan, I overheard an adult suggest that their deaths might have been result of the divine will. "Maybe it was their time; maybe it will bring their parents to God," he piously averred. Another adult glibly noted that their deaths "would remind other teenagers to drive more carefully in inclement weather." Would either one of these adults have been so glib in their reponse, had it been their own child? Was the death of these college students merely a means to an end? Didn't the God whose eye is on the sparrow also notice the beauty of their short lives?

The image of a divine omnipotence that determines every event suggests that the bone cancer that kills a middle-aged single parent, leaving her daughter without either mother or father, was willed by God to strengthen the daughter and her extended family. I cannot accept the notion that God wills cancer and car accidents, and I cannot accept the idea that God predetermined the stroke that left my father paralyzed and mentally compromised.

While it is true that we can grow as persons in the midst of adversity, these theologies of divine omnipotence portray God as an arbitrary and heartless sovereign who ultimately cares little for the well-being of his subjects. Our human pain is merely a means to an end—either the manifestation of divine providence working through passive lumps of clay or a "lesson" to ourselves or others. How many persons have been emotionally destroyed and plunged into hatred of God and all things spiritual by counsels such as "God never gives you burden you cannot carry!" or "God is testing you!" or "This cancer is God's means of getting your attention!"

I believe that God is constantly at work in our world, empowering us to face the burdens of our lives, relationships, and society; but I do *not* believe that God arbitrarily gives us these burdens merely to strengthen us or teach us a lesson. Indeed, I believe that God is the source of good and not evil, health and not illness, transformation and not tribulation. As Jesus himself proclaims, even the smallest of creatures and the least significant things from the human perspective—sparrows, lilies, and grass—are the objects of divine love and caretaking. Ultimately the theological question raised by the problem of evil is personal: "Is God on my side? Does God love me? Do my pain and suffering really matter to God? Can God do anything to relieve my pain? Does God even want to help me?"

When we reflect upon our own pain and the pain of the world, we must avoid simplistic answers that place the responsibility entirely on God or ourselves. At a recent church service on campus a young woman gave her testimony. She had read in the paper that a pedestrian was struck down and killed on a busy intersection in Georgetown, just a moment after she had passed that way. As she gave God the glory for saving her life, I could not help but wonder about the death of the other person. Was she any less privileged than the girl giving testimony? Did God have some mysterious plan for her life that ordained that she die at this crosswalk on a spring day in

Washington, D.C.? Did God care less for the grief of her parents than all the others who passed by unharmed that day? While the blessings and tribulations of life remain a mystery, and while we can find a blessing even in the darkness of tragedy, the image of God arbitrarily picking and choosing in matters of life and death fills me with fear and mistrust of God's true motivations in our lives. The God who saves us one day can equally damn us the next! The God who would hurt to cure, the God who would punish a child to reform a parent, the God who would kill a college student to strengthen the faith of others cannot be trusted with our destiny, either in this life or the next. To glorify divine power rather than love is to place our temporal as well as eternal destiny in the hands of an inscrutable and undependable cosmic despot. Such a vision of power, arbitrarily and vindictively used, not only destroys the spirit of those in pain and grief; it also renders the suffering of Christ an illusion, rather than an icon revealing God's true nature and care for us.

But back to Jesus' healing of the blind man! At first glance, Jesus' own explanation of the man's illness comes perilously close to those life-destroying theologies that have devastated so many lives and rendered faith an offense to so many suffering persons and their families. "He was born blind so that God's works might be revealed in him." If we read this statement apart from the total context of Jesus' healing ministry, the clear implication is that this man's suffering is merely the means to an end, the revelation of God's work in the world. The fact that he has been blind for many years is of no consequence, compared to God's glory or the witness of faith his healing will bring. Yet when we reinterpret this passage in light of Jesus' own image of God as Parent, another image of divine activity and power emerges. When Jesus referred to God as "abba" or "father," he redefined both divine and human parenting. The Divine Father is the best of parents and the model for our own parenting. All the qualities that we prize in healthy parenting—love, patience, forgiveness, concern, listening, support—are complete in God. We can never attribute characteristics to God that we would condemn in a human parent. Yet many persons excuse behaviors in God that would be grounds for condemnation, if not imprisonment, in any human parent: vindictiveness, cruelty, destruction, abuse, insensitivity, narcissism, ethnic cleansing, and murder!

When we read this passage in larger scriptural context, it takes on a whole different meaning. "We must work the works of him who sent me while it is day: night is coming when no one can work. As long as I am in the world, I am the light of the world." From the perspective of Jesus' compassionate incarnation of God, this healing occurs not merely to glorify God or to strengthen the faith of others, but to demonstrate the conflict between light and darkness and healing and sickness, that were central to Jesus' healing ministry. The Word that enlightens every one and that seeks the abundant life of all is at work in all things to bring healing in a world of darkness. To quote Paul: "In all things God works for good" (Rom. 8:28), even those things that God has neither caused nor permitted to occur. As followers of Jesus, we are called to embody the healing work of God. We are called to affirm our partnership with God by challenging illness wherever it is found, regardless of its causes. This may mean initiating prayer groups and parish nurse programs, visiting shut-ins, giving reiki treatments, and driving persons to medical appointments, but it may also mean political involvement in the transformation of the health care system, finding alternatives to the violence in the media and in the streets, and welcoming the homeless and the unemployed.

In the spirit of Jesus' own healing ministry, we are called to make no moral distinction between the self-caused and the apparently arbitrary illness in our concern for the sick. While the light of God's power is at work in our lives and the lives of others, we must work to heal the sick and welcome the outcast. This means today! Care for those who are not whole, ourselves included, cannot be put off until tomorrow. It must be addressed here and now, before it is too late! Even when we must challenge certain unhealthy behaviors, lifestyles, or attitudes, our motivation is not to blame the victims but to enable persons to experience abundant life in body, mind, and spirit.

Many persons today look for a clear, linear explanation for illness and health and the apparently random accidents of life. In their minds, there must be a reason. What better reason is there than the will of God? Indeed, insurance companies have traditionally referred to the damage caused by storms or by trees falling on homes as "acts of God." However, contemporary process-relational and ecological thinking provides an alternative to simplistic one-cause-and-one-effect explanations. In suggesting that the movement of a butterfly's wings in Los Angeles has an impact on the weather in New York, process philosophers, systems thinkers, and ecologists affirm that our lives arise each moment from an intricate and multi-factorial web of relationships and events, each of which makes a difference. In this spirit, rather than seeing cancer or earthquakes as reflections of God's will, we are challenged to see them as the result of the interplay of many factors, including the presence of God, past personal history, human freedom, social conditions, genetic inheritance, and random occurrences. As the inspiration for healing, growth, and abundance in all things, God works within the many factors of our lives to bring about well-being or to ease the pain.

While certain biblical passages exalt the power of God and while Christian hope ultimately depends on God having the final word in our lives and history, I believe that the phrase "God's will" reflects God's beneficent spiritual aim in our world, rather than the arbitrary and coercive use of power. In the best-known biblical citation of the divine will, the Lord's Prayer, the words "Your kingdom come. Your will be done, on earth as it is in heaven" (Matt. 6:10) imply a synergistic partnership between God and humankind to embody the divine ideal in our lives and in the world. The kingdom of God is not a reign of arbitrary power or manipulative technique, but a realm of shalom in which all of creation finds its transformation and fulfillment. In God's reign, the hungry are fed, the sick are healed, and the outcast are welcomed. If Jesus' healing is a sign of God's coming reign, then illness of body, mind, and spirit or injustice in the social sphere cannot be the result of God's will. When we discover that illness and suffering are contrary to God's will, then we are liberated to experience more fully God's aim of healing and new life amid the challenges of pain, illness, personal dislocation, and aging. God is on our side! God wants us to flourish and be whole! God wants us to share this healing with others!

A careful reading of the healings of Jesus clearly demonstrates that Jesus taught no one specific methodology of healing. The touch of God was always tailored to the particular person and situation. In the case of the blind man's healing, Jesus "spat on the ground and made mud with the saliva and spread the mud on the man's eyes" (John 9:6). After applying this common medicinal poultice of his time, Jesus directed the man to "go, wash in the pool of Siloam." As in most of the healing stories, Jesus asked for an action on the part of the person who was to be healed. The man had to take his medicine, as the great Physician ordered. Still sightless, he had to journey toward the healing that lay ahead of him. He had to trust the unseen. Apart from cleansing his eyes, this man would never have been able to see. Yet, as the healing stories equally indicate, without Jesus' compassion and touch, he would have remained blind. In this healing there is little that is at first glance either supernatural or dramatic. Jesus simply uses his healing touch and the medicine of his time to effect a cure, yet the miraculous occurs.

This healing story should lead persons of faith to endorse a holistic medicine that embraces both spirituality and technology. Yet some Christians are still ambivalent in regard to medical care. On the one hand, some persons, such as Christian Scientists, and followers of the new age classic *A Course in Miracles,* see the use of medication and surgery as a spiritual crutch, grounded in our trust of matter rather than spirit. From their perspective, if medications work at all, their success merely reflects our faith in their efficacy. Some conservative Christians, especially certain small fundamentalist sects, assert that faith alone can bring healing. When you consult a physician, you are placing the physician in the place of God and forgetting that all healing comes directly from God's hand. Members of these groups have faced charges of child neglect and even murder when they have failed to get appropriate medical treatment for their children. Their dogmatic adherence to certain scripture passages has blinded them to Jesus' use of any means necessary to bring healing and wholeness to the broken.

On the other hand, many evangelical Christians—like David, whose concern that the use of acupuncture might compromise his faith was cited in the first chapter—are concerned about the dangers of the growing interest in complementary and holistic medicine. From their perspective, the only appropriate Christian medicine is Western biomedicine. First, Western biomedicine claims to be value-neutral and thus does not propagate an explicit spiritual philosophy that might compete with the Christian understanding of reality. Second, many of the complementary forms of medicine carry with them the baggage of new age or Asian philosophy that might contaminate the "purity" of orthodox Christian faith. While I understand the evangelical uneasiness with the philosophical worldviews implicit in certain types of complementary medicine, I believe that a Christian is called to use any form of health care, provided that it does not explicitly deny the witness of God present in Jesus Christ. The inclusive nature of Christian healing is highlighted in Jesus' attitude toward healers who are not among his inner circle of disciples: "Master, we saw someone casting out demons in your name, and we tried to stop him, because he does not follow with us." But Jesus said to him, "Do not stop him; for whoever is not against you is for you" (Luke 9:49–50).

As Christians we are free to believe that wherever healing is present, God is its ultimate source; we are also called to affirm this fact to all we meet by our use of complemetary medicine. Just as early Christians employed Greek philosophy to articulate their theology and the Greek language to express their faith in a global context, today's Christians are invited to use whatever methods of healing relieve suffering and effect cures of body, mind, and spirit. Jesus' use of a mud poultice in his time is analogous to contemporary Christians using antibiotics, chemotherapy, prozac, or hormones to address conditions of body and mind. On the other hand, there is no reason for Christians to neglect the benefits of acupuncture, reiki, therapeutic touch, herbs, or homeopathic remedies, even if the philsosophies that often accompany them are non-Christian in origin. Indeed, some Asian and new age types of healing are actually closer in philosophy to first-century Christianity than somatic-oriented biomedicine, insofar as they recognize the reality of the nonsensible, spiritual world and the interplay of mind and body in health and illness. It is ironic that although Western biomedicine has been adopted by many as the appropriate medical system for Christians, the reigning approach to medicine in the West for three centuries has typically ruled out the influence of the spirit in health and illness and has seen religious commitment and faith in the healing power of God as either intrusive or irrelevant to proper health care.

Fortunately the emerging holistic medicine, as seen in the work of physicians such as Dale Matthews, Larry Dossey, Andrew Weil, Herbert Benson, and Bernie Siegel, is moving toward an integration of spirituality and hard science. Ironically, this growing spiritual transformation of medicine owes as much to the work of agnostic and non-Christian physicians and healers as to that of persons who call themselves followers of Jesus the healer. Today Christians must ask themselves if complementary and non-Western forms of health care can be creatively integrated into the Christian vision of reality in the same way that Greek thought was synthesized with Jesus' own Hebraic tradition. Current discussions on the interplay of *chi* and *pneuma* and the holistic mind-body tradition of the

Hebrews and early Christians and the growing studies in mind-body medicine testify to a faith that includes healing wherever it is found.

Last but not least, regardless of the nature of the treatment, the healing process is never complete until the patient claims her or his role in partnership with the God of healing. As John puts it, the blind man "went [to the pool] and washed and came back able to see" (9:7). Often the healing we need is right in front of us, and all we need to do is follow the directions. The book of Kings (2 Kings 5:1–19) tells the story of the healing of the Naaman, a foreign military commander, of leprosy. When Elisha tells Naaman he will be cured if he simply dips himself in the Jordan seven times, the military commander is angry. He wanted to be sent to a holy place; he wanted some dramatic message from the prophet to bring about his cure. Walking a few feet to the Jordan River seemed far too mundane to bring about a true healing. But that was all that was needed for Naaman to be transformed. Like Elisha, Jesus uses the simplest and handiest remedy, mud, and asks only that the blind man follow directions. Could it be that, for many of us, what we need to find healing is right in front of us and requires only a few steps of effort on our part? Perhaps the remedy for many of us is merely to eat a healthier diet, to exercise more, to decrease our use of alcohol, and to drink more water. Perhaps the remedy is to take a prescription medication such as prozac or paxil and to meditate regularly. As temples of God, our bodies reflect a natural movement toward health, in the proper functioning and recuperative powers of the immune and cardiovascular systems, as well as in the human spirit. Our minds and bodies aim at wholeness. This movement toward wholeness can be enhanced by both spiritual practices and pharmaceutical prescriptions. This movement is divine. It is wholeness in dynamic process. When we open ourselves to this movement of health within us— through methodologies as varied as prayer and mediation, visualization, vitamins, herbs, medications, and exercise—the movement of God toward healing within us only intensifies as it energizes body, mind, and spirit.

An Experiment in Healing and Wholeness

Jesus' use of a mud poultice in the healing of the man born blind reveals the sacramental character of any healing approach. I have found this to be the case in my own life. Whenever I take my daily baby aspirin and maintenance dose of blood pressure medication in order to reduce the risk of heart attack and stroke, I quietly pray that God will be present in my own healing and wholeness.

A young woman who sees me for spiritual direction imagines healing light flowing through her as she receives her monthly chemotherapy infusion. Following her chemotherapy session, she comes to my home for a reiki healing treatment in order to lessen the negative side effects of chemotherapy and balance her system. She takes her medicine in a holy way because she believes that God is at work in chemical as well as complementary medicine.

If you are currently receiving medical treatment, consider seeing your treatment as participation in God's healing touch. As you take your daily medication, pause to thank God for the gifts of medication, and dedicate your evolving health to service to your neighbor. If you are currently undergoing a regimen of chemotherapy, consider the following spiritual discipline during your treatment:

1. As your treatment begins, commit the treatment process to God's care. Thank God for the gifts of medical progress embodied in the chemotherapy.
2. During the time of infusion, close your eyes for a period of time and visualize God's healing light flowing into your body, cleansing and invigorating your body, mind, and spirit. As the chemicals flow through your body, image the light of God surrounding the

cancer cells and gently eliminating them from your body. Visualize your body permeated and surrounded by God's healing light.

3. As your treatment ends, thank God once more for the gift of chemotherapy. Open yourself to God's ongoing healing in your life.

If you are currently receiving radiation treatments, opening to the divine imagination can bring a new healing perspective to your treatments. The following spiritual discipline may enhance your sense of God's healing touch during your treatments:

1. As the treatment begins, quietly thank God for the life-enhancing benefits of medical radiation.
2. As you undergo the radiation treatment, visualize the radiation as a divine light entering your body, surrounding the cancer cells with vital energy, neutralizing their toxicity, and then gently eliminating them from your body.
3. When the treatment ends, conclude with a prayer of thanksgiving for God's healing touch through prayer and radiation.

These exercises can be adapted for any medical regimen and can also become part of your intercessory prayers for persons receiving medical treatment. For example, when a friend or relative is receiving chemotherapy, take time to visualize God's healing light infusing and strengthening their body. For one who is receiving radiation treatments, take time to visualize the divine light radiating throughout the body and surrounding him or her with divine protection.

This same exercise can be valuable in the health enhancement of those who are not undergoing specific medical treatment. For example, you can visualize a healing light centering on your heart and then flowing through your circulatory system, bringing health to your heart and opening your arteries for the healthy flow of blood.

Once, when [Jesus] was in one of the cities, there was a man covered with leprosy. When he saw Jesus, he bowed with his face to the ground and begged him, "Lord, if you choose, you can make me clean." Then Jesus stretched out his hand, touched him, and said, "I do choose. Be made clean." Immediately the leprosy left him. And he ordered him to tell no one. "Go," he said, "and show yourself to the priest, and, as Moses commanded, make an offering for your cleansing, for a testimony to them." But now more than ever the word about Jesus spread abroad; many crowds would gather to hear him and to be cured of their diseases. But he would withdraw to deserted places and pray. One day, while he was teaching, Pharisees and teachers of the law were sitting near by (they had come from every village of Galilee and Judea and from Jerusalem); and the power of the Lord was with him to heal. Just then some men came, carrying a paralyzed man on a bed. They were trying to bring him in and lay him before Jesus; but finding no way to bring him in because of the crowd, they went up on the roof and let him down with his bed through the tiles into the middle of the crowd in front of Jesus. When he saw their faith, he said, "Friend, your sins are forgiven you." Then the scribes and the Pharisees began to question, "Who is this who is speaking blasphemies? Who can forgive sins but God alone?" When Jesus perceived their questionings, he answered them, "Why do you raise such questions in your hearts? Which is easier, to say 'Your sins are forgiven you,' or to say 'Stand up and walk'? But so that you may know that the Son of Man has authority on earth to forgive sins"—he said to the one who was paralyzed—"I say to you, stand up and take your bed and go to your home." Immediately he stood up before them, took what he had been lying on, and went to his home, glorifying God. Amazement siezed all of them, and they glorified God and were filled with awe, saying, "We have seen strange things today."

(Luke 5:12–26)

Chapter Five

Creative Nonconformity

Scientists are currently investigating the faith factor in the healing process. In double-blind studies of cardiac patients in San Francisco and St. Louis, patients who were the objects of intercessory prayer recovered more quickly and had fewer complications than members of the control group who were not the objects of the assigned pray-ers. While this study raises some interesting theological as well as scientific problems, it also points to the fact that health and illness are social as well as individual issues. In other studies, researchers have sought to find a more ideal testing group, that is, a group that would be immune from the placebo effect, on the one hand, and would most likely not be the objects of prayer, on the other hand. They settled on mice, rats, and bacteria! Even under these circumstances, it was found that wounds healed more quickly among mice and rats that were the object of healers' distant prayers and spiritual therapy. Further, it was found that when bacteria were objects of prayer, energy work, and visualization, they grew faster than those that were left to the natural processes of growth. While these studies are still preliminary in nature, they suggest that our own health and well-being may be intimately connected with the good wishes and prayers of persons around us.

These studies also confirm the deep spiritual truth that all things are meant for community and relationship—to speak and be heard, to touch and be touched. As the Genesis accounts of the creation of male and female suggest, "it is not good for a person to be alone." Nor perhaps is it good for a rat or bacterial specimen to exist in solitude either! The Christian doctrine of the Trinity and the belief in angels point to the communal nature of even God. A Stanford University study found that women with metastatic breast cancer who participated in suppport groups lived longer and experienced a better of quality of life than those who were not members of support groups, even though their prognoses and treatment plans were virtually identical in nature. Such studies demonstrate the positive value of healthy community support.

The healing stories of Jesus reveal the communal nature of health and illness. Health invites us to full participation in society, while illness threatens to isolate us from our neighbors and often prevents us from involvement in normal social activities. Health and illness have accumulated personal and collective social meanings and mythologies. Nowhere is the interplay of the social meaning and personal meaning of illness more evident that in our response to cancer. For many persons, the diagnosis of cancer is immediately identified with suffering and death. The medical treatment of cancer is often perceived as worse than the disease itself. Radiation oncologist O. Carl Simonton has challenged the myths that surround cancer by reminding persons that the majority of persons with cancer survive their illness, that persons can take responsibility for their treatment and healing, and that the chemotherapy can be a "friend" whose negative side effects can be minimized through meditation and visualization exercises.[1]

The social meaning of AIDS and HIV is equally obvious in contemporary American society. Many of us steer clear of persons with AIDS and cancer, even when the chance of contagion is infinitesimal or nil. Partly, this is because our society

---

1. O. Carl Simonton, Stephanie Matthews Simonton, James Creighton, *Getting Well Again* (Los Angeles: J. P. Tarcher, 1978).

identifies AIDS and cancer with chaos, debilitation, and death. Orville Kelley, founder of the cancer support group Make Each Day Count, tells of being given a plastic cup at a cocktail party while all the other guests were drinking from cocktail glasses! His host had unconsciously defined Kelley's cancer as contagious and threatening to herself and the other guests. Physicians and nurses, according to hospital time studies, typically spend less time with terminally ill patients and sometimes avoid them altogether. Persons with life-threatening illnesses are often treated as if they are already dead!

The attitudes of friends, family, religious leaders, and physicians and nurses who care for us make a difference in our health and well-being. Physician Andrew Weil notes the damage created by medical language that places limits on the patient's life span or ability to respond to an illness. Often patients conform to their physician's negative prognosis and give up hope entirely. Theological language that invokes divine punishment or the will of God as the source of illness may lead to passivity and depression of the immune system. For those most mesmerized by such theological dicta, the quest for physical well-being defies the will of God and thus places one's eternal soul in jeopardy! On the other hand, religious language and rituals of empowerment and optimism, theological and pastoral care that invokes God's love, healing touch and supportive hugging, and simple acts of kindness and hospitality invite persons to choose life and wholeness rather than death and hopelessness, even when no physical cure is currently available. In a world of relationships, where health and illness arise from a multiplicity of factors, creative countering of the negative impact of social and cultural images of health and disease is pivotal in the healing of mind, body, and spirit.

As the earlier chapters have noted, illness had profound social and spiritual meanings for Jesus' religious traditon. In the ancient world, leprosy was considered a death sentence, even though it was not necessarily fatal. Like many mysterious illnesses, it inspired both fear and contempt. Persons with certain skin conditions, as determined by the Jewish law, were considered ritually unclean. In the words of Leviticus 13:45–46,

> The person who has the leprous disease shall wear torn clothes and let the hair of his head be disheveled, and he shall cover his upper lip and cry out, "Unclean, unclean." He shall remain unclean as long as he has the disease; he is unclean. He shall live alone; his dwelling shall be outside the camp.

By virtue of their skin condition, persons with specific skin disorders were ostracized by their religion and society. As good as dead, they were required to live in isolated places, far from the support of friends and family. As they approached others, persons with leprosy had to announce their presence with the cry "unclean, unclean" as a means of protecting other persons from their contagion, since even minimal contact with a leper caused a person to become ritually unclean. Like many persons with AIDS today, the first-century lepers were abandoned and judged by the religious and familial institutions that were intended by God to provide them with support and comfort.

As objects of social ostracism and religious judgment, no doubt persons with leprosy internalized the judgments placed upon them by their faith and culture. Even when their lives had been upright, they might secretly believe that they deserved divine punishment and that God had turned away from them entirely.

While we do not know the story of this man, who is simply described as being "covered with leprosy" (Luke 5:12), his attitude toward Jesus reveals his status as an outcast and inferior in both the social and spiritual realms. As Luke notes, "when he saw Jesus, he bowed with his face to the ground and begged." Before the healer Jesus, his shame and humiliation overwhelmed him. He had endured the scorn of religious leaders and pious laypersons who blamed him for his illness. He had felt the vindictive spirit of scriptures that defined him as less than human. Could he expect anything different from a religious teacher such as Jesus? Although he had heard that

Jesus had healed other social outcasts and kept company with "sinners," no doubt he wondered if there was a limit to Jesus' compassion and healing power. Had his illness placed him irrevocably beyond the circle of God's people and God's love?

In his entreaty to Jesus, we can feel the tension of both hope and despair. "Lord, if you choose, you can make me clean" (Luke 5:12). Before Jesus he presumed he had no rights, only the impossible dream of a new life. His entire future lay in the Healer's response to him!

Jesus' response to his plea was simple and straightforward. Jesus gave no theological homily on divine punishment or the need to bear patiently the indignities of illness. Jesus was touched by the man's cry, and he touched him in return. "I do choose. Be made clean" (Luke 5:13). In these few words, God's attitude toward health and illness was revealed. God is not a distant, uncaring despot or a narcissistic parent who makes demands but gives little support. Nor is God deaf to our cries and repulsed by our imperfection. Our brokenness does not threaten God's intention for our lives. Rather, God is most present where the pain is: God feels the pain of the leper, the person with AIDS, the child with leukemia, the parent grieving over the accidental death of his child, the young mother shocked with the diagnosis of stage three ovarian cancer. God hears our cries and is touched by our pain.

"I do choose. Be made clean." Jesus' response embodied the aim of the incarnation, "I have come that they may have life, and have it abundantly" (John 10:10). God works in all things to bring forth healing and wholeness by breaking down social and cultural as well as physical and spiritual barriers that prevent humankind from experiencing life in all of its fullness.

"Be made clean." This response reveals Jesus' concern for the whole person, not just her or his physical well-being. In first-century Jewish society, becoming "clean" meant becoming free of the physical symptoms of leprosy. But, as New Testament scholars John Pilch and John Dominic Crossan maintain, Jesus' healing ministry also changed the man's status in the temple and in his community. By giving hospitality to the leper, by acknowledging him as a child of God, Jesus mediated to him the healing of relationships. He no longer needed to see himself as handicapped, unclean, and passive. While the curing of this man was initially physical—that is, he was transformed by Jesus' touch—it was also social, for now he recognized that God cared for him, regardless of his illness and regardless of the taboos of the society.[2] He became the embodiment of the apostle Paul's counsel: "Do not be conformed to the world, but be transformed by the renewing of your minds" (Rom. 12:2). This man was transformed and renewed because he was no longer conformed to his world's understanding of the personal and social implications of his illness. He was free to experience the love of God that challenges every life-denying social system.

This *creative nonconformity* is at the heart of Jesus' healing ministry in our time. Persons with illness can easily be conformed to the world and its negative attitudes toward aging, cancer, AIDS, Alzheimer's, attention deficit disorder, and mental illness. How often do we hear persons speak disparagingly of their age and the limits it has placed on their minds and bodies! Further, we often emotionally and mentally conform to the prognoses that we receive. I think of the tragic example of a physician who virtually pronounced himself a dead man when he was first diagnosed with cancer. He gave up, because he trusted the statistics that suggested that death was inevitable, rather than exploring alternative spiritual and medical approaches to his care and learning about persons who had survived the type of cancer that he faced. He lived by the one-dimensional realities of statistics and the side effects and not the unexpected movements of grace.

---

2. John Dominic Crossan, *Jesus: A Revolutionary Biography* (San Francisco: HarperSanFrancisco, 1994), 76–82, and John Pilch, *Healing in the New Testament: Insights from Medical and Mediterranean Anthropology* (Minneapolis, Fortress: 2000), 57–117.

While medical diagnoses are often accurate, their accuracy is always statistical and pertains to persons in general rather than any particular person such as yourself! Statistical outcomes do not take into account the surprising occurrence of spontaneous and unexpected remissions, the subtle impact of changes in diet, lifestyle, and values, spiritual transformation, the prayers of others, and the quiet touch of God mediated by caring friends and family within even the most deadly disease.

Jesus' mediation of God's transformative love reminds us that we are always "more" than our illness or health. How sad it is, when a young woman introduces herself to a support group with words, "I am a stage two cancer patient." While she *has* cancer, she *is not* her cancer. In her complexity and beauty, she is much more than her cancer cells: she is a mother, daughter, wife, artist, and friend. Indeed, her recognition of the wholeness of her multidimensional life may be the first step toward the spiritual healing that may lead to physical recovery. God's transformaton always calls us to experience the many dimensions of every life—to become *creative nonconformists* who are not limited by our diagnosis or health condition, but who discover wondrous possibilities even within profound limitations.

The transforming touch that Jesus brought into this man's life was not merely verbal. He touched the man with leprosy, even though that touch would render Jesus himself unclean and unable to enter the temple until he underwent ritual cleansing. Filled with compassion, Jesus transcended the mores of his society and the concern that leprosy might infect him. Like Father Damien, a missionary who contracted leprosy even as he ministered to the lepers in Hawaii, Jesus became unclean so that this man might find healing. In his willingness to share this man's suffering and social stigma, Jesus' ministry creatively embodied the truth of Alfred North Whitehead's assertion that "God is the fellow sufferer who understands." God's understanding of our life situation is never abstract or passive: it is bought at the price of God's own compassionate embrace of our pain, sickness, guilt, and humiliation. God becomes an outcast that we may be transformed. God's embrace of pain and brokenness gives new meaning to the traditional understanding of the incarnation of Christ in Jesus as "the lamb of God who takes away the sin of the world." This is the life-changing meaning of the traditional doctrine of divine omniscience: God's knowledge is characterized by an intimacy that allows itself to be touched from the inside—as well as the outside—by the world in all its wonder and tragedy.

In Christ, God touches us and is touched by us. In God's own *creative nonconformity,* God's love creates, transforms, and brings forth new life; but it also receives our deepest cares and bears our deepest pain. God is more innovative than we can ever imagine. God's ability to heal our lives finds its source in the imaginative personal relationship that God has with each one of us in every moment of our lives. The divine plan for our lives is an intimate personal wisdom that takes into account the moment-by-moment uniqueness of our lives and our highest possible good at any given moment. God's personal plan looks toward the future as well as the present. As the source of our hope, God's touch challenges self-limiting concepts and life-destroying prognoses and social attitudes. God's touch invites us to boldly claim the possibility of personal transformation and healing for ourselves and others, despite the social and medical stigmas of illness. The touch of God is not the denial of the prognosis or the adverse impact of social stigma, oppression, and intolerance, but the beckoning of a future that sees these limits as only one small part of our life story, even as it reminds us that we live in an open system where surprise and adventure are everyday realities.

I believe that the order of the gospel stories is as much homiletical and theological as it is chronological. Accordingly, the juxtaposition of these three stories—the healing of the leper, the paralyzed man and his faithful friends, and Jesus' regular retreats into "deserted places" to pray—is quite intentional. As the healing and preaching ministry of Jesus became more well-known, "many crowds would gather to hear him and to be cured of their diseases" (Luke 5:15). No doubt, Jesus had little time to himself for prayer and reflection on his ministry and relation-ship to God. This is also the challenge of any person in the heal-ing professions. When we become fatigued and worn out, the structures provided by our personal and professional boundaries often are pushed to the limit. Burnout, lack of judgment, and even professional misconduct may occur when the demands of helping and healing exceed our resources.

Jesus knew his own limits. Unlike the co-dependent healing professional who is addicted to the healing process and the adulation of parishioners and patients, Jesus was able to dis-engage himself from the need *always* to be of service. In order to bring healing to others, Jesus needed to be constantly open to God's healing presence. By constantly aligning himself with God, Jesus kept his spiritual focus on God's plan for his life and for those who sought his healing touch. In centering on God, Jesus claimed God's choice of him as the healer and intensified his own experience of the healing power of God residing in all things.

In the spirit of Hebraic religious tradition, Jesus sought to integrate the inner and the outer journey. Faced with the con-stant requests for healing and the threat of condemnation from religious leaders, Jesus' external world was often in upheaval. But like the author of Psalm 46, Jesus knew that even when "the mountains shake in the heart of the sea" (v. 2), he could nevertheless "be still" and know that he was in the presence of God. He needed to balance his public and often controversial ministry with the stillness and certainty of his relationship with God the Father. Perhaps, in these quiet days of contem-plative prayer, Jesus even struggled with the fact that he could not heal everyone and that his message of the reign of God brought antagonism as well as affirmation. Jesus knew that the voice of God could be found in the undramatic and quiet

moments of divine inspiration as well as the dramatic transformative power of thunder and lightning.

Those who embody Jesus' healing ministry in the twenty-
first century are challenged to take time to be silent and to let
go of the need always to be a helper. In everyday life, the practical meaning of the graceful omnipresence of God is found by
those who realize that as important as their work may be in
healing the sick or bringing justice to the outcast and
excluded, God is at work even when we rest! A daily sabbath
of quiet meditation or centering prayer and more extended
sabbath retreats on a regular basis replenish the spirit and align
our minds with the mind of God. Although the incarnation
affirms Jesus' metaphysical as well as spiritual unity with the
divine Parent, this oneness was the gift both of God's unique
presence in Jesus' life and Jesus' constant willingness to be
open to the touch of God in every encounter. Like Jesus, when
we take time to align ourselves in silence with the presence of
God in "sighs too deep for words," we also become continually refreshed channels of divine blessing to persons in need.

Within this trilogy of stories, Jesus moves from the quiet of
contemplation to the maelstrom of human need and public
controversy. The story of the healing of the paralyzed man as
a result of his friends' faith begins with Jesus once more in the
public forum, teaching and preaching under the watchful eyes
of the Pharisees and teachers of the law. In describing Jesus'
state of being, Luke simply states "the power of the Lord was
with him to heal" (Luke 5:17). While scripture gives no information about the nature of Jesus' healing power, this passage,
as well as the passage relating to the woman healed of the
hemorrhage, implies that Jesus was a center of divine energy,
pneuma, or *chi,* not unlike a electric power transformer. Perhaps Jesus needed times for quiet prayer in order to harmonize
and refocus the divine energy that flowed through him. No
doubt, Jesus was also susceptible to fatigue that might have led
to a diminishing of his energy. In the spirit of Chinese philosophy and medicine, when Jesus opened himself to God, the

divine *chi* flowed with intensity and balance toward whoever he discerned was in need.

God is the source of the healing energy in all things. Those who seek to embody Jesus' healing ministry in our time must open themselves to divine energy in a healthy, disciplined, and creative fashion for it to flow most effectively toward the needs of others—whether through laying on of hands, words of compassion, leadership of spiritual groups and spiritual direction, or the practice of medicine itself. The potential for burnout and the temptation of unhealthy co-dependence diminish greatly when we remember that we channel, but do not own, this healing energy. When we take time to nurture our own spiritual lives, we enable others to take our place as colleagues in God's healing ministry. In the stillness, we can feel the touch of God that enables us to touch others as well as ourselves with the dynamic energy of healing and transformation.

Sometimes we must rely on the love and faith of others to get us through. When our usual sense of independence and omnipotence crumbles, we must allow others to carry our burdens and shoulder our responsibilities. Sometimes we must even depend upon the generosity and commitment of others for our faith in God. In a world of interdependence, belief is not a solitary possession, but the product of the mutual affirmation of a community living in trust and relationship to God. In this gospel story, we hear nothing about the faith of the paralyzed man; we do not even hear the exact nature of his ailment, other than the fact that he had to depend on the efforts of others in order to see Jesus. But we do hear of the great faith of his friends as the catalyst of his healing.

At the heart of the healing of the paralyzed man is the power of a community's faith to bring healing and salvation to its members. Jesus once said that "where two or three are gathered in my name, I am among them" (Matt. 18:20). Filled with love for their friend, these unknown and unnumbered friends sought to bring him to the teacher and healer. Because so many persons had come to hear the teacher, they could not bring the man into the house. Instead of being paralyzed by the obstacles that lay in their way, they climbed up to the rooftop by using the outside stairway and then proceeded to uncover the thatch, branches, and tiles of the rough-hewn structure. Although their act might have lead to personal embarrassment, ridicule, and even a criminal citation, they would not let the obstacles prevent them from seeing Jesus. These friends were *creative nonconformists,* whose faith enabled them find a path to healing where others would only see a dead end!

In reality, obstacles always lie in the way of every quest for healing of ourselves or others. To seek healing for oneself or another is to enter into a heroic adventure in which there are many obstacles, dangers, temptations, and false turns. Even the most persistent of us may lose heart as we face the giants that stand in the way. When, for example, the Israelite spies canvassed Canaan to gather information about the inhabitants of the promised land, they returned in fear and paralysis, reporting only that the inhabitants seemed like giants and "we seemed like grasshoppers" before them (Num. 13:33). When Jeremiah was called to speak for God, he protested that he was too young, and when Isaiah encountered the divine in the temple, all he could focus on was his sinfulness. Yet, though these future spokespersons of God were initially daunted by the enormity of their limitations, they trusted the divine presence working within their lives to give them the power and insight they needed in order to claim their spiritual calling.

Today we have different, yet equally daunting, obstacles to healing. We must often contend with destructive theologies and medical diagnoses that condemn us to impotence, death, and guilt. Like insensitive teachers and parents, many physicians place artificial and harmful limits on their patients' futures. They demolish what little hope persons with chronic and apparently terminal illnesses may have, with their pronouncements from on high. While the abbreviation "M.D."

may mean "medical deity" to some physicians, no physician can absolutely chart the course of an illness or predict the day of a patient's death with complete certainty. Persons of faith must always remember that even though one's illlness may lead to death, the presence of God and the impact of faith always leaves open the possibility for surprising and unexpected healings of body, mind, and spirit. In the spirit of Jesus' admonition to "knock, ask, and seek," the friends would not give up their quest for healing until their companion was brought before Jesus, and neither should we!

In this narrative, the paralyzed man is a virtual bystander in his own healing process. It is unclear that he even wanted to see Jesus that day. He may have given up the hope for healing, or, as the scripture suggests, his illness may have been related to some form of spiritual dis-ease. Nevertheless, regardless of the source of the illness or the quality of the man's faith, Jesus reached out to touch him spiritually. As the scripture notes, "When he saw their faith, he said, 'Friend, your sins are forgiven you'" (Luke 5:20). Jesus wanted to heal him just as he wanted to heal the man with leprosy, and just as he wants to heal you!

Once again, this healing story is complex and multidimensional. First, the scripture notes that Jesus was filled with healing power. Without the power of God—the life force, *pneuma, chi, prana*—that courses through our veins and permeates our cells, synapses, and thought processes, there can be no healing. Healing in all its forms is a manifestation of the divine power at work in every aspect of our lives. Second, the scripture affirms the faith of the friends. Without their faith, the man would have remained at home. But, more than this, their faith and ours can create a "field of force" that opens a door to the divine power in our lives. Third, the man eventually had to stand on his own two feet in order to claim the divine gift Jesus and his friends sought for him. He had to accept forgiveness, let go of the burdens of the past, and claim his new life as a whole person.

Without a positive spiritual environment, healing is often impeded or prevented. Medical researchers are discovering that patients whose rooms have expansive views tend to recover more quickly and have fewer side effects than those whose rooms lack windows or face out upon dumpsters and parking lots. In this spirit, many hospitals have created gardens and atriums as sanctuaries of beauty for patients, physicians, nurses, and families. Further, we know the power of healing words and thoughts. Physician Bernie Siegel is a pioneer in the holistic approach to health and illness. When a patient's blood pressure becomes irregular during surgery, he often suggests to the sedated patient that her blood pressure return to normal and virtually always the blood pressure becomes stabilized. Whether in an operating room or a church sanctuary, healing begins with the faith-filled perception of an alternative reality to the present state of affairs. Surely these first-century friends, as well as those who advocate for patients today, must be motivated by alternative and nonconforming visions of health, illness, and treatment. No one should go into the hospital alone: the "cloud of witnesses," both near and far at prayer and at the bedside, are called to speak for those who are vulnerable and demand care for those who are powerless. Whether or not a cure occurs, we must have the imagination to the see the possibility of healing and transformation in even the most dire and hopeless situations.

In some way or other, this man's illness was related to his spiritual condition. While Luke's account of Jesus' healing ministry does not see a linear correlation between the tragedies and illnesses persons experience and the quality of their faith, it is evident that this man's illness had an unstated psychosomatic or spiritual dimension. Jesus recognized that regardless of its ultimate cause, all illness is a meaningful invitation to spiritual transformation.

"Friend, your sins are forgiven you." Jesus' words warmed the heart of the friends and gave a new life to the paralyzed man; but they also inflamed the passions of the Pharisees and teachers of the law. "Who can forgive sins but God alone?" they protested. In their minds, for a human to pronounce forgiveness was to claim to speak for God, and such pride is blasphemy. But is it? I am not just talking about Jesus' ability to forgive sins, but our own vocation to be "little Christs," mediating God's healing touch and forgiving presence to others. If, as medical and spiritual experience indicate, guilt and unforgiveness have physiological correlations, then the forgiveness of sin addresses the body as well as the soul.

For many years, at the Ash Wednesday service at Georgetown University, one of the rituals, in addition to the imposition of ashes and the celebration of communion, was the letting go of burdens. Students, staff, and faculty were each asked to write on a 3×5 note card a heavy and life-denying burden they wished to give up during the Lenten season. Often their burdens were deep and paralyzing issues such as guilt, alienation, low self-esteem, abuse, and depression. As they came to receive the ashes and communion, they were invited to place their burden in a basket and to imagine that in so doing they were placing that burden in the hands of God. Many of the participants experienced a sense of peace as they laid down their burdens, for they discovered in that prayerful moment that God would be their partner in bearing these painful and life-denying burdens.

While the benefits of community and caring touch are at the heart of the therapeutic value of church attendance, the church's calling is also to be a community where we bear one another's burdens and mediate to one another the forgiveness of God. In the liturgical interplay of confession, forgiveness, and the eucharist, long-held burdens of body, mind, and spirit may be released. While grounding itself in the recognition of the social realities that surround it, the church is called to imagine and expect surprising outcomes *and* to see even the most guilt-ridden and broken persons with the forgiving eyes of Christ.

Finally, as is the case in most of Jesus' healings, the touch of God invites us to respond to our limitations with faith and courage. The paralyzed man was physically cured, but he was also spiritually healed. Jesus confronted the man in his paralysis of body, mind, and spirit and called him to a new reality. "I say to you, stand up and take your bed and go to your home" (Luke 5:24). For the first time in years, the man himself awakened to his stature before God and his own responsiblity and value: "Immediately he stood up before them, took what he had been lying on, and went to his home, glorifying God" (Luke 5:25). Restored physically, he was also spiritually reconciled with God.

The account ends with the crowd's response: "Amazement seized all of them, and they glorified God and were filled with awe, saying, 'We have seen strange things today'" (Luke 5:26). Rabbi Heschel once stated that the appropriate response of faith is "radical amazement" at the world and the divine presence within it. The reality of healing and transformation makes it impossible to see the world as one-dimensional, secular, and lifeless. For those who encounter God's presence, surprise and adventure are always on the horizon. Awakened to wonder, we proclaim that the heavens declare the glory of God, and so do our kidneys and intenstines. Healing is embedded in each breath and every creative encounter, be it among friends or in the community of faith. With the Navajo holy ones, we proclaim, "With beauty—and, also, healing—all around us, we walk." Life is adventurous, for we never know when God will do a new thing within our lives by using us and our companions as instruments of healing and new creation.

An Experiment in Healing and Wholeness

Healing and wholeness arise in silence as well as action. This is especially true in those of us who are givers. When we are unwilling or unable to hear the still, small voice of God, our actions are often motivated by our need to be a healer or our anxiety to solve another's problems. In spacious silence, we make room for God to give us the insights we need to fulfill our vocation as channels of healing touch.

In this exercise, simply be still with intentionality. Take time to read as a prelude to stillness, the words of Psalm 46:10. Meditate on the admonition "Be still, and know that I am God." In the silence, gently listen to that deep Voice that undergirds the voices of our culture, ego, or compulsion to help. Listen for the deeper Guidance that brings healing to ourselves and others.

If your silence is distracted by wandering thoughts and emotions, simply return to the quiet expectation that within the deep silence God's voice will be heard.

Take time to allow the scripture reading to transform your life. Read over Luke's account of the healing of the paralyzed man. Let the words soak into your spirit. Imagine the following encounter. You have a dear friend who is seriously ill. Her or his illness has manifested itself in a paralysis of body, mind, and spirit. Take a moment to image a person in your life who is currently experiencing one of the many forms of paralysis. You and a few of your friends decide to take the friend you have identified to see the healer Jesus. You gently pick your friend up from her or his bed and place your friend on a stretcher. Together you begin the journey to see Jesus.

As you approach Jesus' house, you notice that a crowd has gathered around his dwelling place. Take note of the scene. Notice the style of Jesus' dwelling place. Notice the people who surround it. Do any of them look familiar? As you come closer, you notice that you have no obvious way to bring your friend to Jesus. How do you feel about this impasse?

Take time to reflect on any obstacle that lies in your way of reaching out to another person, perhaps even the friend on the stretcher. How does this obstacle affect your life? How does this obstacle affect your ability to help that person?

Suddenly you have an inspiration. You guide your friends to the side of the house, and together you climb the stairs to the flat, thatched roof. You begin to tear away at the thatch. How do you feel as you uncover the roof? You create a hole just large enough to lower your friend down. As you begin to lower your friend, you notice that Jesus is looking straight at you and your friends. What expression does he have? What words, if any, does Jesus say directly to you?

Now Jesus addresses your friend, "Your sins are forgiven." What is your response to these words? In the hubbub that follows Jesus' declaration, he challenges your paralyzed friend to "stand up and walk." And your friend walks! Visualize your friend as healed of her or his paralysis. What is your response to your friend's healing?

Take a moment now to let Jesus speak to your own efforts at reaching out to others. Hear him speak words of healing to your own friends and yourself. See them stand up and begin new lives. See yourself overcoming your obstacles to reaching out in love and service. Conclude your time with a brief prayer of thanksgiving for God's empowerment of your own life and God's care for those in need.

After Jesus had finished all his sayings in the hearing of the people, he entered Capernaum. A centurion there had a slave whom he valued highly, and who was ill and close to death. When he heard about Jesus, he sent some Jewish leaders to him, asking him to come and heal his slave. When they came to Jesus, they appealed to him earnestly, saying, "He is worthy of having you do this for him, for he loves our people, and it is he who built our synagogue for us." And Jesus went with them, but when he was not far from the house, the centurion sent friends to say to him, "Lord, do not trouble yourself, for I am not worthy to have you come under my roof; therefore, I did not presume to come to you. But only speak the word, and let my servant be healed. For I also am a man set under authority, with soldiers under me; and I say to one, 'Go,' and he goes, and to another, 'Come,' and he comes, and to my slave, 'Do this,' and the slave does it." When Jesus heard this he was amazed at him, and turning to the crowd that followed him, he said, "I tell you, not even in Israel have I found such faith." When those who had been sent returned to the house, they found the slave in good health.

(Luke 7:1–10: see also Matt. 8:5–13)

Chapter Six

Healing in the Holoverse

Today, a new and adventurous vision of reality is emerging within the Western world. The predominant Western worldview, which held for four hundred years that reality was divided by the sharp boundaries of mind and body, God and the world, and natural and supernatural, is disintegrating before our eyes. The world of insentient "matter in motion," in which all relationships are understood in terms of the external contact of one body to another, is coming to an end. Whether our focus is medicine or spirituality, mind and body can no longer be understood in isolation from one another. In a world of intricate relationships, God can no longer be envisaged as utterly transcendent to the world, an absentee landlord, who intervenes only from the outside in supernatural, law-violating actions for a favored few. Today's images of God focus on immanence and relationship, partnership and reciprocity.

Today physicians, philosophers, theologians, and scientists are exploring the frontiers of a world in which relationship, rather than isolation, is the key to understanding reality. From the perspective of ecology, sytems thinking, and the new physics, the universe is a dynamic community of interconnected energy events in which each unique being arises from the influence of the whole universe. Amid the complex interplay of pattern and novelty, the fluttering of a butterfly's wings in California influences the weather patterns in Washington, D.C. Physicist David Bohm asserts that the universe is a "holoverse," or undivided whole, in which the whole is present and reflected holographically in each part, and the part shapes the character of the whole. Within the dynamic interrelatedness of the holoverse, some vestige of experience—a "within," to use the language of Jesuit paleontologist and theologian Teilhard de Chardin—can be found in all things. Love rather than alienation is essential to reality, according to the emerging metaphysical, theological, and scientific worldview.

Whereas Newtonian physics asserted that influence occurs only through the contact of adjoining entities, this new understanding of the universe affirms the reality of nonlocal or remote causation. In other words, our actions—and even our thoughts and emotions—immediately radiate across the universe without regard to space or time, shaping—albeit minimally—life on other planets and galaxies as well as across the street.

In contrast to the dualistic worldview of Descartes and Newton, which emphasized consciousness as fundamental to human experience while denying meaningful experience or value to nonhuman life or bodily existence, this new understanding of the universe suggests that the most fundamental form of experience shared by all forms of life is nonsensory or unconscious experience. We are constantly shaped by the influence of the universe, both far and near, even when we are unaware of it. This nonlocal or relational understanding of causal interactions opens up a new horizon for understanding phenomena such as intercessory prayer, extrasensory perception, near death experiences, and psychokinesis. Further, this emphasis on nonsensory experience as the fundamental type of experience opens the door for the creative influence of God within all things, even when they are not conscious of the divine presence. We are guided constantly by the those deep-seated "sighs too deep for words" that only occasionally rise to conscious awareness. Prayer, from this perspective, truly changes things, not just in the life of the one who prays; in dramatic and undramatic ways, prayer makes a difference to those for whom we pray. Whether the distance be one foot, one mile, or a thousand miles, prayer shapes the experiences of others at both the unconscious and conscious levels. As studies on the impact of intercessory prayer on humans, bacteria, and mice indicate, within the intimately woven fabric of the holoverse, the process of praying and laying on of hands makes an immediate impact, regardless of the distance.

In a manner comprehensible to today's physicists, the healing ministry of Jesus clearly transcended the immediate boundaries of space, time, and geography. It also transcended ethnic, economic, and political boundaries. The healing of the centurion's slave illumines the all-inclusive, holistic, and unbounded nature of divine healing within the holoverse. The centurion's slave was no doubt a foreigner, who had neither power nor freedom apart from his master's status. In this hierarchical society, slaves were property with little value apart from their usefulness to their owners. Still, this nameless member of the lowest rung of society was the object of Jesus' compassionate, healing power. The healing ministry of Jesus clearly transcended class and station in society, even as it transcended the limitations of space and time.

Jesus' healing ministry also transcended political and ethnic divisions. Although the centurion was a generous supporter of the local synagogue and may very well have become a believer in the one God of Israel, he was still an oppressor and foreigner—a visible manifestation of Roman tyranny and injustice. Though the centurion represented the "kinder and gentler" face of Roman military power, beneath this kind veneer always lay the threat of force if Rome commanded it. Still, despite the fact that Roman power would eventually erect the cross on Calvary, Jesus lovingly responded to the centurion's entreaty that his slave be healed.

Jesus' healing ministry additionally transcended feelings of unworthiness, guilt, and social stigma. Biblical scholar John

Dominic Crossan correctly notes that a significant characteristic of Jesus' healing ministry was its transformation of persons' social and religious status. Lepers were treated as if they were ritually clean; social outcasts were welcomed at the dinner table along with the wealthy and upright; prostitutes were viewed as lovers and friends. As he stood before Jesus, the centurion recognized his own unworthiness and inadequacy. Despite his political and military power, his ethnicity excluded the possibilty that he could make any claim on Jesus' generosity. As a religious teacher, Jesus was no doubt the embodiment, at least in the mind of the centurion, of the tradition of holiness and ritual piety that had insured the spiritual and ethnic survival of the Jewish people. But this piety dictated that any contact with a foreigner or entry into a foreigner's home was inappropriate for a Jew. Conscious that despite his military clout he still remained a religious outsider, the centurion did not even presume to address Jesus directly. Instead, he asked the local elders to intercede on his slave's behalf. In timeless words that have been commemorated in the Roman Catholic liturgy, the centurion asserted his own unworthiness before God and the amazing possibility that Jesus nevertheless might answer the prayer of this military oppressor. "Lord, do not trouble yourself, for I am not worthy to have you come under my roof; therefore I do not presume to come to you. But only speak the word, and let my servant be healed" (Luke 7:6–7).

In the centurion's plea, we hear our own voice and the voices of humanity in all its moral, ethnic, and religious diversity: "After what I have done, how can God possibly love me? Does the God of the universe really care for my problems? Is there any point of contact between my imperfection and God's perfection? Does God really love the poor and dispossessed?" Many persons believe that God cannot possibly care for their welfare as a result of their birth, lifestyle, or past history. In their minds and the minds of their self-righteous accusers, there are definite limits to God's love, and once we have crossed the line morally or doctrinally, all we can hope for is the inexorable working out of God's punitive justice. But the ministry of Jesus demonstrates that God's justice is not some form of impersonal *karma,* working itself out inexorably in a linear rewards-and-punishments fashion. Nor does God's love for us require moral perfection or doctrinal orthodoxy on our part. As the parables of Luke 15 assert, God always takes the initiative in healing and salvation. On the darkest night, the divine shepherd searches for the lost sheep, regardless of how long it takes or how it became lost. With our lives written upon the palm of the divine hand, our wholeness matters to God in such a way that God's own life will never be fully complete until the every last one of the hundred sheep is returned home safely. In the shadows of her hut, the divine housewife searches for that lost coin, the one that has, without any choice of its own, fallen through the cracks of life. In the heat of the day, the divine father (and, we suspect, the divine mother as well!) runs out to greet his son, heedless of the son's immorality and the Hebraic culture's sense of parental propriety. While the healing stories assert the importance of personal initiative in seeking a healing, they more importantly assert that divine healing is a grace, with no personal prerequisites. This healing grace, as revealed in Jesus' care for the man at the pool and the paralyzed man, occurs in spite of all the barriers we place between ourselves and God's presence in our lives.

Although our values and lifestyle may condition the nature and intensity of God's activity in our lives, there are *no moral prerequisites* for being an object of God's love. Even those who have drifted far from the socially accceptable understandings of the kingdom of God—such as the Samaritan woman at the well, twice alienated from God's kingdom as a result of her ethnicity and her immoral lifestyle—are given the living waters of divine refreshment and transformation (John 4:1–41). Jesus' ministry of healing and transformation *was* and still *is* infinite in scope, time, distance, and inclusiveness, for "God is the circle whose center is everywhere and whose circumference is nowhere."

Cynthia believed that she was outside of the divine circle of love. With three abortions in the sixties and a bout of cocaine addiction in the seventies, now in midlife Cynthia felt unworthy despite a fifteen-year marriage and two children. She felt guilty about her youthful abortions and sexual promiscuity. Though she recognized that the abortions may have been unavoidable at the time and affirmed the need for abortion laws protecting women, she mourned the children she never got to know. Over coffee at Starbuck's, she asked me, "Can God still love me anymore? I feel so ashamed of my past." After weeks of spiritual counsel, Cynthia began to believe at long last that nothing could separate her from the love of God—not even her abortions and youthful indiscretions. Like the runaway child in Luke's story, she recognized that she had created the barriers to God's love by her unwillingness to accept God's forgiveness. "God has been running out to meet me for years, but I've been running in the opposite direction," she confessed. "Now, I'm coming home. I'm accepting the love that was always there for me." Months later, Cynthia shared the spiritual healing she experienced at a liturgy for women who had had abortions and their unborn children. She committed her unborn children to God's care, even as she accepted God's infinite care for herself. Months later, she chose to volunteer as a support person for unwed women who have recently had abortions and other unwed women who are choosing to keep their babies. Cynthia remembers how difficult it is to be unwed and pregnant. "Without judgment or a political agenda, I just to want to help out. I want these women to know that I have been in their place and that I will support them regardless of their decision. I want them to know that God loves them, too."

Distance is an existential as well as geographical issue. In everyday life, we can be strangers and enemies to our next door neighbors, whether in Kosovo or the inner city. Recognizing and affirming the radical inclusiveness of the spiritual journey in all of its dimensions challenges every follower of

Jesus and may even have been a challenge to the Healer himself. As scripture proclaims, Jesus "increased in wisdom and in years and in divine and human favor" (Luke 2:52). Indeed, Jesus himself may not have recognized the full extent of divine inclusiveness until he encountered an assertive Syrophoenician woman (Matt. 15:21–28; Mark 7:24–30). The healing of her daughter may have been more than individual and physical in nature; it may even have led to the healing of the rift between Jew and Gentile that was to characterize the emerging faith of Jesus' followers.

As Jesus traveled incognito through the region of Tyre, "a woman whose little daughter had an unclean spirit immediately heard about him, and she came and bowed at his feet" (Mark 7:25). Though she was of a different ethnic group, her desperate search for her daughter's healing drove her beyond the boundaries of her own people. At first, Jesus responded like a typical member of his own ethnic group, "Let the children be fed first, for it is not fair to take the children's food and throw it to the dogs" (Mark 7:27). Many commentators do their best to deny the apparent racism of Jesus' remarks by suggesting that he was merely testing her faith in order to discover how much she really wanted her daughter's healing. While this may be one possible explanation of the text, what doctor or nurse would make such a reply to a patient in need? Jesus' remarks are reminiscent of the "white only" and "black only" drinking fountains, churches, swimming pools, and hospitals of the the segregated South. But the desperate mother is not daunted by Jesus' rebuff: "Sir, even the dogs under the table eat the children's crumbs" (Mark 7:28). This woman was willing to do anything, including accept ethnic insult, for her daughter's well-being.

While we cannot fully decipher Jesus' initial response to the Syrophoenician woman, it clearly reflected the common racism of his own people. In comparison to the Jews, the Gentiles, Phoenicians, and the Samaritans were "dogs." Sadly, the exclusivism reflected in Jesus' words still echoes in our time.

A number of years ago the president of the Southern Baptist Convention asserted that God does not hear the prayers of Jews. Today many pious Christians doubt if God hears the prayers of Hindus, Buddhists, Muslims, or new agers. In reflecting on the current interest in healing among new agers, conservative Christian author Douglass Groothuis maintains that "if someone is healed of cancer through the laying on of hands by biblically discerning Christians, this is a sign of the kingdom. Yet, if a psychic healer heals a person of cancer, this is not from God, even if the result—in the short run—is similar."[1] While we may easily suspect the orthodoxy of new agers and appropriately note the theological differences between Christians, Jews, and Hindus in our quest for interfaith understanding, it is my belief that Christians must affirm the presence of God in every authentic healing, regardless of its source.

Fundamentalists of all traditions and theologies share one thing in common: a linear and local understanding of reality that clearly demarcates orthodoxy and heresy, friend and foe, saved and damned, sacred and profane. They live by linear doctrinal abstractions, rather than the concrete and often iconoclastic experience of the divine touch in human life. By contrast, the relational, ecological, and nonlocal vision of reality that I affirm suggests that God is actively present in *all* things and *all* persons, regardless of their status or progress in the spiritual journey. Whether or not we know it, we are all seekers after God. In the spirit of Augustine's description of the divine-human relationship, each person is unconsciously responding to the divine grace that is luring toward wholeness: "Thou hast made us for thyself, and our hearts are restless until they find their rest in thee." In a world of intimate and nonlocal relatedness, there are really only two kinds of persons: those who are in God's hand and know it, and those who

---

1. Douglass Groothuis, *Confronting the New Age* (Downers Grove, Ill.: Inter-Varsity Press, 1988), 44.

are in God's hand and don't know it! There are no "outcasts" and "outsiders" in the relational world of grace.

Could the Syrophoenician woman have taught Jesus a lesson? Could she have been an instrument in the healing of the Healer's own attitudes toward foreigners? At the very least, Jesus' responses to the woman and to the centurion represented a radical break from the racial exclusivism characteristic of his time. From then on, there would be no boundaries in the message of healing and transformation initiated by Jesus. Nothing would be unclean to Jesus and his followers. This same inclusive healing power is at work in the world today! And it is at work in our own lives and the lives of our own outcasts and strangers.

In both accounts, Jesus' healing is distant in nature. Neither the slave nor the little girl is responsible for their own well-being, nor did Jesus have to touch them physically to bring about the healing. Within the divine holoverse, all Jesus needed to do was say the word and intend the healing of one he had never met. The healings of slave and child arise from Jesus' response to the love of two foreigners—the centurion and the Syrophoenician woman. Had either one of them let the impediments of ethnicity or distance get in the way, the healings they sought would not have occurred. As Mark's Gospel notes, "Then he said to her, 'For saying that, you may go—the demon has left your daughter.' So she went home, found the child lying on the bed, and the demon gone" (Mark 7:29). The effect of Jesus' words of exorcism is immediate; the demon is vanquished and the young girl regains her true self. Today, as in centuries past, the healing words of Christ cannot be bound by space or time: they radiate across the boundaries of nations and peoples, they brought new life to persons in the first century; and they transform the past, present, and future of persons in our time. As I stated in the last chapter, the possibility of distant healing is now being studied in the laboratory: the health of rats, mice, fungi, and even humans is shaped to some degree by the "distant intentionality" of spiritual healers. If Christ is

alive today, there can be no separation or isolation of the hurt-
ing or sick from the healing touch of God.

For many persons, the impact of past experiences is the
source of their greatest pain and disease. Virtually all of us are
imprisoned by certain attitudes and fears whose origins are to
be found in the pivotal moments in our family life, early childhood education, or relationships. These events not only shape
our self-images and sense of worth, but also are the ground of
self-imposed limitations. As a middle-aged man looks back on
his life, he remembers a teacher's critical comments about a
picture he had drawn. From then on, he chooses to draw simple stick figures and juvenile images in order to avoid the possibility of further criticism. Only when he is invited at a
friend's fiftieth birthday party to use tempera paints as an exercise in creativity and play does he discover a long-submerged
interest and aptitude for art work. An intelligent and beautiful
young woman constantly diets and obsessess about her weight,
because in her youth her father regularly pointed out her
weight and called her Fatso. Only when she lets go of the hurt-
ful past can she experience the beauty and wholeness that is
her authentic reality.

The distant past can be source of inspiration and giftedness,
but it can also bring anguish and paralysis as moments of
physical, psychological, and sexual abuse, racism and sexism,
and social ostracism are relived consciously or unconsciously
in the present moment. Distant though these events may be,
they contaminate the present moment and structure the type of
self we become. As we look at the burdens of the past, we ask
ourselves, "Can these moments be healed and transformed?
Can these deep memories be healed?"

In recent years, Roman Catholic priests Dennis and
Matthew Linn have described the significance of "the healing
of memories" in the context of a pastoral care or liturgical setting. Through guided imaging, persons are asked to go back to
their painful memories with Christ as their loving companion.
As we review our lives, "the healing of memories" involves

inviting Christ to be present in the place of our pain or, if we cannot locate the origin of our brokenness, to open ourselves to whatever forgotten experiences God wants to heal in our lives. The process of the healing of memories is simple but profound: "Christ must enter the scene, take the hurt, and touch the sore spots with his words and actions." As we surround the pain with Christ's love, we are called to pray for the one who has hurt us. Yet such forgiveness is an impossibility for many of us: the pain is too deep, and its impact is too great, for us to let go on our own. In such moments, we turn our lack of forgiveness and pain to a power greater than ourselves. We pray for Christ within us to forgive what we cannot forgive on our own. In a world of relationships, there is no ultimate distance in space and time. In openness to Christ's healing touch, our experience of the past and its continuing impact on our lives can be transformed and become the foundation for our new creation in the present moment.[2]

While there is no ultimate boundary between past, present, and future, we often find ourselves anxious and dis-eased in body, mind, and spirit within the present moment. If we are to find wholeness in our lives, it must be gained one moment at at time. Vietnamese Buddhist monk Thich Nhat Hahn invites us to breathe mindfully and peacefully whenever our personal center is threatened. "Breathing in, I experience peace; breathing out, I smile."[3] In that same spirit, when I become anxious at meetings or in difficult encounters, I often utilize a Christian breath prayer—"I breathe the spirit deeply in, and blow it gratefully out again"—releasing tension, alienation, and anxiety with each exhaling. As I become open to God in the present moment, my perception of the encounter is transformed.

---

2. Dennis Linn and Matthew Linn, *Healing Life's Hurts* (New York: Paulist Press, 1978).

3. Thich Nhat Hahn, *Interbeing: Fourteen Guidelines for Engaged Buddhism* (New York: Parallax Press, 1998) and *Being Peace* (New York: Parallax Press, 1987).

Now I see my colleague and antagonist as a partner and companion in the body of Christ. Like myself, my antagonist is also seeking God. As my experience becomes more spacious in nature, the encounter itself is transformed from one of alienation and dissonance to one of partnership and healing. Freed of the constrictions of past brokenness and present fear, the present moment becomes a surprising adventure in partnership with God and others. Old enmities are overcome, and new partnerships are forged.

The transcendence of distance is most obvious in prayers of intercession. When we discover that the divine center is everywhere, then we can affirm that "in the twinkling of an eye" our prayers radiate across the street or the nation, creating an opening or a " force field" for the divine presence. While we can never quantify these prayers, we can trust that they make a difference within the many factors that make up each moment of experience. While our prayers are neither magical nor omnipotent, our prayers and the prayers of others can change the outcome of a meeting, surgery, or a job interview. If "the body of Christ" is created in such a way that the joys and sorrows *and* successes and failures of each "part of the body" contribute to the well-being of the whole, then we can be certain that our attitudes make a difference to the whole in the same way that optimism, faith, and positive thinking add to the health of our bodies (1 Corinthians 12).

While the future remains open and uncertain in many ways, I am convinced that our attitudes and prayers about the future have an impact upon what will be. The future is undecided, open, and surprising, not only to ourselves but also to God. While God's aim working within all things is to promote beauty, wholeness, and abundance, this aim is woven through the intentions and actions of all living things as they contribute to their own spheres of influence. When we pray that there be healing and that "God's will be done" in reference to a future event, we do not fully determine that future event, but we creatively shape the world from which the future will arise. Our prayers become the raw materials, along with many other influences, utilized by God in the creation of the future universe. They help open the door to the God who "stands and knocks" in every moment of life. In praying for the future, we become conscious partners with God in bringing about God's reign in individual experience as well as for the planet as a whole.

The healing of the centurion's slave did not require Jesus' physical touch. But through the interplay of the friend's intercession, the centurion's faith, and Jesus' loving power, the touch of God transformed the life of that unknown and socially unimportant slave. As Jesus' healing partners, we too can touch persons at a distance, and by our touch the divisions—of time and space; of ethnicity, gender, and sexual orientation; of memory and hope; of body, mind, and spirit—are brought together in the dynamic holoverse, the surprising circle of God's healing love.

An Experiment in Healing and Wholeness

Within the divine holoverse, our prayers of intercession shape the realities of those for whom we pray. While there is no one model of intercessory prayer, I have found the image of divine light effective in my own prayer life. As I pray for another, I hold them in God's healing light in the following manner:

1. I begin with a moment of quiet centering in order to open to the "sighs too deep for words" that join me and the one for whom I intercede.
2. As I gently focus on my breath, I image the one for whom I am praying.
3. With each exhaling, I envisage the divine healing light surrounding and permeating their lives, bringing their lives to wholeness. (Although I am humble in terms of the best outcome, I choose to image the

other in terms of success and wellness rather than in terms of pathology.)

4. After a few moments of soaking prayer, I close with a prayer that the divine light continue to surround them and that they experience this healing light in its fullness.

In your own personal petitions, especially as these involve future events, you may find the following exercise helpful.

1. After spending a few moments in quiet prayer, image the particular situation that is of concern to you.
2. Let the light of God permeate and surround this situation. Experience yourself whole and successful within the divine light.
3. Let the light of God also permeate any other persons that are involved in this situation. Experience them as whole and successful within the divine light.
4. Conclude with a few moments of thanksgiving for God's presence in your life and for God's aim at wholeness for all persons in the situation.

Ruth Carter Stapleton and Dennis and Matthew Linn have been pioneers in using creative visualization for the healing of memories. While there are many approaches to the healing of past events, I have utilized the following visualization in order to transform the impact of a past event from alienation and negativity to reconciliation and affirmation.

1. Take a few minutes to be still in the presence of God.
2. Ask for divine guidance to discern a past event or encounter that weighs heavy upon your emotional or spiritual life.
3. Visualize the particular event or encounter, remembering the emotional injury and experiencing its current impact on your life.
4. Invite Jesus to join you in this moment of pain. Experience his deep love and abiding protection.

5. Share with Jesus your feelings about this event or encounter.
6. Allow Jesus to surround this situation with his love. Place your burden in Jesus' hands. Let Jesus carry it for you. Allow Jesus to bring his healing power to this situation. (As you listen to the deep sighs of the Spirit, let the process of healing emerge intuitively: Jesus may protect you from danger by surrounding you with an impregnable force field. Jesus may, on the other hand, invite you to forgive the offender by helping you find the appropriate words of forgiveness. Jesus may join your hands with the one who has hurt you, overcoming the alienation that you have long felt toward another. In this situation, you may give and receive forgiveness.)
7. Conclude your time of healing with a prayer of thanksgiving for God's presence in your life and a prayer of empowerment for the courage and insight to continue the process of healing.

*They came to Bethsaida. Some people brought a blind man
to [Jesus] and begged him to touch him. He took the blind
man by the hand and led him out of the village; and when he
had put saliva on his eyes and laid his hands on him, he
asked him, "Can you see anything?" And the man looked
up and said, "I can see people, but they look like trees,
walking." Then Jesus laid his hands on his eyes again; and
he looked intently and his sight was restored, and he saw
everything clearly. Then he sent him away to his home,
saying, "Do not even go into the village."*

(Mark 8:22–26)

Chapter Seven

Patience with Prayer

*J*esus once told the parable of a woman who continuously sought the assistance of an unconcerned magistrate (Luke 18:1–8). Day after day, she begged him to intercede on her behalf, and each time he sent her away empty-handed. Finally, although the judge was neither moral nor sympathetic, he decided the case on her behalf just to get rid of her. Jesus used her to remind his disciples that God was very different from the unjust judge. God will answer our prayers, but will we have the faith to persist until we hear God's response?

Everyone who prays regularly has had the experience of apparently deferred and unanswered prayers. Some of us come before God with the same prayers of intercession or petition hundreds of times in the course of a lifetime. The same diseases of body, mind, and spirit burden us or ones we love day after day and month after month. Though we may experience temporary relief from our pain and distress, often the burden remains just outside of consciousness until the moment it overwhelms us once again. Under such circumstances, we are tempted to become cynical about the power of prayer. While we may concede that prayer provides some relief, we may also admit that prayer doesn't really change things. We may be tempted to become angry and hopeless, especially when we hear the claims of confident and self-satisfied Christians and new agers who witness that God or the universe has supplied all their financial needs, delivered them from anxiety, restored their marriages, and healed their children. While we may take heart at such confessions of faith, these witnesses may also become a challenge to our own faith, since most of the time prayer is *not* answered in a direct and immediate manner. More often than not, we discover that the prayers that, at first, seem to be fully answered may in time be found to be only partially answered. We must understand the nature of *unanswered prayer* and *partially answered prayer* as well as *gradually answered prayer,* if we are to persist in prayer through all the seasons of life. While many persons claim "instant answers" to their prayers, Jesus knew that spiritual commitment does not always insure success; his own ability to heal varied from time to time and place to place and was often related to the faith of others (Mark 6:5–6).

The cures we seek through prayer and spiritual discipline as well as medical technology can be gradual, partial, or entirely unsuccessful in result. Early one morning, when the phone rang with the news that my father had just had a stroke, I immediately turned to prayer for his healing and well-being. When it became clear that he would survive the stroke, I thanked God for the presence of divine healing power in my father's life. But after months of physical therapy, accompanied by prayers and the laying on of hands, my father still remains paralyzed. Although he can feed himself and communicate with some difficulty, his diapers must be changed several times a day and he can no longer read his beloved Bible or manage his personal affairs. There is little likelihood that his condition will improve enough for him to return to the garden he so much loved. In the weeks that followed the stroke, I often asked myself, "Did my prayers really make a difference? Why didn't they restore my father to health? Or was his

survival and rate of recovery simply a matter of his con-
stitution and the severity of the stroke?" From time to
time, I wonder if my father would have been better off had
I chosen not to pray! Sometimes the *partially answered*
prayers are as challenging to our faith as those that appear
to be unanswered.

A promising young man is critically injured after being
hit by a drunk driver. For weeks he hovers between life and
death, sustained only by life-support systems and the
prayers of his church family. At one point, the doctor hopelessly pronounces, "I can do nothing more. Now, it's in God's
hands." When unexpectedly he regains consciousness, many
of those who had prayed for him rejoice: "It's a miracle,
God has done mighty things. God has faithfully answered
our prayers." But, as months go by, the glow of the healing
loses its lustre, as the young man, who had planned to enter
medical school, plateaus emotionally and intellectually in a
preadolescent state. He struggles just to get out of bed. His
speech is often slurred and peppered with profanities. His
friends and family now wonder, "Will he ever be the same
again? Why did God bring him back to life and start this
healing process only to bring it to a halt?" Others piously
suggest that God has a plan: Although we cannot fully
understand it, God is teaching us a lesson through the apparently partial healing. Perhaps God is reminding us to count
the blessings of our own health.

There are times when our prayers appear not to be
answered at all. When a beloved priest is diagnosed with
non-Hodgkins lymphoma, healing services and masses are
celebrated on his behalf both at the university where he
teaches and in churches throughout the country. Buoyed by
the prayerful support, the young priest shows improvement
in body, mind, and spirit. "God will work a miracle!" a
friend confidently suggests. But just a few months later, as
he lies dying, the faithful wonder. "Why didn't God heal

him? If anyone deserved to be healed, it was him!" Some are even angry that he died and not someone less valuable to the community of faith!

At the evening service of a Presbyterian church in southern California, two sets of parents ask the congregation to pray for their teenage children, both of whom have been diagnosed with brain tumors. The prognoses of their disease are similar: a 50-50 chance of recovery. A few months later, one family rejoices, for their son is in remission and is now looking forward to college; the other mourns, for their daughter has just died. Many in the church now wonder, "Why did God heal the boy but not the girl? Were her parents stronger in the faith? Does God have a great plan for the survivor?" Some even ask if the one died because she did not have a sufficient number of persons praying for her. Feeling a sense of guilt, they wonder if this young woman would have survived, had they remembered to pray for her more regularly. Afraid to raise their doubts in public, others ask in the quiet of their hearts, "Maybe our prayers didn't really matter. Perhaps it was entirely a matter of luck or divine predestination. Maybe God doesn't really get involved in our concerns." The joy of the family whose son has survived has been muted by their sadness at his friend's death.

There is a mystery to the healing process that often challenges our faith and calls us to challenge popular images of divine power. For those who see God as both loving an all-powerful or engaged in a constant battle with the demonic sources of illness, unanswered or partially answered prayers often bring about a crisis of faith. A controversial Episcopal bishop, John Shelby Spong, reflects on his own crisis of faith and his attempt to fathom the nature of divine power in light of his wife's diagnosis with cancer. When she appeared to be in remission from the disease that would eventually kill her, Spong notes that "the people who were most concerned and whose prayers were most intense began to take credit for her longevity. 'Our prayers are working,' they claimed. 'God is using our prayers to keep this malevolent disease at bay.'" In his own reflections, Spong reveals many of the problems inherent in the traditional understandings of the power of prayer and the role of God in health and illness.

> Despite my gratitude for the embracing love that these people demonstrated, . . . I could not help but to be troubled at their explanations. Suppose . . . that a sanitation worker in Newark, New Jersey, . . . has a wife with the same diagnosis. Because she is not a high-profile person, well connected to a large network of people, socially prominent, or covered by the press, the sickness of his wife never comes to public attention. Suppose he is not a religiously oriented person and thus prayer groups and individual petitions in hundreds of churches are not offered on his behalf. Would that affect the course of her sickness? Would she live less time from diagnosis to death, endure more obvious pain, or face a more difficult dying? If so, would that not be to attribute to God not only a capricious nature, but also a value system shaped by human importance and the worldly standards of social elitism? Would I be interested in worshiping a God who would treat my wife differently because we had had opportunities in life that the sanitation worker had not had? Do I want to attribute to the deity a behavior pattern based on human status?[1]

Spong concludes his ruminations with the confession that "if prayer is to continue to be part of my life, I must start in a new place that requires, first of all, a new way of envisioning

---

1. John Shelby Spong, *Why Christianity Must Change or Die* (San Francisco: HarperSanFrancisco, 1998), 141–42.

God." While I cannot fully accept Spong's re-visioning of God, this collection of healing stories is an attempt to address the need for a transformed and re-visioned image of God. The multifactorial approach to health and healing articulated throughout this book affirms a divine-human partnership at work within a complex and intricate matrix of events, each of which makes a difference in the immediate and final outcomes of health and illness. Further, throughout this book, I have sought to distinguish between the *curing of the body* and the *healing of the whole person*. God seeks the healing of the whole person, even when a physical cure is not always possible.

In everyday life, the most common experiences of healing and curing are gradual rather than dramatic in nature, whether they occur as a result of medical interventions, prayer, laying on of hands, the use of affirmations, or a combination of biomedical and complementary healing approaches. In real life, most cures and healings can be understood as the natural working out of our body's own healing processes, which can be enhanced or weakened by the quality of our spirituality, lifestyle, diet, and medical care. The heavens declare the glories of God, and so also do our immune and cardiovascular systems. In undramatic, gradual, and absolutely necessary ways, the immune system protects us from the majority of the threats to our physical well-being. Intricate in nature, the immune system recognizes unwanted invaders, whether they be random cancer cells, germs, or bacteria, surrounds the potential threats, and then eliminates them from the body before they can cause harm. The immune system is so effective in the preservation of life that we must depress the immune system if a heart, lung, or kidney transplant is to be successful. While once physicians and scientists believed that the immune system operated automatically, today we now know that the immune system can not only be depressed and deactivated by "invaders" such as HIV, but it can also be compromised by attitudes such as hopelessness and depression and the ongoing experience of stress and the "fight or flight" response. Conversely, the immune system can be enhanced by certain homeopathic and herbal remedies and pharmaceutical interventions, as well as by physical exercise, music, dance, positive affirmations, imaging, and prayer and meditation. A growing number of studies suggest that loving relationships, service to the community, and even viewing films of holy persons such as Mother Teresa positively influence the effectiveness of the immune system. *Seen from a spiritual perspective, the immune system is a revelation of God's gentle and all-encompassing care for humankind in often gradual and nonintrusive ways.*

For the most part, the spiritual techniques that enhance the immune sytem, cardiovascular system, and other body systems operate in an equally gradual and nonintrusive fashion. While the practice of meditation or the utilization of reiki, therapeutic touch, and laying on of hands brings an immediate sense of peace and well-being, physical and emotional transformation of a particular ailment may take months and often involves an equally diligent use of medical technology. We experience the impact of our spiritual disciplines and healing practices in incremental improvements rather than dramatic interventions. The same gradual and often unobservable healing occurs in the human spirit and emotional life: healings of memories, emotions, and psychological imbalances most often occur quietly and unobtrusively. Like the incremental growth of a plant, sometimes the transformation cannot be recognized until months have passed and the bloom of new life appears.

Many of us, however, grow impatient with the gradual processes of physical, emotional, and spiritual healing. We want instant answers and quick solutions to the deepest problems of our lives, even when these problems are the manifestation of years of unhealthy lifestyle habits, negative thought processes, dysfunctional relationships, and habitual disregard of God's presence in our lives.

Often, when a student comes to me with a serious theological question, such as "Does God answer prayer?" or "Is the Bible the word of God?" I respond with a question myelf: "How much time do you have?" The deepest spiritual, theological, emotional, and physical issues can seldom be solved overnight. Healing the wounds of body, mind, and spirit; bereavement and grief; and the pain of broken relationships require patience and time for transformation. While we can enhance the process of healing by our attitudes, behaviors, and spiritual commitments, we must nevertheless trust the quiet working of God in the healing of our woundedness. Though some people hope for a dramatic revelation of God that will solve all our problems, end injustice, and reveal the truth to all, Jesus identifies the kingdom of heaven with "a grain of mustard seed," the smallest of seeds, whose growth gradually eventuates in the revelation of God's presence in all and to all.

After her husband died, Edna wanted to give up. Now in her eighties, Edna saw the future as a grim solitude that would not lift until the day she died. Her husband Hugo had been her constant companion since her teenage years. He was her other half and soul mate. Without his presence, she felt incomplete and lost. "I'm not sure that I can go on," she confessed to me one afternoon. "I have no energy, no passion, no vitality, and no hope. I don't even want to eat anymore. I wish I would just go to sleep and not wake up. I want to be with Hugo. Will this grief ever end?" I suggested that she see a physician, just to check out any physical issues that might be bothering her. But I also suggested that she see her grief as a wound, just like the ankle she had broken a decade before. "Healing is painful and slow," I told her, "but if you listen to the pain and cherish the love you have, even the pain can be a blessing." I told her that while it was important to affirm the reality of her loss, it was also important, whenever she struggled with the pain of missing Hugo, to thank God for the love they had for one another. I also reminded her that her grief and her healthy response to it would be a gift to her children and grandchildren. They would learn by her patient struggle that healing is possible, even in the most difficult personal situations.

Months later, Edna called me with great joy in her voice. "I still miss Hugo terribly. But I discovered that I have a life on my own. Each day I thank God for our love and for the slow healing that God is working in my life." Today Edna volunteers at the hospice where Hugo died. Her grief has become a gift to other grieving spouses. She is a witness to the fact that as painful as grief may be, life and love can still go on.

In the gradual healing of the blind man, the gentle spirit of divine healing was revealed. Gradual healing is a process requiring a number of steps if the spiritual and physical growth that has begun is to remain consistent and positive. First, Jesus "took the blind man by the hand and led him out of the village" (Mark 8:23). No doubt, this man needed to leave his familiar surroundings in order to open himself to Jesus' healing presence. In his usual environment, his blindness no doubt dominated his attitude toward himself and the attitudes of his friends and family toward him. The blind man needed to "see" himself in a new light if he was to receive the benefits of Jesus' healing touch.

In a multifactorial understanding of healing, the environment can either promote or negate the healing process. When we are lifted out of our typical environment and its expectations, we can experience the world in a novel and adventurous manner. In our opening to novelty, God's presence can break through in unexpected ways. But once again I want to make clear that the power of God is not just breaking through from the outside, but also acting from within the many causal interactions of our lives.

In the quiet of their one-to-one encounter, Jesus invited the man to go beyond the past and its negative impact on his life, in order to experience new sight and new life. The recovery of sight would involve not only the touch of God but also the man's willingness to let go of his previous self-understanding. He had to become a *creative nonconformist* in order to be fully healed. In his healing of the blind man, Jesus combined first-century medicine and the spiritual technique of the laying on of hands. Jesus used this interplay of first-century "medical technology" not only to heal this blind man but also to heal a deaf man with a speech impediment (Mark 7:31–37). In the case of the blind man discussed in the last chapter (John 9:1–11), Jesus used a combination of dirt and saliva to effect a healing. I believe that the divine healing touch complements and enhances the effectiveness of other healing modalities—medication, chemotherapy, pain killers, herbology, acupuncture, and reiki, for example. If God's aim of abundant life is reflected in our bodies as well as our minds, then *anything* that enhances physical well-being in the context of our deepest spiritual needs comes from the creativity of God, *whether or not the name of God is explicitly invoked.*

As we reflect on this healing, we can easily be perplexed. Why wasn't this man healed immediately and decisively? After all, in other contexts, such as the healing of the woman with the hemorrhage, the paralyzed man at the pool, and the demon-possessed man, the healing was immediate and, for those who observed or experienced the healing, dramatic in nature. The text gives us no answer to this question. It simply states that it took two tries for Jesus fully to heal this man of blindness. "When he had put saliva on his eyes and laid his hands on him, he asked him, 'Can you see anything?' And the man looked up and said, 'I can see people, but they look like trees, walking.'" Undaunted, Jesus tried one more time: "Then Jesus laid his hands on his eyes again; and he [the man] looked intently and his sight was restored, and he saw everything clearly" (Mark 8:23–25).

Were there factors involved in this man's healing process other than his expectation and Jesus' integration of healing touch and first-century medicine? Was the man's lifetime "habit" of blindness an impediment? Or was the nature of the healing similar to eye surgery today? Following significant eye surgery, the patient is not allowed immediately to gaze upon the brightness of the world. Gradually, she must be prepared both psychologically and physiologically for the novel, colorful, and complex sights of the world.

In a world in which health and illness arise from many causes, some that help and others that hinder the healing process, we cannot always expect the healing process to be immediate or observable. Learning a new art or mastering a field of study takes time, and so do the transformations of body, mind, and spirit. Opening to the divine healing in our lives calls us to patience, hopefulness, and, above all, trust in the unseen. It calls us to a subtlety of spiritual vision that asks us to intuit and build upon even the most gradual transformations in ourselves and others. It calls for a persistence in petition and intercessory prayer and other means as diverse as guided visualization and healing music by which we "soak" the chaotic and desolate parts of our lives and others, time after time, in images and rhythms of order, beauty, and wholeness. Indeed, we may first need to grow spiritually in order to appreciate and utilize the physical healing in a manner that benefits ourselves and others. We are cured, not to go back to old behaviors that may have contributed to our disease, but to manifest innovative spiritual, emotional, and physical approaches to life.

Even when we do not fully understand the nature of God's presence in our lives, we are called to trust the wisdom of the divine process of wholeness, working within the ecology of our lives. In certain spiritul teachings, it is said that "when the student is ready, the teacher appears." Perhaps the same can be said of healing: "When we are ready, the healing appears." Our lives arise from an intricately connected dynamic system, not unlike the ecological systems that characterize the nonhuman world. In this ecology of life, we shape and are shaped by the constantly changing matrix of creativity. God's own aim at healing may be conditioned by our own ability to appreciate and appropriate the healings that lie upon the horizon. A change that occurs at the wrong time may not only be overlooked and repressed; it may also cause harm in ourselves and our relationships. While God is not entirely in control of the healing process, God aims for the healing at the "right" time, in the "right" place, and in the "right" context, given all the factors of our life and our environment. God's healing aim works by *kairos* time and not *chronos* time, by *synchronicity* rather than *linearity.* Even in times of struggle, we can affirm that God gently and quietly works for good within all things.

Even the unanswered and partially answered prayers point to the significance of an environment of healing. Jesus' own ability to heal was conditioned, in part, by the faith and lack of faith of persons in his environment. In certain situations, the disease may have progressed beyond the possibility of a cure, or dysfunctional and destructive relationships and attitudes may close the door on the intensifications of divine healing energy needed to bring about wholeness. Still, even when the cure is not possible or is impeded by our physical condition or environment, God remains present, seeking the healing of the whole person that can be attained in this situation. Always, we must remember that divine healing ultimately maximizes the good of the whole person and also the good of the greater whole (the family, community, and planet), and not merely physical symptoms of an isolated individual or even the span of one lifetime.

Healing is ultimately aimed toward service to others. Out of our experiences of wholeness, we become partners and cocreators in the ecology of life that encompasses our lives. Further, those who do not receive a cure in this lifetime are challenged to look at their spiritual adventure from the widest perspective. As resurrection faith proclaims, God's graceful care and healing touch extend far beyond the grave.

Although the interplay of medical and spiritual techniques restored this man to sight, the scripture infers that his healing was still not complete. He had to ground his healing in an extended retreat from his community. As the scripture notes, "Then [Jesus] sent him away to his home, saying, 'Do not even go into the village'" (Mark 8:26). Some scholars suggest that Jesus' admonition reflects Mark's understanding of the messianic secret, that is, Jesus' desire to keep his divine nature hidden from all but his closest followers. But perhaps there is a deeper meaning to Jesus' counsel that the man return home. Healings of mind, body, and spirit unsettle our lives and require a period of internal adjustment. In order to be fully healed and not merely physically cured, this man needed to reflect on the many dimensions of his new sight and his former blindness. His spiritual transformation needed to catch up with his physical transformation; often this healthy transformation requires a time of retreat and solitude. After all, as Jesus suggested in John 9, physical sight may be accompanied by spiritual blindness. Persons can be physically healthy and yet be the prisoners of a victim mentality or other negative attitudes such as envy, hatred, and poor self-image. We need to grow into the healings and insights we are receiving. We need to use our sight rightly so that we will be able to see the truth of our lives and God's presence within them. Jesus the healer—who himself needed to meditate in solitude to refresh his spirit and to align himself with God's vision—may well have known that this man also needed a "retreat" from the public eye so that his life in its totality might truly become a life of sight and not blindness.

Times of solitude and retreat are necessary for us to remember and maximize the forces of healing that God has implanted in our very neurons, cells, emotions, and spirit—to bring us the healing that we truly need. Ideally, the effectiveness of divine energy coursing through our lives and our environment complements our own commitment to the healing process and is enhanced by our own openness to God. Still, we must be patient when the results of our prayers remain uncertain. More than that, we need trust that there is an ever-present healing energy within us that will not—in this life or the next—abandon us to entropy but will push our lives forward toward wholeness and companionship with God

An Experiment in Healing and Wholeness

Spiritual, emotional, and physical healing is often so gradual that it is virtually unobservable. Still, through imaginative prayer we can visualize and enhance our own or another's personal healing process.

In this exercise, take a few moments to reflect upon a part of your life that is in need of the healing touch of God. Explore your experience of this area of dis-ease. Do you discover any deeper meaning to the pain or struggle you are experiencing? As you visualize this part of your life, image a divine healing light surrounding and nurturing this part of your life. See the light emerge in your life gently, quietly, and gradually. Visualize the particular part of your life gradually healing as it is permeated by this gentle light. See the physical, emotional, relational, or spiritual wound gradually being transformed. Experience the wholeness that God has intended for you. Conclude this time of visualization with a prayer of thanksgiving for God's unobtrusive presence in your life.

This exercise can be repeated as a form of intercessory prayer by focusing the gentle healing light on a person who has identified a particular wound to you. As part of their life ecology, your visualizations are a positive nonlocal contribution to their environment. Simply identify the expressed problem without judgment. Surround the one for whom you intercede with God's healing light. Visualize this light bringing wholeness to every aspect of their lives. Then focus the healing energy on the particular part of their life that is in need of transformation. Let the light bring forth the gradual healing resources of mind, body, emotion, and spirit. See their own woundedness being healed gradually until the wound is utterly transformed. Conclude by thanking God for working creatively within the life of your friend.

*On the way to Jerusalem Jesus was going through the
region between Samaria and Galilee. As he entered a
village, ten lepers approached him. Keeping their distance,
they called out, saying, "Jesus, Master, have mercy on us!"
When he saw them, he said to them, "Go and show
yourselves to the priests." And as they went, they were made
clean. Then one of them, when he saw that he was healed,
turned back, praising God with a loud voice. He prostrated
himself at Jesus' feet and thanked him. And he was a
Samaritan. Then Jesus asked, "Were not ten made clean?
But the other nine, where are they? Was none of them found
to return and give praise to God except this foreigner?"
Then he said to him, "Get up and go on your way; your
faith has made you well."*

(Luke 17:11–19)

Chapter Eight

Curing and Healing

*T*oday medical anthropologists distinguish between curing and healing. *Curing* is related to the alleviation of the symptoms of a disease, while *healing* relates to the whole person—mind, body, spirit, and relationships. From this perspective, a person can be cured physically while still remaining diseased emotionally, relationally, or spiritually. For example, long after a person has recovered mobility after a broken hip, he may still be afraid to go down steps or resume activities that were normal before the fall. Following successful heart bypass surgery, a woman may still hesitate to return to her formal exercise routine, for fear that she might put too much stress on her heart. On the other hand, persons may experience healing or wholeness even though their physical condition is deteriorating. Their joy is not dependent upon their ability to walk or even take care of matters of basic hygiene, but is grounded in their relationship with God, their commitment to friendships within a creative community of faith, and their sense of personal vocation even in the most challenging of situations. Despite ongoing infirmity, they are profoundly grateful for the graces of everyday life—a phone call or card from a friend, the companionship of a faithful pet, the bloom of a rose outside the window, the touch of a spouse's hand, and the quiet assurance of God's presence.

The healing of the Samaritan leper brings together curing and healing in the context of the experience of gratitude. Of the ten lepers who were physically cured, Jesus attributes wholeness or healing to only one of them, because he alone gives thanks to God.

When the ten men came to Jesus, they sought to be cured of the disease of leprosy. In biblical times, leprosy referred to a number of skin conditions. It could involve pain in the joints and the ulceration of the skin; it could also involve the loss of sensation in the limbs, which often led accidently to serious injury; or it might be a combination of these two ailments. In addition, leprosy could refer to something like psoriasis, a common disease of the skin whose symptoms involve scaling or itching. Any significant skin ailment was classified as leprosy. While disease to the Hebrews often was perceived as related to sin, guilt, or divine punishment, they specifically considered leprosy as one of the most spiritually, emotionally, physically, and relationally destructive illnesses. Leviticus 13:2–3 outlines the appropriate religious response to leprosy for the practicing Hebrew:

> When a person has on the skin of his body a swelling or an eruption or a spot, and it turns into a leprous disease on the skin of his body, he shall be brought to Aaron the priest or one of his sons the priests. The priest shall examine the disease on the skin of his body, and if the hair in the diseased area has turned white and the disease appears to be deeper than the skin of his body, it is a leprous disease; after the priest has examined him, he shall pronounce him ceremonially unclean.

Leprosy might involve ailments as diverse as raw flesh, a skin ailment that turns the hair white, an unhealed burn that changes color, diseases related to the hair or the beard that involve itching, or skin diseases of balding persons. Because leprosy was identified with divine displeasure, the community often responded with fear and anxiety. The "cure" for leprosy was a combination of social isolation and ostracism that was often far worse than the disease itself.

> The person who has the leprous disease shall wear torn clothes and let the hair of his head be disheveled; and he shall cover his upper lip and cry out, "Unclean, unclean." He shall remain unclean as long as he has the disease; he is unclean. He shall live alone; his dwelling shall be outside the camp. (Lev. 13:45–46)

In the event of a cure, the Mosaic law prescribed that the person receiving a cure fulfill certain ritual cleansings. These cleansings provided the ritual purity that was essential for the leper's restoration to the community.

> He shall be brought to the priest; the priest shall go out of the camp, and the priest shall make an examination. If the disease is healed in the leprous person, the priest shall command that two living clean birds and cedarwood and crimson yarn and hyssop be brought for the one who is to be cleansed. The priest shall command that one of the birds be slaughtered over fresh water in an earthen vessel. . . . The one who is to be cleansed shall wash his clothes, and shave off all his hair, and bathe himself in water, and he shall be clean. After that he shall come into the camp, but shall live outside his tent seven days. On the seventh day he shall shave all his hair: of head, beard, eyebrows; he shall shave all his hair. Then he shall wash his clothes, and bathe his body in water, and he shall be clean. (Lev. 14:2b–5, 8–9)

The process of regaining ritual and social cleanliness was concluded by the sacrifice of two male lambs or, among the poor, two turtledoves or pigeons as a guilt offering.

The diagnosis of leprosy placed a person outside the realm of society in terms of status and rights and denied one the ability to worship with his or her family and friends. In a social order where relationship with the larger community rather than individual achievement defined the self, the leper was a nonperson—a virtual corpse—until he or she once more regained health.

To be a leper was a double curse within the context of Jewish society. A leper lost not only health but also social status; he or she was presumed to be the object of divine punishment for previous sinful behaviors. The man Jesus healed had a third curse to bear. From the Jewish perspective, to be born a Samaritan was to be a victim of divine displeasure and visible symbol of spiritual uncleanliness. While moderns speak naïvely of "good Samaritans," the notion of a good Samaritan was a contradiction in terms among the majority of Jews in Jesus' time. In their estimation, the Samaritans were the sinful descendants of the Jews who remained in Judah and intermarried with the pagan locals during the time of the Babylonian exile. As a result of their compromise with the pagan culture within which they lived, the Samaritans were accused of perverting the true faith of Israel. They could never, within the precincts of the Jewish community, claim social or religious equality.

That day, in despair over their physical and social isolation, the ten lepers cried out to Jesus, "Jesus, Master, have mercy upon us!" Jesus' response was simple and straightforward, "Go and show yourselves to the priests." Such a directive could have only one meaning to these desparate men—they would be cured of their leprosy! Their skin would again be unblemished, and their bodies would be normal once more. Free at last, they could return to home, family, and work.

As the Samaritan leper joyfully raced toward the temple, we may suspect that two sudden realizations brought him back to Jesus: (1) as he ran, he felt a power surge through him and noticed that his skin was being restored to its normal complexion, (2) as he experienced the healing power, he also remembered one thing that had not changed, his identity as a Samaritan. While their common affliction bonded the ten lepers together, now that they were healed, they would once more be divided by centuries of ethnic mistrust and hatred. As he ran, the Samaritan leper realized that he had nowhere to go except back to Jesus. With his heart filled with gratitude and relief, he returned to the Jew whose healing words had literally brought him back to life and restored him to family, society, work, and worship.

At first glance, Jesus' response to the Samaritan seems puzzling. After all, the other nine lepers were also following his directions. They were returning to the priests to receive validation of their physical cure and to be pronounced clean and eligible to return to society. But only this foreigner, who had every earthly reason to mistrust Jesus because of his own ethnic background and the centuries-long enmity between their peoples, returned to the source of his cure. He received not just a cure but a healing, too! Perhaps his physical healing gave him a new vision of his life and his relationship to God and enabled him to transcend the historical and social separation of the Jews and Samaritans. In that moment of healing, he became "a new creation." As the Samaritan praised God for his healing, Jesus asked about his companions, "Were not ten made clean? But the other nine, where are they? Was none of them found to return and give thanks to God except this foreigner?" (Luke 17:17–18). Then, Jesus pronounces a healing as well as a cure. "Get up and go on your way; your faith has made you well" (Luke 17:19).

The others were made ritually clean. They received the physical cure that they had asked for. They no longer experienced the physical pain and social isolation of leprosy, and they no longer were barred from religious rituals because of their uncleanliness. But this foreigner, who could not even enter the temple to show his new cleanliness to the Jewish priests, was "made well," that is, "healed" in body, mind, and spirit because of his gratitude to God.

There is a profound difference between curing and healing. Healing reconnects us with God, ourselves, and others. To be healed is to experience God's shalom and wholeness, regardless of one's physical or social condition. Nelson Mendela was a free man even when he was imprisoned in South Africa! He demonstrated his free spirit by seeking reconciliation rather than retribution when he became leader of the newly constituted country. Paul was a free person when he discovered that, despite the pain of chronic illness, God's grace was sufficient for him (2 Cor. 12:9). While there are many dimensions of healing, the healing of the Samaritan leper reveals the close connection between thanksgiving, grace, and healing.

The German mystic Meister Eckhart once proclaimed that "if the only prayer you make is thank you, this will be enough." While disease isolates and disconnects persons physically, if not socially and spiritually, thanksgiving reconnects us with the source of life and wholeness, regardless of our place in society. In experiences of thanksgiving, we recover our sense of the whole. We no longer see ourselves as isolated minds, bodies, persons, or nations. We experience ourselves as part of that vast web of relationships that scripture describes as the body of Christ. Thanksgiving roots us in our interdependence with the nonhuman world, our bodies, our friends, and God. In moments of thanksgiving, we recognize the truth of Jesus' words, "I am the vine, you are the branches. Those who abide in me and I in them bear much fruit" (John 15:5). In this doxological consciousness, we discover that life is a gift and that within the divine holoverse we are giving and receiving from one another all the time. Even when we may feel most diseased, the healing energy of the vine still flows through us.

From the perspective of many of his contemporaries, Larry has little for which to give thanks. This once promising athlete is now confined to a wheelchair as a result of a skiing accident. Paralyzed from the waist down, he can no longer participate in the golf, basketball, baseball, and soccer that characterized his high school and college days. Although he was angry and depressed at first, the counsel of another paraplegic changed his life. His friend reminded him that although he was limited, he was not dead! He had much to be thankful for and could choose to explore a whole new set of activities. Larry returned to school for a graduate degree and now spends his time counseling other physically challenged persons. This past year Larry participated as a wheelchair contestant in his first marathon. He regularly competes in 10K races and has organized a wheelchair basketball league in his community. Each day Larry gives thanks for what he has—meaningful work, good friends, an optimistic spirit, a beautiful fiancée, loving parents, and the companionship of God. Larry admits that "sometimes life is difficult, but even when I'm struggling to get around, I remember that I can be witness to God's love and the power that comes from an affirmative faith. I thank God that I can make a difference to someone every day."

Thanksgiving roots us in our bodies as well as our spirits. During times of sickness, our bodies seem no longer to be benign; our naïve sense of invulnerabilty is shattered; and our familiar, seldom complaining friend becomes an enemy, inconvenience, and threat to our well-being. But when our spirits are restored to well-being, we experience the grace of God's energy flowing within and around us anew, and the only appropriate response is gratitude—gratitude not only that the heavens declare the glory of God, but that our intestines, immune system, cardiovascular system, and nervous system also reveal God's wisdom and care.

Rabbi Abraham Heschel once described the nature of religious experience as "radical amazement," not only at the fact that we exist, but also at the wonder and beauty of our wild and precious world. In Thornton Wilder's play *Our Town* the protagonist is given the posthumous opportunity to relive a typical day of her life. She returns to her companions at the cemetery overwhelmed at the beauty of the simplest things and filled with regret at how often she failed to recognize the wonder of every day. In everyday life, few persons recognize how wonderful it is just to be! The spirit of gratitude is embodied in the Native American saying, "With beauty all around me, I walk."

Gratitude enables us to awaken each day and drink deeply of the beauty of the sunrise or sunset. Without gratitude, we never fully experience grace and wholeness in our lives. A world of grace and gratitude is a transformed world, in which all things, even the negative, are icons though which we may see the divine, and all moments are potential epiphanies in which God speaks to us. Suffering and disease often constrict the spirit as well as the body, isolating persons in self-absorption, but gratitude expands the spirit to include the cosmos. In moments of thanksgiving, we discover the vast web of relationships and the God "in whom we live, move, and have our being." Though the cancer may remain or financial problems persist, they pale in comparison to the simple abundance of God that nurtures us in every moment. At such moments, when our lives in all of their pain and joy become icons revealing the divine, we can chant gratefully, "I thank you, God, for the wonder of my being."

Yet any reflection on gratitude must recognize the dark and shadowy side of the discipline of gratitude. Is it possible to be grateful to God when the pain of terminal cancer makes it impossible to sleep at night, when we can no longer go to the toilet on our own, or when we must face social ostracism in addition to the indignities of illness? Can we live doxologically when our spouse is diagnosed with Alzheimer's? In Madeleine L'Engle's *A Ring of Endless Light,* Vicki Austin's grandfather is dying of acute leukemia. Although his condition has now made it impossible for this once-vibrant adventurer to leave his bed, he still believes that God has a purpose for his life. Physically weak and occasionally mentally incoherent, he tells young Vicki, "Perhaps, now, my vocation is simply to pray." Vicki's grandfather reminds us that weakness of the body need not debilitate the spirit. With the apostle Paul, who himself suffered from a chronic disease, he can gratefully claim, "whenever I am weak, then I am strong" (2 Cor. 12:10). In light of recent studies on the power of prayer, we can only imagine how our world might be transformed if nursing, assisted-living, and retirement homes became cathedrals of the spirit, in which elders kept round the clock vigil in joyful intercessory prayer for the healing of our world. We can only imagine the self-esteem that would radiate from these often dismal warehouses of body and spirit!

Disease can constrict the spirit, but it can also open the heart and the spirit to experience the holiness of the ordinary in amazing ways. A young person dying of AIDS proclaims that, for the first time in his life, God is no longer a distant, vengeful figure, out to punish him for his lifestyle; instead, he sees the face of Jesus and touch of God in the members of the rather traditional Presbyterian church who bathe and bring him meals daily, a friend who gives him reiki healing touch twice a week, and a caregiver who patiently walks him to the bathroom. "Waking up each day is a miracle for me now. I rejoice in the taste of orange juice and the coolness of water. I feel God's presence in the touch of a friend. I am so grateful for the blessings of each day."

A forty-year-old woman, undergoing an extensive regimen of chemotherapy, discovers God's presence in the daily doses she receives. "Each day, when I take my medication, I think of it as the eucharist, the body and blood of Christ. I feel God's healing light permeating my spirit and flooding my body along with the medication. I am thankful for God's love manifested in the friend who sits with me during chemotherapy, my pastor who gives me a reiki treatment afterward, and the medication that is giving me a chance to live long enough to see my grandchildren grow up."

Despite the emotional, mental, and physical limitations my father has experienced since his stroke, he still tries to pray for his nursing home care givers and gives them a kind word as they perform tasks that would be unpleasant for the rest of us.

A young girl, imprisoned during the Holocaust, gazes beyond the gates of the camp and rejoices in the beauty of an ordinary field flower growing just outside the wall. In another concentration camp, Viktor Frankl prayerfully remembers his wife and family and begins to write one of the most influential psychological texts of the twentieth century. As the film *Life Is*

Beautiful suggests, a love song playing over the loudspeaker system can drown out the voices of hatred and fear. Stephen, the New Testament martyr, looks into the heavens in prayer, asking God to receive his spirit and forgive his tormentors, even as his persecutors' stones deal their deathblow. For all these persons, thanksgiving is a profoundly creative counter-cultural act and a manifestation of the divine imagination, for it affirms most powerfully, in the midst of oppression and pain, that divine love and beauty are the ultimate and unextinguishable realities of life. The spirit of thanksgiving has transformed them from victims to celebrants of the life they have.

The same attitude of thanksgiving that broadens the spirit and connects us to God may also transform our experience of pain and bring us greater well-being. If we see ourselves from the infinite divine perspective, then pain is no longer the *only* reality, but just *one reality among many!* Our thanksgiving opens us to new possibilities of seeing the light amid the darkness and holiness amid the ordinary. Current scientific studies are pursuing evidence that such God-centered moments may even release the endorphins that bring greater comfort to the body and stimulate the immune system. In living doxologically by giving thanksgiving in every encounter, we discover that everywhere is home and all places are holy, for grace abounds and grace surrounds us in all of life's seasons. We thank God for the wonder of all being, for despite appearances to the contrary, God is working gently in all things. Thanks be to God!

An Experiment in Healing and Wholeness

Thanksgiving, like love, is a matter of intentionality and commitment, as well as emotion. Gratitude depends not on the environment but on our perception of beauty and grace. In many ways, believing is seeing! We can begin living doxologically by practicing certain spiritual exercises.

A friend of mine spends her morning walk praising God for the gift of life and the beauty of the earth. In the spirit of her daily doxology, I invite you to experiment with a walking prayer. As you take your daily walk or run, simply recollect the many graces in your life. In a brief walk around the block in my neighborhood recently, I took time to give thanks for health, a good marriage, my son's happiness, the home in which we live, the beauty of the park that adjoins our home, the care my father receives at his nursing home, the ability to write and think creatively, the opportunity to participate in the intellectual and spiritual formation of students and parishioners and workshop participants, the love I received from my parents. As I walked through the neighborhood, it occurred to me that I could walk for hours and not exhaust the blessings I have received.

At the Shalem Institute for Spiritual Formation in the Washington, D.C., area, I learned a prayer that can either become the heart of quiet centering prayer or become a chanted prayer. It simply goes, "I thank you, God, for the wonder of my being." This prayer can be generalized to "I thank you, God, for the wonder of all being" or particularized to express your gratitude for a particular blessing: "I thank you, God, for the wonder of Matt's being (my son)," "I thank you, God, for the wonder of this morning," and so on.

Finally, healing is a social as well as individual issue. In the micro worlds of our daily lives, we can begin to live doxologically by expressing our thanks verbally to everyone who assists us. Gratitude is contagious. It lifts our spirits and expands our horizons. How would your office change if you practiced and expressed the spirit of gratitude in every encounter? How would your family life change if you and your family constantly expressed appreciation for the graces of communal life? How would your attitude toward life change if you lived by words and thoughts of thanksgiving rather than faultfinding or criticism?

When Jesus had crossed again in the boat to the other side, a great crowd gathered around him; and he was by the sea. Then one of the leaders of the synagogue named Jairus came and, when he saw him, fell at his feet and begged repeatedly, "My little daughter is at the point of death. Come and lay hands on her, so that she may be made well, and live." So he went with him. . . . While [Jesus] was still speaking, some people came from the leader's house to say, "Your daughter is dead. Why trouble the teacher any further?" But overhearing what they said, Jesus said to the leader of the synagogue, "Do not fear, only believe." He allowed no one to follow him except Peter, James, and John, the brother of James. When they came to the house of the leader of the synagogue, he saw a commotion, people weeping and wailing loudly. When he had entered, he said to them, "Why do you make a commotion and weep? The child is not dead but sleeping." And they laughed at him. Then he put them all outside, and took the child's father and mother and those who were with him, and went in where the child was. He took her by the hand and said to her, "Talitha cum," which means, "Little girl, get up!" And immediately the girl got up and began to walk about (she was twelve years of age). At this they were overcome with amazement. He strictly ordered them that no one should know this, and told them to give her something to eat.

(Mark 5:21–23, 35–43;
see also Matt. 9:18–26, Luke 8:40–56)

Chapter Nine

The Healing Affirmation

*O*ne of the greatest tragedies a parent can experience is the death of her or his child. In the natural order of things, parents dream of their child's marriage, vocational success, moral growth, and the possibility of grandchildren to nurture and affirm. Just the threat of a child's death can overwhelm a parent spiritually and emotionally. When our only son was a senior in high school, looking forward to applying to colleges, fulfilling his duties as student body president, and enjoying the fun of senior year, a tumor was detected in his sphenoid sinus, just a hair's breadth from his brain. The possibility of cancer hovered near, until the surgery itself confirmed the tumor as a rare type of invasive, but nonmalignant, tumor called an angiofibroma. With our only son on the verge of the adventure of adulthood, the news threatened to devastate us, as it challenged our expectations for his future. When his surgery at the Georgetown University Hospital stretched from the expected four hours to nearly eight hours, with no word from the surgeon, we would have been in a near-panic, had it not been for the comforting presence of our closest friends and colleagues. When the surgeon finally appeared in the waiting room with news that the lengthy surgery had been successful, we were relieved and overjoyed. Although we had spiritually and emotionally prepared ourselves for the surgery, it was virtually impossible to maintain a positive attitude during those hours of anxious waiting. Visions of cancer and death on the operating table crowded out the positive images we had maintained in the weeks before surgery. But we were able to maintain an attitude of gratitude for the presence of our friends, the advances in skull-based surgery, the availability of a highly skilled and God-believing surgeon, and the discovery of the tumor in the first place. Our gratitude to God and the exhausted surgeon gushed forth and triumphed quickly over our fatigue and our "worse case scenario" images of paralysis or blindness. We were blessed with friends who were a visible sign of God's presence as they reminded us that the length of the surgery could be a positive as well as a negative sign.

In the wake of our son's surgery, our family has committed itself anew to living more intentionally in doxological awareness of the beauty and wonder of life. Through the process of discovery, surgery, and recovery, we each have committed ourselves more explicitly to living by our spiritual affirmations and opening ourselves to God's vision of possibility, rather than by our own negative and fearful thinking. Our son came to a more mature sense of responsibility for maintaining the health of his immune system, which for him meant resisting peer pressure to smoke and taking on a daily regimen of rinsing out his sinuses, where mucous membranes and cilia had been removed. Now a college student, our son Matt volunteers as a "big brother" for a child with leukemia. We have committed ourselves to embodying the spirit of Jesus' healing of Jairus's young daughter by recognizing that affirmative or negative thinking can be a matter of life and death for the mind, body, or spirit.

The interplay of the healing of Jairus's daughter and the healing of the woman with the flow of blood within the gospel narratives is hardly accidental. These healing encounters witness profoundly to the synergy of divine healing and human faith. To the woman with the hemorrhage, Jesus proclaimed, "Your faith has made you well; go in peace, and be healed of your disease" (Mark 5:34). By focusing on the healing possibilities of touching

Jesus, this woman opened a pathway between her faith and God's transforming energy. But in order to do so, she had to free herself from the negative spiritual, emotional, and physical power of her disease. In like manner, the healing of Jairus's daughter involved her parents' faith in God's vision of reality, rather than the negative images of friends and family.

Today physicians recognize this same dynamic in the contrast between the placebo and nocebo effects. Faith in the positive value of medication engenders a healthy physiological response in 30–35 percent of the patients, even when the medication is of no pharmaceutical value. In contrast, persons who are told of the negative impact of a medication often experience negative side effects, even when the treatment they receive has no medicinal content. Whether in clinical trials or everyday life, our attitudes shape our reality and possibilities. Our thoughts, habits of mind, and social environment can either limit or expand our vision of health, healing, and human possibility. Indeed, sometimes the healing of mind, body, or spirit requires us to leave negative family, medical, and cultural environments in order to experience the positive presence of divine energy in our lives.

The healing of Jairus's daughter began with the plea of her father. How often have parents cried for relief and healing at a child's bedside or hospital room! "My little daughter is at the point of death. Come and lay your hands on her, so that she may be made well, and live," the father pleaded (Mark 5:23). Whatever antagonism or misunderstanding may have stood between Jairus, the leader of the synagogue, and the radical teacher Jesus must have paled in comparison to his daughter's need. Though Jesus himself was often in conflict with the Jewish religious leaders, any previous conflicts were put aside in light of this young girl's well-being. It is clear from Jesus' response to Jairus that there are no prerequisites to the healing of his daughter. Everyone is welcome within God's healing circle, even those who oppose him theologically and question his claim to be God's chosen one. As the twelve-step movements proclaim, even when we hit rock bottom and recognize how far we have strayed from God, abused others by our addiction, and squandered our own or others' resources, that healing "power greater than ourselves" still reaches out to touch us where we need it the most. The grace of God does not require spiritual perfection or previous commitment to Christ or the church in order to transform our lives. God's surprising grace seeks our transformation, even when we have denied completely God's existence and care for our lives, and it will—like the shepherd in search of the lost sheep—venture forth into whatever darkness we have created in order to bring us home to God's healing circle. While the completion of our healing process may require significant personal transformation and a radical break with past behaviors and thought patterns, the initiation of this process is a gift given to each one of us, regardless of our lifestyle choices, negativity, or brokenness. For this we can and should be grateful.

In recognition of God's unconditional love, the church as a healing community must place no personal, ethical, or lifestyle limitations on its ministry to the broken. Around the healing circle, the homosexual with AIDS, the alcoholic with liver disease, and the drug user with bipolar disorder are just as welcome as the infant with spina bifida, the child with leukemia, or the elder with Alzheimer's disease. In a world that places limits on what we can accomplish and who should receive our love, God proclaims that "all things are possible" within Christ's all-inclusive healing circle.

As they walked toward Jairus's home, Jairus—and, we suspect, his wife—heard the chilling words, "Your daughter is dead. Why trouble the teacher any further?" These same words echo in the corridors of hospitals, emergency rooms, and nursing homes, "Now is the time to give up hope. There is nothing more we can do." Recently, a young man visited me with the report of his dying mother. Each year, she and her husband flew from Chicago to see the Grand Canyon and the red rocks of Sedona, Arizona. But this year, after the diagnosis of stage three ovarian cancer, they canceled their trip, even though she was not yet in debilitating pain. The young man questioned the wisdom of their decision. To him, the decision meant, not only that they had given up on physical survival, but they had also given up on enjoying the months that remained for her. He was right!

After receiving the news of a potentially terminal illness, many families are devastated. The negative diagnosis becomes the defining reality of their lives. But defining realities are often confining realities! The only possibility that they can envisage is simply to keep the patient comfortable and sedated by medication and television until inevitable death arrives. But the diagnosis of terminal illness does not mean the patient is already dead!

Other patients and their families refuse to submit to the grim negativity of their medical diagnosis. Athough they recognize that death is an imminent possibility, they commit themselves to making each new day count by seeking alternative remedies, sharing words of love, going on spiritual and geographical adventures, and passionately claiming and filling each day with gratitude. They do not deny the possiblity of death, but they place it in a wider perspective where transformation of spirit, mind, and relationships—and maybe even the body—is always a possibility for those who choose life. If we live within a divinely inspired, open system of relationships, then there is always "something more" we can do, even at the descending edges of life.

At the descending edges of life, when a terminal illness has been diagnosed or when a lifetime of mental or physical pain and disability seems to lie ahead, we have only the most fragile strand of hope upon which to hang our future. In such dark moments, we may pray that we hear the still, small voice of God's spirit, echoing the words of Jesus to this desperate couple: "Do not fear, only believe." In the biblical tradition these are the words of a theophany, a divine revelation; these are the words spoken by the angels to the perplexed and anxious Mary and Joseph when the news of an unexpected and life-transforming birth was announced, and later to the amazed and frightened shepherds when the glory of the Lord enveloped them to announce Jesus' birth. These are the words God speaks to each of us when all hope for deliverance seems lost: "Do not be afraid." Our hope in such moments may be not for a physical cure or the deliverance from a chronic ailment but for the courage and serenity to face the future. This affirmative attitude opens our eyes to an adventurous and constantly surprising world in which the presence of God surrounds us and makes us whole in many unexpected ways.

As they listened to the Healer's words, Jairus and his wife most likely did not fully understand the meaning of Jesus' counsel "to believe," but they trusted that Jesus would hold the future of their daughter and themselves in loving and protective hands. Jesus did not urge them to repress their worries or deny the possibility that their daughter might be dying; but he invited them to place their greatest fears in the hands of God and allow God to bring forth healing in those places where mortals give up hope.

As I wrote in an earlier chapter, the healing of body, mind, spirit, and relationships often requires solitude, detachment, and letting go. The everyday world can easily overcome us with its narrow vision of divine and human possibility and its negativity regarding certain health conditions. In solitude, a Native American youth goes on a vision quest and receives a new name and role in his community. He must let go of his community's images of himself in order to find his emerging true self. A middle-aged man goes on a two-week retreat, accompanied only by inspirational books and the occasional presence of the retreat center's spiritual director, in order to hear the voice of God that has been drowned out by the loud and demanding voices of his profession, family, colleagues, society, and everyday, preoccupied self. A woman diagnosed with breast cancer takes a daily twenty-minute mini-retreat by imagining a divine, healing light like the glow of sunshine at the seashore flooding her body and washing away the toxic cancer cells. While she trusts the accuracy of the medical diagnosis, her times in guided prayer remind her of the deeper reality of healing and courage that counters the negative social images of breast cancer. A college freshman chooses to spend more time in prayer and meditation and bonds with new spiritually oriented friends in order to overcome the peer pressure to drink excessively and experiment with casual sex each weekend. And Jesus, amid the crowd that proclaims the little girl has died, takes the family and his chosen disciples on a mini-retreat in order to gain a new perspective on the girl's health situation. Perhaps even Jesus had to liberate himself from the negativity of the environment of death in order to address the needs of the young girl and her desperate parents. As the scripture notes,

> he allowed no one to follow him except Peter, James, and John, the brother of James. When they came to the house of the leader of the synagogue, he saw a commotion, people weeping and wailing loudly. When he entered, he said to them, "Why do you make a commotion and weep? The child is not dead but sleeping." And they laughed at him. Then he put them all outside, and took the child's father and mother and those who were with him, and went in where the child was. (Mark 5:37–40)

As well-meaning as the mourners may have been, their disbelief was an impediment to the healing process. In Jairus's house, a war was raging between the "realists" who saw only the diagnosis and the surface reality of death and the "faithful" who intuited a deeper life-giving power within the context of the community's understanding of illness and death. Indeed, Jesus may be accurately assessing her physical condition when he states, "The child is not dead but sleeping" (5:39). Even in our modern world, we often have difficulty determining the boundary between life and death. Recently in northern Virginia a controversy erupted over whether to withdraw life support machines from a man who was diagnosed with an irreversible coma. Hooked up to machines that maintained the functioning of his cardivascular and pulmonary systems, his appearance gave the impression of life and the hope that someday he would awaken.

Yet apart from the intervention of medical technology, the life of this man, whose brain had already died, could not be sustained. In the context of advanced medical technology, the quest for healing involves openness to discerning the actual medical condition of the person in need. Fidelity to the healing Christ involves a spiritual realism that affirms the most loving possibility for healing, given the medical realities of the situation. This may involve the prayer for a dramatic recovery, but it may also involve the prayer for a peaceful death and the courage to discontinue medical interventions.

While many persons see the healing of Jairus's daughter as the resuscitation and restoration of a corpse to physical life, similar to the raising of Lazarus, Jesus' own words point to another possibility. The girl may have been in a deep coma. This naturalistic explanation of her condition and the healing that ensues in no way challenges the power of God present in Jesus' healing ministry. It merely locates the healing in another context—the synergy of Jesus' own faith and healing power *and* the faith of the family and disciples, in contrast to the negativity of the world that defined the young girl as dead. Surely the one who could heal at a distance could also intuitively diagnose the young girl's health condition. Even in our time, biomedical physicians and alternative and spiritual healers occasionally make a wrong diagnosis of an illness or an inaccurate prognosis. To the closed-system thinker, the results of a blood workup or pathology report tell the whole story. But to one who believes in a dynamic, open system of divine and human partnership, novelty, surprise, and adventure are always a posssibility. The future is always open!

In response to their laughter and disbelief, Jesus "put them all outside" with the exception of the family and disciples. Clearly, in an environment characterized by negativity, Jesus needed to create a healing environment. The apostle Paul proclaimed, "Do not be conformed to this world, but be transformed by the renewing of your minds" (Rom. 12:2). Nowhere is this transformation of the mind more powerful than at the intersection of health and illness *and* life and death. While we can never underestimate the positive power of evil and the reality of sickness and death, we often succumb to the negativity grounded in the pervasive influences of our culture, family of origin, professional setting, and personal history. For example, when given the option in a friendship or marriage to interpret our spouse's or friend's behavior in a positive, negative, or neutral matter, many of us succumb to negative interpretations, even though in a similar situation, *we* would want to be interpreted positively by our loved ones. This proclivity toward negativity can make the difference between life and death in ourselves and others. In that moment, Jesus created a healing circle that embraced Jairus and his family and the disciples in the healing light, even as it protected them from the negativity of their environment.

Pioneering psychiatrist and founder of the attitudinal healing movement, Dr. Jerry Jampolsky has demonstrated for over three decades the power of positive thinking in finding wholeness in the context of cancer. Jampolsky advises his patients to let go of all negative language. Words such as *can't, never, impossible,* and other stereotyping and negative vocabularly are not only inaccurate in an open system; they also limit the infinite presence of the divine in our lives.[1] In the course of medical history, countless patients have exceeded their physician's prognosis. Others have experienced what physicians describe as spontaneous remissions, even though they may interpret them from the spiritual vantage point as the presence of God or an answer to prayer. When the apostle Paul proclaims, "I can do all things through [Christ] who strengthens me"(Phil. 4:13), he is challenging us to break through the cultural, medical, and familial limitations that bind us. He is affirming that within the positive circle of divine healing, miraculous manifestations of divine and human energy abound.

---

1. Jerry Jampolsky, *Love Is Letting Go of Fear* (Milbrac, Calif.: Celestial Arts, 1979), 39–41.

Just think for a moment of a limitation that you have placed upon yourself, be it mundane or dramatic in impact. A college student recently came to me with feelings of worthlessness. For all his life, he had carried the burden of being an "illegitimate child." He had never even met his "deadbeat" dad. Even though his whole life had been an attempt to prove that, unlike his father, he was responsible to God, his mother, and his values, he still felt alone. He still needed to prove himself. His burden was lifted when he discovered the simple truth that from God's perspective there are no illegitimate children. Regardless of how he got here, he now knows that he is a child of God. His life is "written on the palm of God's hand." At the end of each pastoral care session, I reminded him to affirm every day the deepest truth of his being: "I am a child of God. Nothing can separate me from the love of God."

Faced with fears of aging and death, a recently retired seventy-year-old takes up hiking and writing, publishes her first book of short stories, and feels better than she has in years. Inner-city children, surrounded by violence and despair, plan the funerals they expect to occur before they reach adulthood. To counteract the hopelessness of their toxic environment, the Rev. Jesse Jackson invites them to visualize themselves as infinitely valuable by teaching them the affirmations "I am somebody" and "Yes, I can!" In a time of marital dissonance, my wife and I chose to focus on the positive and not the negative in each other. In the spirit of Jampolsky's work in attitudinal healing, we chose to be "love finders rather than fault finders." A year later, we renewed our marriage vows, and we still take time for affirmations, especially in times of conflict.

While we may think ourselves as modern persons far too sophisticated to succumb to voodoo curses, physician and prayer researcher Larry Dossey suggests that our own words and beliefs may be just as destructive. One of the most celebrated cases of a modern medical "voodoo" death involves the case of a man whose condition improved or worsened depending on his information about the medical benefits of the drug

Krebiozen that he was taking. In 1957 a patient of Dr. Bruno Klopfer was diagnosed with advanced untreatable lymphoma and was expected to die within a few weeks. However, he was injected with an experimental drug. Although the drug was later found to be ineffective as a treatment for cancer, the results were an amazing tribute to the power of the mind to cure or kill. Following the injection, Klopfer notes:

> What a surprise was in store for me! I left him febrile, gasping for air, completely bedridden. Now, here he was, walking around the ward, chatting happily with the nurses, and spreading the message of good cheer to all who would listen. . . . The tumor masses had melted like snow balls on a hot stove, and in only these few days they were half their original size! This is, of course, far more rapid regression than the most radiosensitive tumor could display under heavy x-ray given every day. . . . And he had no other treatment outside of the single useless shot.[2]

After ten days, the man was practically disease-free and was able to resume his normal pastimes. His improvement continued until he read reports that questioned the medicinal value of the drug he was taking. After reading them, he acted as if he had been cursed; his mental and physical state deteriorated markedly. In order to counter the impact of the negative news, Dr. Klopfer urged him not to pay attention to the reports and then injected him with a "super strength" version of the drug, which was, in fact, only sterile water. Once more, the patient returned to a state of physical well-being and hopefulness. As physician Larry Dossey notes, "the de-hexing worked." However, he was hexed once again when he read that the American Medical Association deemed Krebiozen to be worthless in the treatment of cancer. He returned to the hospital and died two days later.

Physicians Larry Dossey and Andrew Weil both point out the possibility of medical hexing. Andrew Weil, director of the

---

2. Larry Dossey, *Be Careful What You Pray For . . . You Just Might Get It* (San Francisco: HarperSanFrancisco, 1997), 70.

Program in Integrative Medicine at the University of Arizona, states that "too many doctors are deeply pessimistic about the possibility of people getting better and they communicate that to their patients and families." The interplay of disease-oriented medical training and an objectivity that leaves little room for unexpected transformation in their understanding of illness and recovery can be harmful to their patients. Many physicians have forgotten the innate healing tendencies within each person, as well as the heightening of the healing process through the divine-human synergy. As authority figures, not unlike shamans and priests of traditional cultures, physicians by their words often define the medical realities of their patients. According to Weil, physicians need "to use extreme care in the words they speak to patients" and be "more conscious of the power projected onto them by patients and the possibilities for reflecting that power back in ways that influence health for better rather than worse."[3] Weil and Dossey note the most common complaints they hear of medical negativity include judgments such as the following:

"They said there was nothing they could do for me."
"They told me it would only get worse."
"They told me I would just have to live with it."
"They said I would be dead in six months."
"You are living on borrowed time."
"You are going downhill fast."
"Your next heartbeat may be your last."

As medically accurate as these counsels may be to the physician, they deny even the most realistic forms of hope for the patient, which in turn may only further depress the immune or cardiovascular systems, and thus accelerate the process of deterioration. To such medical realists, one might easily respond, albeit with a degree of irony and gentleness, in the words of Jesus to Peter, "Get behind me, Satan!"

---

3. Andrew Weil, *Spontaneous Healing* (New York: Alfred A. Knopf, 1995), 64.

As an example of medical hexing Larry Dossey describes a letter he received from a woman with AIDS. Her doctor, who believed in presenting a "realistic" picture of his or her chances to each patient, reminded the woman that since AIDS is "uniformly fatal," she should follow his treatment to the letter. In her own words, she describes her own discovery of this toxic counsel:

> I began to realize my doctor doesn't *believe* I'm going to live. . . . It takes two weeks to recover from a visit to him. He leaves me depressed and feeling sick. But after two weeks have passed, I always begin to feel terrific. Then, when it's time to return for an appointment, a feeling of dread overwhelms me. I have to make myself keep my appointment. After the visit the cycle repeats itself. . . . Why do I feel like my own physician is *killing* me? [4]

If our health and illness is the result of many factors, including the beliefs of our culture, family, and physicians, Weil is absolutely correct when he states that "it is not a good idea to stay in treatment with a doctor who thinks you cannot get better."[5] In the spirit of Jesus' attitude toward the mourners at Jairus's house, we should "put out" such a physician and find one who integrates medical realism with openness to human possibility, the power of prayer and affirmations, and the surprising presence of God. In addition, we should fire ministers, counselors, and new age spiritual/medical guides who see our illnesses as "divine punishment for sin," "a result of our lack of faith," or "reflection entirely of our thoughts." Our spiritual and physical survival may depend upon it!

In order to create an environment of healing and transformation, Jesus isolated the little girl and her parents from everything that would prevent them from trusting God. In that moment, the parents needed to hear just one voice—the healing voice of the

4. Dossey, *Be Careful What You Pray For*, 74.
5. Weil, *Spontaneous Healing*, 64.

divine spirit. They needed a respite from their culture's voices of negativity and death. In providing that healing voice, Jesus demonstrated his prophetic vocation to embody an alternative reality to the forces of death and destruction in his culture. To the realist, Jesus' statement that the girl still lived was an illusion. In terms of their one-dimensional, closed-system vision of reality, Jesus' words were counterfactual. But Jesus' deeper perception brought a dying girl back to life.

The visualization of an alternative reality can make the difference between life and death of the flesh and the spirit. In his counsel to persons diagnosed with cancer, radiation oncologist O. Carl Simonton challenges them to question three medical and social myths that often demoralize persons diagnosed with cancer: (1) cancer is synonymous with death; (2) cancer is something that strikes from without, and there is no hope for controlling it; and (3) treatment is always drastic and has negative side effects. Simonton invites persons to explore alternative realities that often transform their lives. In recognizing the emotional and spiritual aspects of health and illness, Simonton reminds his patients that (1) the majority of persons diagnosed with cancer survive and persons may survive even the most virulent of cancers; (2) persons are not passive victims of their cancer, but can marshal resources for the healing of mind and body through meditation and visualization, changing negative habits of thinking, and claiming their own unique power; (3) the medicine is meant to help the patient, and its side effects are not uniform and may depend on one's attitude.[6] Simonton sees the diagnosis of cancer as an opportunity to choose life and to find new spiritual power. Even if death is the final outcome, Simonton's process of spiritual empowerment enables persons to die with dignity, hope, and reconciliation. From his own observation of persons with cancer, Simonton asserts that a "positive

---

6. O. Carl Simonton, Stephanie Matthews Simonton, James Creighton, *Getting Well Again* (Los Angeles: J. P. Tarcher, 1978), 78.

attitude toward treatment was a better predictor of response to treatment than the severity of disease."[7]

At one level, the effective use of affirmations involves the exercise of the power of the imagination. Today many of us utilize guided meditation and visualization exercises to awaken the healing presence of God in our lives. When I feel the flu coming on, I take time to "center" on the divine light surrounding my body and permeating every cell within it. As I inhale, I embrace God's healing light, and as I exhale, I release the toxins within me. A young mother diagnosed with cancer visualizes the chemotherapy as healing waters entering her body and renewing its strength. She images herself as actively raising her children and serving God, despite the intrusive treatments. While she experiences some of the side effects of chemotherapy, her discomfort is minimized by her belief that in all things God is working for good.

In the Still Point meditation group at her church in Washington, D.C., my wife, Dr. Katherine Epperly, begins each group meeting with a guided visualization of the flow and absorption of God's healing and cleansing light and love into the body with each inhalation. Beginning with the head and moving down the body, with particular attention to any points of dis-ease, she invites the participants to image the body as embraced by the empowering "flow state" of God's light and love. Sometimes the visualization is expanded to include the group as a healing circle of light radiating outward for the healing of each member and the wider community.

A profound example of the creative power of the mind to transform reality is portrayed in the award-winning film *Life is Beautiful*. Set in the context of a dehumanizing Nazi concentration camp, the film reveals how an alternative vision of reality can make the difference between life and death. When a

---

7. Ibid., 7.

father and his young son are sent to a concentration camp, the father hides his son in the dormitory and then artfully tells him that the concentration camp is a giant game; the child who behaves, hides himself, keeps a positive spirit, and doesn't ask for snacks even when he is hungry will win a wonderful prize—a life-sized tank. With death, fear, and insecurity all around him, the boy survives the camp precisely because he believes his father's alternative interpretation of reality. While this film may seem overly simplistic in its description of the young boy's survival, psychiatrist Victor Frankl, also a Holocaust survivor, proclaims that those patients who transcended the indignities of the concentration camp as a result of their hope in the future, faith in God, or the dream of reuniting with their families tended to survive, while those who gave up hope soon died of illness. Which interpretation of experience most deeply reflects the nature of reality—the demonic forces of Hitler or a father's creative love, the realism of the weeping crowd or Jesus' vision of a child made well, the brutality of the cross or the mystery of the resurrection? Even within the concentration camp, there is a divine beauty and a deeper voice of truth that will long outlast the Hitlers of our world. Even in the cancer ward, there is the inspiration of new life, transformed behaviors, and reconcilation with God and loved ones. This *creative nonconformity can be a matter of life and death!*

In the privacy of the healing circle, Jesus reached out to the comatose child. Jesus touched her and then awakened her with the simple command, "Little girl, get up." Jesus created a "field of force," a divine energy field, in which life was stronger than her environment's image of death. Had the parents, the disciples, or even Jesus focused on the realism of the mourners, the little girl would never have been revived. Jesus' affirmation of God's presence in her life included the reality of her tenuous health condition, but it was not limited by it—for within her coma, she could still experience the touch that would make her well.

Of course, even the creation of a physical or spiritual healing circle or the imaging of the God's healing light does not insure physical recovery. Within the multidimensional and multicausal nature of life and divine activity, not all illnesses are cured, the process of aging is not always arrested, and death is not always vanquished. Still, those who suffer from chronic illnesses may discover the abiding peace that lies beneath the social stereotypes of disability. Although he experiences the debilitation of chronic illness and still mourns the death of his wife of fifty years, the aging widower may discover the true meaning of the "golden years" as a time to nurture a meaningful and generative relationship with his grandchildren.

For the dying and the chronically ill, there is always the possibility of another kind of healing environment and another kind of healing. Dying need not be a "lost season," but can be an opportunity for sharing one's story and discovering the meaning of life. In their response to the physical and spiritual pain of dying, churches and hospices can enable persons to celebrate their lives by planning memorial services and sharing their life histories on audio or video tape. They can also confront the emotional and spiritual pain of dying with media as simple as crayons or as elaborate as oil paints, music, drama, and dance. But always the healing occurs when we are surrounded by "the circle whose center is everywhere and whose circumference is nowhere," in the embodiment of God's love in the loving care of family, friends, and compassionate caregivers.

This past week I officiated at the memorial service of a woman whose belief in the power of the mind and the wellspring of divine creativity enabled her to face her cancer with courage. As the service ended, the congregation at the Unity church was moved by the singing of Louis Armstrong's rendition of "What a Wonderful World." The community that gathered at the service remembered that cancer and death were not the whole story of Jean's life nor are they whole story of our own lives. Jean's life and our own lives were and are knit together by a continuous flow of beauty, imagination, love, surprise, and joy. Even in her final days, this woman could still proclaim, "What a wonderful world!"

The healing of Jairus' daughter challenges us to create holistic healing environments on both the physical and spiritual levels. Today many hospitals are planting gardens and enhancing the environments of their patients, in light of findings that patients whose rooms provide pleasant views recover more quickly than those who lack lovely and open vistas. Hospices and churches are constructing "memory trees" to honor the deceased. Patients request the music of their choice and recorded spiritual affirmations to be played during surgery and are decorating their hospital rooms with familiar and aesthetic objects. Patients and families are increasingly "countercultural" as they choose not to define their lives in terms of medical limitations.

Churches and hospices are called to be places of creative spiritual noncomformity, where persons can test alternative visions of reality pertaining to the health of body, mind, and spirit. Churches in particular should become beacons of hope and empowerment, advocating holistic health and wholeness and enabling persons to be creatively transformed from hopelessness to authentic hope. Within God's healing circle, followers of the healing Christ are called to challenge the medical profession, insurance system, and culture as a whole to facililate positive progams for healing at every level of life. With full awareness of the accountant's bottom line, they can still advocate creatively for a health care system based on compassion and abundance rather than scarcity. Jesus "put out" the negative so that the positive might emerge. He called the parents to see their daughter as alive! We are equally called to live by the divine affirmations so that God's wonderful world may break forth for all whose lives are imprisoned by suffering and death.

An Experiment in Healing and Wholeness

Jesus' life was the embodiment of his affirmations of faith. Many people today are learning to change their lives through the conscious dwelling on affirmations of faith. Virtually any limiting situation can call forth a transformative affirmation. In my own spiritual life, I regularly recite biblical affirmations as a means of renewing and retraining my mind so that it may be more closely aligned with the imaginative and transformative mind of Christ. My regular affirmations of faith include statements such as these: "Nothing can separate me from the love of God." "I can do all things through Christ who strengthens me." "God will supply all my needs." "I am strong in the Lord." "God's light shines in my life." As I live with these and other affirmations, I begin to see the world from the perspective of creativity, abundance, and possibility. New insights emerge where previously I saw only dead ends. Behaviors change, and thought patterns evolve.

Take time to reflect on your own life. What situations are limiting your sense of possibility? What obstacles lie in your path to abundant life? What gift of God would you need to overcome these obstacles? What divine promise from scripture or worship addresses your need for transformation?

Take time to let these creative affirmations emerge. While these affirmations may at first seem unrealistic or counterfactual, they may become the catalysts for a new vision of reality and a new life itself for you. You may also come to experience the truth of Paul's own affirmation, "Do not be conformed to this world, but be transformed by the renewing of your minds" (Rom. 12:2).

After leaving the synagogue [Jesus] entered Simon's house.
Now Simon's mother-in-law was suffering from a high fever,
and they asked about her. Then he stood over her and
rebuked the fever, and it left her. Immediately, she got up and
began to serve them. As the sun was setting, all those who
had any who were sick with various kinds of diseases
brought them to him; and he laid his hands on them and
cured them. Demons also came out of many, shouting, "You
are the Son of God!" But he rebuked them and would not
allow them to speak, because they knew he was the Messiah.
At daybreak he departed and went to a deserted place. And
the crowds were looking for him; and when they reached
him, they wanted to prevent him from leaving them. But he
said to them, "I must proclaim the good news of the
kingdom of God to the other cities also; for I was sent for
this purpose." So he continued proclaiming the message in
the synagogues of Judea.

(Luke 4:38–44, see also Matt. 8:14–17, Mark 1:29–34)

Chapter Ten

The Healing of the Ordinary

*M*y wife tells the story of a prayer request by a recently born-again Christian. Following her conversion, the young woman found herself backsliding into her old habits of marijuana and alcohol use. In the parking lot following a service at Calvary Chapel in southern California, she invited a number of bystanders to gather in a circle to pray that she find a new place to live, where she would be free of the temptations of drugs and alcohol, and the fortitude to maintain her commitment to a substance-free life. As the prayer ended, she swooned in ecstasy and then opened her eyes and made one more prayer request: "Could we pray for one more thing? Could someone pray that I get a cheeseburger, coke, and french fries?"

While this girl's attitude about prayer may reflect the superficial and naïve understanding of prayer character-istic of much popular Christianity, the young woman's prayer request still raises an important issue for anyone who prays regularly: are any of our needs too small or insignificant to be of concern to God? Is God concerned about our next meal, our job interview or promotion, or the relief of minor headache or flu?

At first glance, Jesus' healing of Peter's mother-in-law from a high fever seems of little consequence compared to Jesus' exorcism of demons, healing of lepers, and restoration of persons with chronic illnesses. But if we take a closer look at Jesus' healing ministry, within that very modest healing story we see God's intimate interest in even the "least of these."

Although there are obvious gradations in the impact of various diseases of mind, body, and spirit on a person's health, no disease or discomfort is unimportant *when it affects our lives*. For a number of years, I was afflicted once or twice each year with debilitating headaches. They would follow a pattern: a headache and fever, nausea, and throwing up. Although the headaches would eventually subside, they took up the better part of a day and prevented me from fulfilling my family and professional responsibilities. When I finally broke the cycle of headache and nausea through a combination of centering and breath prayer, I felt a sense of physical and spiritual deliverance. As unimportant as these occasional headaches might have seemed to an outsider, I had experienced a healing!

There are no small ailments: a case of the three-day flu can prevent us from attending a college friend's wedding; arthritic pain can make a lifetime hobby such as golf or knitting a virtual torture; a sprained ankle on the eve of a marathon can delay a long-term dream; a pimple on the eve of the senior prom can temporarily ruin a teenager's life; the anxiety of encountering a difficult person can cloud our joy of attending a dinner party. Relief from even the smallest ailments lifts and broadens our spirits, for now once more we can plunge into life with a sense of vitality and confidence. Even as I write these words, I am recovering from a spring cold that left me weary, unfocused, and sleepless at a time when I was looking forward to a few extra hours for writing, hiking, and socializing. For me, this inconvenience was no small matter. I wanted to feel my best during my spring break. I took extra time for meditation and self-administered reiki healing touch in order to accelerate the healing process. I also prayed for God's healing presence to be the catalyst for the most creative outcome. If God truly is "the circle whose center is everywhere and whose circumference is nowhere," then no problem is either too small or too large to ask for the touch of God.

Have you ever become sick on the eve of a dinner party at your home? If you have had this experience, you know what Simon's mother-in-law felt as the visitors arrived: the groceries have been purchased, the floors cleaned and furniture dusted, the flowers arranged, the liquor cabinet stocked; but now you're not sure if the party can go on. As the day progresses, you wonder if you should call your friends with apologies and plans for another day.

In Jesus' culture, hospitality was a fine art. Even in the humblest of homes, guests were greeted as if they were angels in disguise. Special foods were prepared, and the best wines were purchased. In the patriarchal society of Jesus' time, such preparation fell to the women, and the quality of hospitality and cuisine reflected on the senior woman of the house. With the coming of Simon's good friend and teacher, Jesus, Simon's mother-in-law's illness was for her a social catastrophe. The intensity of her feelings of disappointment and failure matched that of her high fever.

When Jesus arrived at Simon Peter's home, Simon Peter and his wife simply asked him to look in on her and see if anything could be done to relieve her symptoms. Although Simon Peter's mother-in-law's fever was not a serious illness, Luke's account implies that it was related to the activity of a demon. As we will see in the next chapter, Jesus' contemporaries often viewed the activity of demons as the source of physical and mental disturbances. Jesus' exorcism of the fever followed the same pattern as his exorcism of the demons at the synagogue in Capernaum: "He stood over her and rebuked the fever, and it left her" (Luke 4:39). The earlier account of this healing found in Mark's Gospel identifies Jesus' healing of the fever with the touch of God: "He came and took her by the hand and lifted her up. Then the fever left her" (Mark 1:31). Whether mediated by word or touch, divine healing is available even for the smallest of things.

Regardless of the methodology of Jesus' healing or whether demons were, in fact, involved in the illness, one thing is certain: Jesus' concern for wholeness embraced not only persons experiencing chronic illness, social ostracism, and demon possession; it also included persons suffering from the minor, self-limiting ailments that diminished the quality of their lives. If Jesus came that we might have abundant life, then anything that prevents us from living fully is a proper object for God's care and our own.

Often, when persons come to see me, they apologize in advance for taking up my time with their small problems. After all, a relational breakup, a torn ligament, or everyday stress seems hardly worth taking up the pastor's time, in light of the pressing needs of mental illness, divorce, injustice and racism, and global warming. Yet at such times I remind my visitors of God's omnipresent care. The divine circle embraces even the smallest of problems. As Jesus proclaims in the Sermon on the Mount, "If God so clothes the grass of the field, which is alive today and tomorrow is thrown into the oven, will he not much more clothe you—you of little faith? Therefore, do not worry, saying 'What will we eat?' or 'What will we drink?' or 'What will we wear?' . . . Your heavenly Father knows that you need all these things" (Mat. 6:30–32). Like the good parent, the divine Parent is concerned about the ordinary events, as well as the dramatic decisions of our lives, for in the ecology of human life the smallest details can be of great significance. A chance comment can change a person's life forever. The proper functioning of an inexpensive O-ring can make the difference between a successful space mission or the crash of the Challenger. God is in the details of our physical as well as our spiritual lives.

> Ask, and it will be given to you; search, and you will find; knock, and the door will be opened for you. For everyone who asks receives, and everyone who searches finds, and for everyone who knocks, the door will be opened. Is there anyone among you who, if your child asks for bread, will give a stone? Or if a child asks for a fish, will give a snake? If you then, who are evil [imperfect as parents], know how to give good gifts to your children, how much more will your Father in heaven give good things to those who ask him! (Matt. 7:7–11)

The God "to whom all hearts are open and all desires known" is at work in each and every situation of our lives. As the apostle Paul notes in his desciption of the body of Christ in 1 Corinthians 12:26: "If one member suffers, all suffer together with it; if one member is honored, all rejoice together with it." This intricate web of relationships, dynamically creative of one another, radiates throughout our persons, relationships, and communities. The restoration of wholeness to any aspect of our lives can bring harmony and well-being to every other aspect of our lives, relationships, family, and community. If, as a Vietnamese Buddhist monk asserts, "peace is every step," then any small step of peace and wholeness transfigures our planet.

The healing of mind, body, and spirit is a call to service. Luke's Gospel simply states that "immediately she got up and began to serve them" (Luke 4:39). While some might suggest that her return to the kitchen is a reflection of the paternalistic bias of her society, there is a deeper meaning to her response than merely fulfilling a woman's role in a sexist culture! Author Frederick Buechner once stated that a person's vocation is where his or her gifts and passions meet the world's needs. In this situation, Simon's mother-in-law possessed the gift of service and hospitality. When the fever abated, she could once more fulfill her deepest desire and giftedness within her social and family context. In like manner, our own healings call us to mediate healing and wholeness to others.

Our own process of spiritual discernment will reveal to us the form of service that is our vocation in the present moment. Just as the healing of the leper was completed by his expression of gratitude to Jesus, our own healing process remains incomplete apart from our reconnection with others through grateful service to God's creation. Simon's mother-in-law's healing reminds us that we are "blessed to be a blessing," channeling the healing we have received to those around us.

Many commentators note that Luke 4 is a literary device whose purpose is to describe the rhythm of a day in the life of Jesus. In the course of that chapter Jesus teaches at the synagogue, heals a demon-possessed man, enjoys a meal with friends, and then at day's end cures persons of a variety of diseases. But as the new day begins, Jesus "departed and went into a deserted place" (Luke 4:42). As our model of ministry, Jesus reminds us that we need to take time for spiritual recreation as well. The quality of Jesus' own ministry required that he take regular time for prayer, meditation, and refreshment. Jesus needed to reconnect consciously with his divine Parent in order to have the guidance and power to respond to the spiritual, emotional, and physical needs of those who constantly sought his care. In centering on God, Jesus maintained his own personal center amid the maelstrom of sickness and controversy that defined the external quality of his daily life.

We should take note that in the midst of his ministry of healing, Jesus also does something quite remarkable. When the townspeople ask him to stay, Jesus asserts that he needs to reach out to others: "I must proclaim the good news of the kingdom of God to the other cities also; for I was sent for this purpose" (Luke 4:43). One of the greatest problems that caregivers encounter is the temptation to become indispensable to their patients and parishioners. Often healers feel that persons in need cannot live without their care and that they must constantly immerse themselves in the needs of the parish, community, or hospital. In the quest to be the perfect and essential helper, many caregivers may come to need their patients as much as the patients need them. Family life, personal relationships, marriages, and self-care are neglected in order to care for just one more person. Often the caregiver is convicted of her or his own dependence on being a healer when a spouse or child cries out, "I wish I were sick, so that you would take care of me."

It is an important act of faith to leave your work unfinished and to let go of those who have been the objects of your care. The stability of the familiar and the notoriety of success have a tremendous allure. The need to be productive and helpful can become addictive, especially when our self-worth depends on our constant caregiving. But, Jesus let go of the need to be a helper when he left the adulation and comfort of Capernaum to journey toward new and surprising encounters along the Sea of Galilee. Perhaps, in the quiet of the morning Jesus struggled with his own temptation to co-dependence, his own need to solve everyone's problem, and his concern about leaving so many persons still in pain. No doubt Jesus realized that he could have a lifetime's work just caring for the spiritual and physical needs of the people of Capernaum. But as compassionate as such care would be, it would have left his neighbors in a position of dependence and restricted the impact of his own ministry to a limited geographical area. In leaving the successful work at Capernaum, Jesus trusted that indigenous healers would emerge and that those whom he had healed would share his healing power with others. Jesus also trusted that God would continue the good work that he had begun in Capernaum. In leaving an ideal healing setting in order to face the controversies ahead, Jesus empowered his followers in Capernaum to grow in wisdom and in divine and human favor, just as Jesus himself had grown (Luke 2:52).

Jesus no doubt experienced grief over leaving those he had healed. Every caregiver experiences this same grief, and many are tempted to maintain a relationship of dependence in those they treat, in order to avoid the pain of saying good-bye and to maintain their superior status in the healer-patient relationship. Further, we want to see the fruits of our spiritual labors blossom into healthy and whole persons. But such clinging, hierarchical relationships eventually weaken the energy that had been instrumental in the healing process and stand in the way of the patient's own well-being. God always calls us to greater adventures!

Difficult as it may be to accept, the adventure of life always involves the experience of "perpetual perishing," as the philosopher Alfred North Whitehead maintains. While this constant reality of perishing elicits the experience of grief and can cause undue clinging to familiar situations, it also brings the gift of novelty, surprise, and growth. Educators, pastors, and healers are "transitional persons," whose vocation is lived out best by giving "roots and wings" to those they encounter. In the midst of the challenges of our own perpetual perishing, clinging to even the most creative healing relationships disempowers both the caregiver and the patient. It prevents the caregiver from experiencing God's call toward the future, and it prevents the patient from claiming her role as a healer and agent of God's love. If we are, in the spirit of God's promise to the aged pilgrims Abraham and Sarah, blessed to be a blessing (Gen. 12:2), then the greatest ambition for any parent, pastor, professor, caregiver, or healer is that those for whom they have cared may grow in freedom, stature, and service, and thus become healers themselves. In contrast to those who see obedience to rules or infantile adulation as the primary form of the divine-human relationship, the image of an adventurous partnership inspires us to creativity, freedom, and novelty in our relationship with the divine Parent. God delights in freedom and surprise. Partnership with God requires us to imitate the divine adventure in our own commitment to creative freedom.

In taking time for quiet reflection and reconnection with God, the caregiver learns to live with the grief of letting go and find new adventures in the vocation that God has planned for her. When Jesus left Capernaum, he followed the will of God to reach out to other cities and towns. When the caregiver attends to God's often unsettling and adventurous voice, he is also beginning a new journey with the trust in the synchronicities—meaningful coincidences and everyday epiphanies—that will bring him into contact with new persons who will share in the mutual process of healing and transformation. She is also on the edge of discovering new dimensions of her own life and vocation as a partnership with the divine adventurer for whom nothing is ordinary and whose care embraces all things, large and small.

An Experiment in Healing and Wholeness

A healing spirituality makes sacred the ordinary and everyday realities of life. God is working for wholeness and abundant life in the smallest details of our lives. Most of the time, however, we are blind to God's presence. A prayerful imagination enables us to discern God in the ordinary. In this exercise, we will imaginatively seek God's unobtrusive presence in the undramatic events of our lives.

1. Take a moment to be still and know that God is with you.
2. In the quiet, ask God to reveal God's presence to you in a particular ordinary event. Let the event emerge without judgment.
3. As you reflect on the event, explore it from many perspectives. Open to God's presence within that particular event. Glimpse signs of divine guidance and creativity in yourself and in others.
4. Then, surround the event with the light of God. Let the divine light permeate and transform the event into an icon or epiphany of God's presence.
5. Thank God for being with you in the ordinary moments of life.

This meditative prayer can be done for a future event in which you desire to be attuned to God's presence by simply substituting, in step three, a future event for a present or past event.

Life is a perpetual perishing. As the Buddhists note, clinging or attachment to the ever-changing is the source of unhappiness. In this exercise, identify some event, possession, relationship, or position to which you are particularly attached. Observe the nature of your attachment. How does it manifest itself in your life? Is it a source of anxiety or pain? Then, as significant as this role or possession may be, place it in God's hands. Let go of the familiar. Explore what it is like to live without this possession. Give your future to God's care. Ask God to reveal to you the gifts of letting go of this familiar situation. In your mind's eye, experience the edges of a new adventure God has planned for you. With confidence in the future, you can let go and let God!

Then they arrived at the country of the Gerasenes, which is opposite Galilee. As they stepped out on land, a man of the city who had demons met him. For a long time he had worn no clothes, and he did not live in a house but in the tombs. When he saw Jesus, he fell down before him and shouted at the top of his voice, "What have you to do with me, Jesus, Son of the Most High God? I beg you, do not torment me"— for Jesus had commanded the unclean spirit to come out of the man. (For many times it had seized him; he was kept under guard and bound with chains and shackles, but he would break the bonds and be driven by the demon into the wilds.) Jesus then asked him, "What is your name?" He said, "Legion"; for many demons had entered him. They begged him not to order them to go back into the abyss.

Now there on the hillside a large herd of swine was feeding; and the demons begged Jesus to enter these. So he gave them permission. Then the demons came out of the man and entered the swine, and the herd rushed down the steep bank into the lake and was drowned.

When the swineherds saw what had happened, they ran off and told it in the city and in the country. Then people came out to see what had happened, and when they came to Jesus, they found the man from whom the demons had gone sitting at the feet of Jesus, clothed and in his right mind. . . . The man from whom the demons had gone begged that he might be with him; but Jesus sent him away, saying, "Return to your home, and declare how much God has done for you." So he went away, proclaiming throughout the city how much Jesus had done for him.

(Luke 8:26–35, 38–39)

Chapter Eleven

Healing the Shattered Self

*A*round the corner from my office at Georgetown University are the famed "Exorcist Steps." While Georgetown University is world-renowned for its academic excellence, many visitors to the university find its connection with the movie *The Exorcist* of greater interest than its libraries, chapels, and classrooms. Although presentations of the *The Exorcist* have been dropped from the university orientation schedule as a result of the terror many students experienced during their first weekend on campus, still each Halloween the grand lecture hall is filled to capacity for showings of this drama of spiritual warfare.

In spite of the big-screen obsession with the topic of demon possession, Luke's account of the healing of the demon-possessed man has been an embarrassment to many modern Christians. For persons who are committed to the modern world's focus on one-dimensional, closed-system, and reductionistic explanations of illness and misfortune, serious speculation on the possibility of demon possession borders on archaic superstition and magical thinking. Indeed, the notion of demon possession has itself been "exorcized" from the modern world, first, by medical explanations such as multiple personality or other dissociative disorders, which are then to be addressed only by the right medications and, second, by the de-mythologizing of Bible scholars who interpret such accounts as poetic and metaphorical descriptions of existential angst and the challenge of achieving authentic, centered selfhood.

Still, despite the modern worldview's emphasis on the supremacy of conscious control and scientific explanation, sometimes even modern persons recognize how precarious their sense of control and normalcy may be. From time to time, ordinary language betrays the fracture within the rational unity of the self through explanations for atypical behavior such as "I'm just not myself today," "What possessed me to say that to her?" "Why did I do this?" and "What's gotten into her?" While psychiatrists such as Freud and Jung speak of the power of unconscious drives and archetypes to shape conscious intentionality, the unsettled first-year college student may still quite irrationally fear that a demon lurks in the shadows along the dimly lit hallways of gargoyle-protected buildings, following his Halloween viewing of *The Exorcist*.

Despite the modern exaltation of rationality and conscious control of the psyche, there has been a growing interest in the nonrational and mysterious demensions of the universe. A fascination with angels, demons, and spirit beings is demonstrated by the popularity of television programs such as *Touched by an Angel* and *The X-Files* and the best-selling new age narratives of "channeled" communications described in Neal Donald Walsch's *Conversations with God* or actress Shirley MacLaine's autobiographical narratives. The *Star Wars* saga celebrates the transformative power of following our inner, intuitive voice and the ongoing battle between the "light" and "dark" sides of the Force. At the local bookstore, books on ESP, tarot cards, contacting spirit guides, and white and black witchcraft are stacked right beside the various translations of more traditional inspired texts, such as the Bible, the Koran, and the Bhagavad Gita. Spirits of good and evil seem to be speaking from every street corner!

While the power of evil is often downplayed in mainline Christianity and the new age movement by identifying it with ignorance, illusion, the absence of good, metaphysical lessons we need to learn, or simply an outmoded worldview, the words of the twentieth-century Pope Paul VI challenge us to rethink our understanding of both personal and global evil: "Evil is not merely a lack of something, but an effective agent, a living spiritual being, perverted and perverting." About sixty years ago, in the most sophisticated literary and scientific culture of its time, the demonic broke forth in the rantings of an evil leader and the willingness of millions of average citizens to support the "final solution" of the Holocaust. As we witness the reemergence of ethnic cleansing in the former Yugoslavia, swastikas painted on the walls at Columbine High School in Littleton, Colorado, and the rebirth of murderous apocalyptic religious cults and hate groups in the United States, Japan, and Africa, the power of the demonic seems much more tangible than the idyllic new age dream of the dawning of the Age of Aquarius.

In the shadowlands of consciousness where things go bump in the night, even the sophisticated and skeptical modern wonders if there really are powers of evil at work in the compulsions and irrational behaviors of persons and nations, as well as in his or her own random musings. While the idea of a literal Satan, attired in red tights and horns and brandishing a pitchfork, has been banished from all but the most conservative churches and clichéd movie scripts, the evils that today confront us point to the existence of a vast uncontrolled world, inhabiting the twilight zone beyond the boundaries of conscious experience. As we ponder the reality of altered states and parallel realities, our much-vaunted human consciousness may be merely a flickering candle enveloped by the gloom of unconscious drives, personal and corporate demons, and irrational compulsions, on the one hand, and brightness of angelic hosts and divine guidance, on the other.

In Luke's Gospel, the account of the Geresene demoniac is juxtaposed with the narrative of a storm at sea, as if to remind us that in real life the storms of the spirit and the flesh mirror one another. With waves crashing all around them and their ship on the verge of sinking, the disciples panicked. "Master, Master, we are perishing!" they cried out. In the midst of the maelstrom, they forgot that Jesus was present with them. When Jesus awoke, he rebuked the storm and once more the sea was calm. Jesus' rebuke, similar in pattern to his exorcism of the Geresene demonic, banished the disciples' fear, as well as the threatening storm. As the waves ceased to buffet their boat, Jesus simply asked, "Where is your faith?" In the spirit of Psalm 46, Jesus reminded his followers that although the earth may shake and the mountains fall into the sea, God still remains our refuge. Even when the tumult of life threatens to shatter us, there is a deep place of peace within each one of us—Jesus is in the midst of the storm as our deepest reality and source of strength. Whether the storms are internal or external—whether our bodies are perishing or our emotional lives out of control—there is a place within the storm where we can be still and know that God is with us.

In real life, the inner storms of spirit and flesh are often more frightening than the external storms of wind and rain. When the self is shattered and out of control, there is no escape to a place of quiet and peace. The mind has become its own worst enemy, unpredictable and irrational in its thought patterns and interpretations of reality. This experience of inner tumult has, from the very beginning of human history, been a source of both fear and awe. It has been the pathway to both transformation and disintegration. Among the ancient Greeks, epilepsy was described as the sacred disease, because its symptoms mimicked the ecstatic and self-transcending experiences of divine possession. The calling and designation of the shaman involved the experience of trancelike states that dissociated the shaman from everyday experience. Hebraic prophets often were caught up in divine frenzy as they became the mouthpieces of God. Today charismatic speaking in tongues and new age channeling of spiritual entities involve the voluntary or involuntary setting aside of the rational self so that higher powers may utilize the self as a means of divine communication. Yet for many persons the setting aside of the conscious self by other spiritual or psychic influences is involuntary and leads to terror and the loss of the self. Encounter with the transrational or nonrational edges of life can cure or kill the spirit, depending on the strength of the centered self and the nature and intentions of the nonrational spirit. When the self has lost control entirely to negative forces beyond itself, then we need a spiritual exorcism, the touch of God, to deliver us from the demonic and return us to wholeness.

The description of the demon-possessed man has a clinical quality to it: "For a long time he had worn no clothes, and he did not live in a house but in the tombs. . . . For many times it [the unclean spirit] had seized him; he was kept under guard and bound with chains and shackles, but he would break the bonds and be driven by the demon into the wilds" (Luke 8:27, 29). Although the demons reveal themselves to be multiple in identity, Luke's account implies the existence of a master demon or ultimate cause of the disintegration of the man's self. Perhaps the trauma of some experience had enabled the many demons to enter into his life, or perhaps he was controlled by an evil spirit that sought out the companionship of other demonic entities. Whether we demonize or medicalize this man's ailment, it is clear that he is powerless to deliver himself from the influence of his unwelcome guests, be they conflicting subpersonalities or demonic multiple personalities. By any description, such a state is diabolical, that is, disintegrating and shattering of the intended wholeness of the self. Isolated from his family and community, this man is powerless to defeat the forces of evil that have invaded his psyche.

When Jesus asks about the identity of these spiritual beings, the demon's response is direct: "I am legion," as if to say "I am many selves and the one I possess no longer has a personal center of his own any more." While few of us can relate from personal experience to the notion of demon possession or multiple personality disorder, we have all experienced the reality of the uncentered self. Like the apostle Paul, we search for identity and integrity of spirit, only to discover how fragmented and self-contradictory we really are. As Paul confesses, "I do not do the good I want, but the evil I do not want is what I do. . . . Who will rescue me from this body of death?" (Rom. 7:19, 24) Even those of us who consider ourselves spiritually and mentally healthy often discover how little control we have over our emotions and reactions to life situations. Often these voices shout loudest in moments when we seek the silence of meditation or centering prayer. Buffeted about by conscious desires and unconscious drives, we become "practical polytheists," worshiping the god of the moment, with only the barest strand of self-possession to give our lives coherence and clear direction. In such moments we confess with the poet Walt Whitman, "I am large, I contain a multitude."

While such complexity and breadth of experience can be the source of adventure and beauty, the unintegrated multiplicity can bring about aimlessness, chaos, and moral disorder. As Maurice Nicoll avers, "A multitude of different people live inside of each of you. These are different I's belonging to each personality. . . . Not one of you has a real permanent unchanging "I." Not one of you has a real unity of being."[1] Each of our "many selves" worships at the altar of a different God, often forgetful of that still, small voice of God's spirit, which is the deepest reality of our lives.

The spiritual healing that brings integrity to our many selves involves the commitment to listen to and follow the guidance of that deepest self, the Christ within, moving gently and persistently in the storm of conflicting voices to give unity and guidance to the psyche. Such healing involves our willingness, or the willingness of another who speaks on our behalf, to embark on the prayerful quest for the divine center that speaks within us in "sighs too deep for words."

---

1. Quoted in Elizabeth O'Connor, *Our Many Selves* (New York: Harper & Row, 1971), 35.

When we look closely and honestly at ourselves, we know that our selves are multivalent, protean, and manifold in nature. The manifold self we discover can be so frightening that we scale down our experience, limiting our experience to the socially and spiritually acceptable sides of our nature, or, after realizing our inability to do the good toward which we aim, plunging ourselves into the darkness of evil, unconsciousness, and addiction. Our experience can be so protean and unstable that we focus only on the clearly defined self of our conscious roles and responsibilities. In so doing, we become alienated from the wellsprings of creativity that also lurk beneath the conscious mind. As we confront the dark and light, the abyss as well as the heights, of our self's complexity, we may also discover that our manifold self is the inspiration to adventure as we seek to become the artists of our own experience. As a poster inspired by the thought of Carl Jung notes, "All the wonders you seek are inside yourself." But this adventure in healthy creative synthesis of the prismatic and protean self occurs only when our personal center of experience is aligned with the divine center whose center is everywhere, even including the manifold and mysterious self.

In the quest for spiritual and personal integrity, many persons have been inspired by Roberto Assagioli's theory of psychosynthesis. According to Assagioli, spiritual and emotional well-being emerge when we bring the fragments of our lives into synthesis. Apart from such a creative synthesis, the self languishes in painful disorder: As Assagioli's interpreter, Piero Ferrucci notes:

> A great deal of the psychological pain, imbalance, and meaninglessness, are felt when our diverse inner elements exist unconnected side by side or clash with one another. . . . When they merge in successively greater wholes, we experience a release of energy, a sense of well-being, and greater depth of meaning in our lives.[2]

---

2. Piero Ferrucci, *What We May Be* (Los Angeles: Jeremy Tarcher, 1982), 22.

In everyday life, the many facets of the self, described by Assagioli as "subpersonalities," vie with one another for dominance, taking on their worst or most intrusive characteristics until they are embraced and given their proper place within the self:

> Subpersonalities are psychological satellites, coexisting as a multitude of lives within the medium of our personality. Each subpersonality has a style and motivation of its own, often strikingly dissimilar from those of the others. . . . Each of us is a crowd. There can be the rebel and the intellectual, the seducer and the housewife, the saboteur and the aesthete, the organizer and the bon vivant—each with its own mythology, and all more or less crowded into one single person. Often they are far from being at peace with one another. . . . Several subpersonalities are continually scuffling: impulses, desires, principles, aspirations, are engaged in an unceasing struggle.[3]

This ongoing struggle within the self is not always a sign of mental illness—although it can often lead to tremendous inner turmoil and ambivalence—but a recognition of the complexity, mystery, and variety of each person's personality. Spiritual health arises, first, when we simply become aware of our many subpersonalities. In mindful and accepting prayer, we literally listen these selves into wholeness and integrity. Often we recognize these subpersonalities through the particular roles we take on in life, regardless of the situation, or through a habitual response or an inner voice that often addresses us. Raised to a spiritual level, each of these subpersonalities contributes to the dynamic formation of a healthy and life-affirming self. Through psychological, physical, and spiritual techniques, involving imaginatively addressing and harmonizing each aspect of the self, the personality becomes a healthy synthesis in which each subpersonality reflects its highest characteristics to the benefit of the whole person.

---

3. Ibid., 47.

Assagioli recognizes that beyond all the various subpersonal-ities is the higher self or divine center, which seeks wholeness and balance in every aspect of our lives. When we place the many selves within the context of the divine center within each one of us, each of the subpersonalities finds a creative role within the divine matrix of experience. Rather than nar-rowly emphasizing one aspect of the self, we embrace the totality of the self in terms of the integrity of God's healing love. The process of integration is the result of a dynamic and lifelong commitment to aligning our own multifaceted self with the ever-creative divine center of experience within us. We become artists of our own experience, creating something of beauty in partnership with "the One to whom all hearts are open and all desires known."

Yet there are deeper sources of dissonance and disintegra-tion within the self. Whereas the ancients may have spoken of the "legion" that divides the self, today psychiatrists speak of multiple personality or dissociative disorders. Persons with this condition often compare their experience to demon possession, insofar as they experience a variety of discrete personalities or centers of experience that share neither consciousness nor memory with their host personality. The various personalities rotate in their control of the center of experience, almost always ignorant of and competitive with the other personalities. When a particular personality is dominant, it controls the per-son's attitudes and behavior, even to the extent that different personalities have differing psychosomatic characteristics. For example, one personality may limp, while another is kinetic; one personality may be allergic to strawberries and break out in hives in proximity with the allergen, while another personality relishes the taste of these luscious berries with absolutely no negative side effects. Medical studies have shown that different personalities may even have different pulse rates and levels of blood pressure.

Today we recognize that the development of these differing personalities is a survival mechanism for a self under siege.

Nearly 90 percent of persons diagnosed with dissociative disorders were subject during childhood to beatings, physical and sexual abuse, burning and cutting. Tragically many of these abuses were perpetrated by persons claiming to follow the dictates of God. By dividing into many selves, the central personality is better able to deal with the pain of abuse. The centered self "believes" that the abuse is happening to someone else. While such splitting of the self is ultimately dysfunctional, it provides a temporary refuge from the torment the child is experiencing. Indeed, such shattering of the self may be the "best for the impasse," as the philosopher Whitehead notes, given the reality of parental abuse. Yet there comes a time when the fractured self is no longer functional. The enemy whose abuse led to the "splitting off" of the self no longer is present. Possessed by unpredictable powers beyond itself, the fragile-centered self seeks healing and integration of various dominating personalities. Such healing is lifelong and hard won and occurs only as God's spirit moves through the interplay of psychotherapy, medication, the acceptance and affirmation of friends and a healing community, and the willingness of the one who suffers to recognize that God loves even the many dissociative selves.

Still, the question of demon possession—that is, possession and domination by forces outside the self or from a demonic spiritual self—remains mysterious to the modern world. While we do not typically attribute diseases of body, mind, and spirit to malevolent forces in search of a spiritual home, Jesus' healing of this man drives us to reflect on the possibility that the spiritual world contains malevolent as well as benevolent beings, self-interested messengers of evil as well as supportive and life-giving messengers of God. When Jesus instructed his disciples to pray, "Deliver us from evil," he recognized the power of forces beyond the self to wreak havoc with our lives. Whether Jesus' temptations in the desert can be explained through psychosynthesis or demonic powers and principalities, it is clear that certain realities defy our conscious control. If we cannot find a healing place for them within the constellation of the self, they will come to control us, sapping our energy, vitality, and spiritual focus. In his ministry Jesus regularly confronted the evils of sin, physical disease, injustice, and spiritual malevolence. As Mark's Gospel proclaims, "And [Jesus] went throughout Galilee, proclaiming the message in their synagogues and casting out demons" (Mark 1:39). Jesus' own quest to bring about authentic existence, wholeness, and the just reign of God's shalom involved his commitment to carrying out a hard-fought battle against realities whose goal is to dominate and destroy the divine center in each person. This same sense that human life exists in an ambiguous spiritual environment, populated by demons as well as angels, is captured by the apostle Paul's confession: "For our struggle is not against enemies of blood and flesh, but against the rulers, against the authorities, against the cosmic powers of this present darkness, against the spiritual forces of evil in the heavenly places" (Eph. 6:12). Only the power of God can prevail against such forces.

Recently a friend of mine related the story of attending a new age meeting where the participants gathered in a circle, calling upon the powers of titans and ancient deities such as Zeus and Hera. As he viewed the spectacle, he wondered how the supplicants would respond if these often arbitrary and violent spirits actually appeared in their midst. While we as Christians should not fear these powers of evil or ambiguous legendary figures, we should be careful when relating to the "supernatural" world either by word or deed. Although I believe that there is wisdom and truth in many of today's new age groups and in the messages of certain channeled spiritual beings, many persons have found their mental well-being jeopardized through naïve or intentional contact with these "spiritual beings," including Satan, as they played with Ouiji boards or sought to channel higher beings. As the biblical tradition rightly notes, the lack of physical embodiment is no assurance of moral goodness or spiritual benevolence. Persons should "test the spirits" to see if they come from God or are concerned with their own self-aggrandizement.

While persons can learn from channeled materials such as *A Course in Miracles* or Neale Walsch's *Conversations with God,* they should also subject these materials to the highest canons of reason and spiritual discernment. Many persons follow channeled advice that would be deemed foolishness if it became their embodied next-door neighbor.[4] The search for wisdom and guidance, I believe, is best undertaken by opening oneself to the highest unambiguous good we can envisage, Jesus Christ, rather than finite, ambiguous, and relative spiritual beings. Although divine protection constantly surrounds us, Christians still should not naïvely pray for the deliverance of persons who claim to be possessed by demonic spirits. If these demonic powers truly exist, contact with them at any level is fraught with danger. One must do battle with the forces of evil only if one has a spiritual gift to respond to the powers of darkness. While many of us feel called to pray for emotional and psychological healing of others, we should always clothe ourselves and those we pray for with "the whole armor of God" whenever there is a possibility that the problem's source is the spiritual realm. Liturgical churches such as the Roman Catholic and Episcopal have wisely placed the responsibility for such exorcisms in the hands of trained exorcists, who act in full awareness of the power of the demonic realm. Because of spiritual power and protection of healing circles, such confrontation with the demonic is best done by exorcism teams rather than isolated individuals.

In dealing with our fears of the demonic or the brokenness of our own personalities, we can find no better advice than that of the apostle Paul: "Therefore take up the whole armor of God, so that you may be able to withstand on that evil day, and having done everything, to stand firm" (Eph. 6:13). In my own

---

4. For an extensive discussion of channeling and its relationship to revelation within the Christian tradition, see Bruce Epperly, *Crystal and Cross: Christians and the New Age in Creative Dialogue* (Mystic, Conn. Twenty-Third Publications, 1996), 65–96.

daily spiritual discipline, I prepare myself to face the brokenness within myself and the challenges of the world, first, by
imagining God's healing light permeating every cell of my
body and empowering my immune and cardiovascular systems; then, I see the light flooding my mind, cleansing it from
stress, guilt, and anxiety; finally, I envisage this same light surrounding my body, covering it with a spiritual armor so that
although my heart and my mind will be open, my whole being
will be enveloped in God's protective love. I then place the
conflicts of life within that same healing light, trusting that
God will heal those persons or situations that I perceive as
threatening to myself and others. No demonic force can ultimately threaten or lead me astray when I place my life in the
hands of the healing Christ.

Having said all this, I believe that far too much power is
given to the manifestations of the demonic in our midst. While
we cannot underestimate the powers of evil operative in
Kosovo, Auschwitz, and Littleton, Colorado, in the deviant
behavior of certain religious leaders, and the brokenness in
ourselves, we can also overestimate these influence powers in
our world or our lives. As we fight the good fight for personal
and global healing, we would do well to remember the words
of Martin Luther's great hymn "A Mighty Fortress Is Our
God." Besieged from forces within his psyche and threats from
his religious and secular opponents, Luther knew the power of
divine protection that comes from spiritually affirming the
name of Christ and the protection of God. The living Word of
God incarnate in Jesus Christ unambiguously represents the
ever-present power of God's healing touch over all the perceived powers of inner and external darkness. When we struggle in the darkness, the spirit of Jesus Christ, whose presence
embodies the touch of God in each moment, will serve as our
strength and protection from every foe and fear.

Further, despite the power of evil in our midst, this is and
always will be God's world—the divine healing impulse is
"centered" and "flows forth" in all things, even those beings

who turn away from God's intention for them. The battle between the divine and the demonic is not between two equal powers, nor is there a dualism in the universe between good and evil, light and dark, and spirit and flesh. In the midst of the conflict with the evils within and beyond ourselves, we must claim with the Psalmist the unquenchable power of God's healing light: "If I say, 'Surely the darkness shall cover me, and the light around me become night,' even the darkness is not dark to you; the night is as bright as the day, for darkness is as light to you" (Ps. 139:11–12). With creation theologians from all religious traditions, we must affirm that beauty, love, and wholeness are the natural state and the natural end of all things, regardless of their current condition in relationship to God.

Although few of us will be called explicitly to emulate Jesus' healing of the demon-possessed man, Jesus' deliverance of the man gives an insight into God's response to the powers of evil. While many of Jesus' contemporaries did not recognize his uniqueness as the embodiment of God's love, the demons clearly identify his authority and power. The chief demon calls out to Jesus, "What have you to do with me, Jesus, Son of the Most High God?" (Luke 8:28). Confident in his spiritual centeredness, Jesus is even willing to listen to the demonic beings. Jesus is willing to grant their supplication that they be allowed to enter the herd of pigs. Could Jesus, even in his opposition to the demonic, have sought the healing of these misguided and malevolent beings? Would they be recreated by God in the abyss? Does God love Satan and his demonic minions, seeing them as ultimately broken, disordered, and lost children—like the chaotic cancer cells that some persons surround with divine healing light—even as they seek to pervert the universe? Is it possible that the same healing transformation that we need is available to these beings, but they have continually turned away from the healing touch of divine reconciliation? To use the language of the Luke Skywalker in describing his "evil" nemesis and father, Darth Vader, "There is good in him." While we cannot expect to answer these questions, we can be assured that God loves the lost and broken parts of us and will not rest content until we experience spiritual integrity and wholeness, whether in this life or the next. I equally believe that God calls us to be instruments of divine healing as we, surrounded by the whole armor of God, seek to bring healing (and this healing may, at times, require conflict with the forces of evil) to a world of ethnic cleansing, racial hatred, psychological and physical violence, ritual abuse, and pastoral misconduct. Yet as we contend with such powers, we must remember that our ultimate protection is twofold—the conscious recognition of our own potential to become instruments of evil, even in the process of fighting against evil, and the amazing power of God's grace to touch with healing our lives and even the lives of our enemies.

The healing of the demon-possessed man concluded with the promise of a new life and new home. When the man begged Jesus to let him become a disciple, "Jesus sent him away, saying, 'Return to your home and declare how much God has done for you'" (Luke 8:38–39). Like the healing of Peter's mother-in-law, this man's healing had as its completion a return to the normalcy of everyday life. From now on, he would be a living witness for spiritual well-being and would, by his transformed life, claim his household as a haven of God's love, perhaps even a place of welcome for other "sick souls." Like the Samaritan leper, he would live doxologically from now on, "proclaiming throughout the city how much Jesus had done for him." The healing of our psychological and spiritual brokenness sends us, like this man from Gerasene, home to the lively adventure of gratefully bringing forth the beauty of our own lives as we contribute to the beauty and well-being of our children, spouses, relatives, and neighbors.

An Experiment in Healing and Wholeness

In a world where evil and violence constantly bombard us in the media, it is tempting to see ourselves as helpless victims of malevolent powers beyond ourselves. While we need to be prudent in our care for ourselves and others, it is essential that we claim the basic trust that is our God-given heritage. Clothed in the divine armor, we can creatively and carefully face the powers of disintegration and destruction. In this exercise, take time to experience the meaning of the armor of God for yourself and for others.

After a few moments of relaxed mindfulness, notice your breath as you inhale and exhale. As your breath becomes calm, visualize the light of God entering your whole being, cleansing, strengthening, and protecting. Experience this powerful, protective, and healing light restoring order and power to your mind and the various bodily systems. Then image this healing light surrounding your body like an impregnable field of force, protecting you from evil action and intent, while still admitting every kind thought, inspiration, and action. Affirm to yourself that you are protected by the whole armor of God.

If you are anticipating a conflict situation in the future, visualize yourself in that situation, surrounded by the divine light in such a way that any potential foe is powerless to hurt you. Image yourself responding to any threat with calm courage and openheartedness. Visualize your potential adversary also permeated by the divine light in such a way that he or she will respond creatively in this conflict situation.

As an antidote to our fears for others and as an inspiration for our nonlocal intercessory prayer, take time during your mediation on the protecting light of God to visualize your child, spouse, or friend surrounded by this same impregnable and healing divine force field. Affirm that they are also surrounded and protected by the whole armor of God.

Many persons have found the process of psychosynthesis to be helpful in nurturing a sense of self and personal integrity. While these exercises are not substitutes for personal or group psychotherapy or medication if these are indicated, they help center the self and provide a means for appreciating and creatively empowering the many aspects of our personalities.

A simple excercise in spiritual centering involves an ongoing mindfulness of the many personalities vying for attention in your life. As you recognize a decentering self emerging or a constant voice of fear or need, simply take time to notice what this subpersonality is saying. What does this subpersonality really want? Does it have any redeeming qualities that can be transformed for the well-being of yourself or others? Let your divine center listen to the voice of the particular subpersonality (for example, a self that always makes excuses, becomes easily angered, or whines about its misfortunes). As you listen, let the divine healing light surround and permeate that subpersonality, delivering you from its domination and purifying it for service to the whole self. Let God place this self in communion with the totality of your self. Commit this healing self to God's care, protection, and wholeness.

Piero Ferrucci's *What We May Be* (Los Angeles: J. P. Tarcher, 1982) and Roberto Assagioli's *Psychosynthesis* (New York: Viking, 1971) provide excellent guides to self-discovery. Nevertheless, this adventure in self-discovery should be accompanied by an openness to the touch of God and a commitment to use your self-knowledge for service to others.

But Mary stood weeping outside the tomb. As she wept, she bent over to look into the tomb; and she saw two angels in white, sitting where the body of Jesus had been lying, one at the head and the other at the feet. They said to her, "Woman, why are you weeping?" She said to them, "They have taken away my Lord, and I do not know where they have laid him." When she said this, she turned and saw Jesus standing there, but she did not know that it was Jesus. Jesus said to her, "Woman, why are you weeping? Whom are you looking for?" Supposing him to be the gardener, she said to him, "Sir, if you have carried him away, tell me where you have laid him, and I will take him away." Jesus said to her, "Mary!" She turned and said to him in Hebrew, "Rabbouni!" (which means Teacher). Jesus said to her, "Do not hold on to me, because I have not yet ascended to the Father. But go to my brothers and say to them, 'I am ascending to my Father and your Father, to my God and your God.'" Mary Magdalene went and announced to the disciples, "I have seen the Lord"; and she told them that he had said these things to her.

(John 20:11–18)

Chapter Twelve

Is There an Answer to Death?

We have heard the Easter stories so often that they contain little dramatic or theological tension for us today. Both critics and believers have domesticated these stories, by denying that the resurrection occurred and thus restricting the Easter message to the disciples' subjective experience, on the one hand, or by objectifying, harmonizing, and literalizing and thus negating the ineffable mystery and contemporary impact of Jesus' resurrection, on the other. We are so familiar with the Easter story that when we reflect upon the bibical accounts of the resurrection, we anticipate a happy ending even as we read the passion narratives. Though the resurrection and postresurrection narratives may still amaze and inspire us, the accounts of Jesus' resurrection seem no more surprising to us than the yearly Christmas ritual of watching Frank Capra's *It's a Wonderful Life*. Before the film even begins, we know that despite the lost money and George Bailey's feelings of despair, eventually the whole town will rally behind him and gather around the Bailey Christmas tree with pockets full of money to save his business. In our familiarity with the Easter story, we often forget its transformative power in the lives of Jesus' first-century male and female followers, and we overlook the possibility that this event can unexpectedly transform our own lives twenty centuries later. In locating Jesus' resurrection in past history, either by fundamentalist literalism or liberal rationalism, we consign the resurrection to the irrelevance of one-dimensional fact or ancient legend. We forget the deeper message: Christ is alive and still overcomes the death that threatens to engulf persons in all ages. We forget that the Risen Christ may come to us when we most need the power of God to raise us from the dead!

Martin Luther once stated that "in the midst of life, we are surrounded by death." Indeed, in the midst of life, when after years of struggle we have reached our personal goals and can now look forward to the leisurely enjoyment of the pleasures of marriage, family, and financial affluence, we hear our physician's shattering words, "You have cancer! It's time to get your affairs in order!" In our shock we protest, "This can't be happening to me. I have so many things to do. I have my whole life ahead of me! I planned for a carefree retirement!" But as we numbly prepare for a regimen of chemotherapy that may save our lives, the reality of the prognosis begins to set in. Though our spouse and friends may surround us, we feel alone and isolated as we contemplate the uncertain journey that lies ahead.

In the middle of the night, the phone rings, startling my wife and me wide awake with the news, "Your mother has had a stroke and is dying." As I gather my wits and pack my suitcase, I wonder if I will have the strength to plan the funeral, pay the bills, or even survive the cross-country plane trip.

A young man with the "Midas touch" has succeeded at everything, but now he is desperate. His life is emotionally flat and he can barely make it out of bed each morning. His corner office at the law firm, Mercedes sports car, and growing stock portfolio mean nothing as he struggles with the inner darkness of depression.

A college student, emotionally shattered by a breakup with her first true love, wonders when she will quit crying and if she will ever love a person so fully again. "Is this all there is to love," she confides to me. "When will this deadness of spirit lift? When will I feel alive again?"

While we may be able to domesticate that first Easter story, the death-filled moments of our own lives do not always promise a happy ending. Although we can theologically breeze from Palm Sunday to Easter morning with little thought given to the God-forsakenness of Good Friday or the emptiness of Holy Saturday, our own lives tell a far different story: In the darkest night, there is no promise of sunrise; in the deepest depression, joy seems a phantasm; after days of chronic pain, a day of rest and relief seems as unlikely as the imminent return of Halley's comet; in the wake of a child's death, the long valley of grief stretches on to infinity. In such moments, when we can no longer control the forces of death that dominate us within and without, and when all of our socially acceptable buffers against mortality and brokenness have collapsed, we need a resurrection. We need a risen Christ. We need to experience firsthand the empty tomb and the angelic witness of a living Christ as realities in our own lives. We need to experience a personal Jesus who is alive, not just in the subjective experiences of a few disciples in the first century, but in the transformation and rebirth of all that has died within our own bodies, minds, spirits, and relationships.

The modern world has often sought to explain away the resurrection of Jesus. The Easter event is far too raw and unexpected—far too astonishing—to fit into the rationalistic, closed-system, one-dimensional worldview of modern humankind. From the vantage point of modernity, the cross and the resurrection alike seem like foolishness. To some skeptics, the first witnesses to the resurrection must have been liars, inventing the story of the living Jesus so that they would not have to return to their former mundane occupations as fisherman and tax collectors. To others, the disciples and women followers suffered a communal hallucination, the result of their intense feelings at having lost their teacher, lover, and spiritual guide. Others, who seek to make sense of what can never be encompassed fully by human reason, impute good faith to the disciples and women, but still see this event purely as existential or subjective in nature, reflecting the first followers' experience that Jesus lived on in their hearts in their transformed lives, the stories they told, and the meals they shared.

In contrast to agnostic scholars and existentialist theologians, other Christians, claiming to be the authentic proponents of orthodox Christiantiy, render the resurrection irrelevant by locating it entirely in a literal understanding of the words of scripture. In attempting to literalize the risen "body of Christ" as a revived physical body or a supernatural intervention, they neglect the diversity, complexity, and mystery of the seemingly contradictory and polyvalent resurrection stories. To objectify and corporealize Jesus is to limit him entirely to first-century Jerusalem and render the risen Savior existentially meaningless and spiritually dead to agnostics, seekers, and persons of other faiths.

The healing Christ we need today cannot be reduced to the stark polarities of subjectivity and objectivity, nor can Christ be limited to one-dimensional, linear explanations. From the holistic perspective of this book, the resurrection of the healing Christ must embrace the intricate web of interconnectedness that joins mind, body, spirit, emotions, and relationships. As revelation of the living touch of God for all times and places, the resurrection must be nonlocal and universal in its transformation of the totality of life. The touch of God, revealed in these surprising resurrection stories, must be contemporary as well as ancient. Only then can we answer yes with life-transforming conviction when we sing, "Christ the Lord is risen *today*!"

Most contemporary Christian accounts of the resurrection and afterlife suffer from the same lack of imagination that plagues their explanation of the healings of Jesus. In a time when new agers, alternative physicians both East and West, and popular magazines proclaim the significance of spirituality and prayer in transforming our health, the mainstream church lags far behind the secular and non-Christian culture in articulating a holistic Christian vision of the mind-body connection. While non-Christians research and write about near death experiences and angelic visitations, mainstream Christian visions of the afterlife and spiritual world often appear stunted, one-dimensional, and unimaginative in nature. Mainstream and liberal Christians have too often reacted against the linear and exclusivistic interpretations of the afterlife proclaimed by conservative evangelicals and fundamentalists. In their embarrassment over the literalistic, linear, and morally suspect images of heaven and hell and saved and unsaved, which consign Muhammad, Gautama, Gandhi, and the Dalai Lama to damnation, many liberals and mainstream Christians have given up any serious attempt to imagine our future beyond the grave. This failure of the imagination has robbed persons of hope for this life, as well as the next. If there is no hope for transformation as we face death, can there be any meaningful transformation within the challenges of disease of mind, body, and spirit; relational brokenness; or the power of the past to overwhelm the present?

As we ponder the resurrection and the afterlife, we are challenged to reclaim the Christian imagination and to see our world as a multidimensional, interconnected, holographic, open system in which, as C. S. Lewis proclaims in *The Lion, the Witch, and the Wardrobe,* there are deeper and more ancient—indeed, more powerful—laws within the natural world than we have yet discovered. If, as Lewis suggests, "Aslan is not a tame lion"—that is, God is not a domesticated and predictable God—then within the matrix of relationships we must always be open to the surprise, adventure, and radical amazement that is inspired by each moment's marriage of time and eternity, ordinariness and wonder. This alone can heal us when death is all around us.

The Psalmist's confession captures the desperate quest for transformation and healing that confronts us at the descending edges of life:

> Be gracious to me, O Lord, for I am in distress;
> my eye wastes away from grief,
> my soul and body also.

> For my life is spent with sorrow,
> and my years with sighing;
> my strength fails because of my misery,
> and my bones waste away.
> I am the scorn of all my adversaries,
> a horror to my neighbors,
> an object of dread to my acquaintances;
> those who see me in the street flee from me.
> I have passed out of mind like one who is dead;
> I have become like a broken vessel.
> For I hear the whispering of many—
> terror all around!—
> as they scheme together against me,
> as they plot to take my life. (Psalm 31:9–13)

Stricken with terminal cancer, AIDS, physical disfigurement, and mental illness, we may experience ourselves as alone in the darkness with terror all around. When the world has shrunk to the dimensions of a dying child's hospital room, our imagination fails us. When, with Tolstoy's Ivan Illych, we experience the "shock of nonbeing" as we ask a silent universe and bankrupt self, "Where will I be when I am no more?" we fear that there will be no answer.[1] When we, with Simone de Beauvoir, hear our helpless cancer-ridden parent cry out, "Don't leave me to the power of the brutes!" or discover that our dynamic and intellectual spouse no longer recognizes us as he obsessively plays with a pajama button all day long, our hearts and spirits sink into their own region of helplessness.[2] At such moments, with Jesus and the psalmist, we may cry out in the darkness of personal and cosmic abandonment: "My God, my God, why have you forsaken me? Why are you so far from helping me, from the words of my groaning? O my God,

---

1. Leo Tolstoy, *The Death of Ivan Illych and Other Stories* (New York: New American Library, 1960).
2. Simone de Beauvoir, *A Very Easy Death* (New York: Warner Books, 1973).

I cry by day, but you do not answer; and by night, but find no rest" (Ps. 22:1–2).

God-forsaken, with no help in sight, we hope against hope that there will be a resurrection and that God will hear our prayers and bring wholeness to the shattered body, mind, and spirit. In the depths we pray for refuge, "But I trust in you, O LORD; I say, 'You are my God.' My times are in your hand. . . . Let your face shine upon your servant; save me in your steadfast love" (Ps. 31:14–16). At such moments, we become companions of those women who grieved hopelessly at the foot of the cross and trudged wearily to the tomb. Hoping against hope, as we search for spiritual empowerment, we need a resurrection *today* just as much as Jesus' first-century followers.

Now the reality of the resurrection is a mystery, always lying just beyond our comprehension and control. The scriptures give us no technology of the resurrection event, nor can we assume that a video camera would have captured the moment of Jesus' rising. As we face the enveloping darkness, we need more than flesh and bones, and so did the first disciples! The resurrection of Jesus was no mere resuscitation of a rotting corpse, nor was it bringing back to life one recently dead, like Lazarus or the son of the widow of Nain. Although we cannot absolutely deny such physical resuscitations, they are of little importance in the struggles we face. When the EEG is flat, all hope for personal resuscitation is lost: even to pray for the revival of a person in a irreversible vegetative state would be to commit spiritual malpractice and to demand that God suspend the laws of the universe to bring back one solitary life. There must be something more—there must be the hope for healing, even when the hope of physical survival is gone.

While the much-publicized near-death experiences are reminders that there is more to reality than our present lifetime or embodied existence, these images of hope cannot fully provide the spiritual transformation we need at the edges of

life. Whether we are revived technologically by heart paddles
or spiritually by the touch of Jesus, we still must face our mortality and grieve the loss of love. As C. S. Lewis muses in *A
Grief Observed,* Lazarus had to die twice! All those who have
had near-death experiences will eventually face the "real
thing," from which there will be no escape and no return. The
dying need the hope of a resurrection that is more than just the
resuscitation of flesh and bone or the extension of physical
life, and so do we, as we face life without their familiar presence! We need God's enlivening touch so that we may experience the trustworthiness of eternity when all human hope has
been eclipsed.

As a holistic and contemporary reality, the resurrection can
never be disconnected from the abandonment of the cross. Elie
Wiesel describes the death of a young boy at the hands of the
prison guards during his imprisonment at Auschwitz. As the
boy struggled for breath, a man standing behind Wiesel asked,
"Where is God now?" His neighbor responded, "Where is he?
Here He is—He is hanging on this gallows!"[3] These words
join despair and hope. On the one hand, when suffering is
intense and without spiritual redemption, the God we once
believed in now appears to be dead, distant, or disinterested.
"My God, my God, why hast thou forsaken me!" is our cry of
hopelessness, as well as the last gasp of Jesus! But there is
also a glimmer of hope: the God who struggles for breath on
the cross and who is hung by merciless tyrants is also the God
who experiences our deepest suffering. In God's apparent
helplessness, God is, as the philosopher Alfred North Whitehead asserts, "the fellow sufferer who understands."

In its deepest dimension, the doctrine of the atonement,
God's reconciliation of a broken, sinful, and dying world, is
not—as some have described it—the act of an abusive parent
who would sacrifice his own son to restore God's own lost

---

3. Elie Wiesel, *Night* (New York: Avon Books, 1971), 75–76.

honor and placate the divine wrath against human imperfection. Rather, the atoning cross is God's embracing of the pain and sin of the world as essential to God's own experience. If the image of the body of Christ reflects God's relationship to the world, then our pain and joy really matter to God. God feels our pain as a loving parent feels it, from the inside, by identification and incarnation. The "One to whom all hearts are open and all desires known" rescues our pain from oblivion by sharing it with us and by bearing it on our behalf. Like the Risen Christ, God is known in woundedness, as well as in triumph. Surely this is what Luther meant when he proclaimed the centrality of the "theology of the cross" for our salvation. When, on the verge of his own execution, Dietrich Bonhoeffer wrote that "only a suffering God can save," he embodied the ancient affirmation that "God's power is made perfect in weakness," which embraces and then transforms our pain within the matrix of God's suffering love.

The suffering of God has always been a problem for those who define God's perfection in terms of unchanging bliss. A blissful, perfect, and unsullied God, however, cannot save us from the terror of death and debilitation, for such a God cannot act within our lives in any way that can deliver us from the ever-present and all-conquering darkness and death. This God cannot touch us with the healing that we need when a cure is no longer possible and relief is unlikely. On the cross, God dies so that God may be reborn in our lives and in our world. The whole universe is cruciform in God's transformation of the perpetual perishing wreckage of our lives into the bright mystery of Easter morning. In our pain and hopelessness, we need a God for whom even the darkness is as light, precisely because God has been there too! God is with us!

The meaning of the resurrection in our lives today must be as experiential as it is theological. It must reveal the touch of God in the midst of pain and helplessness for persons, at all stages of life, and not just for the righteous, the faithful, or the Christian. In reflecting on the healing power of the resurrection,

I cannot claim to be exhaustive in my analysis of the biblical texts or the theological doctrines, nor will I attempt to adjudicate the theological culture wars and litmus tests that have alienated Christians from one another and denied to certain persons the resurrecting touch of God at those times when it is most needed.

As is often the case, theologians err as much in what they deny as in what they affirm. To paraphrase Augustine's comment about the dangers of claiming to know God fully, "If you think you fully know the resurrection, it isn't the real thing!" With the conservative scholars, I affirm the reality of the resurrection as an event of history as well as faith, although I do not claim to define the nature of Jesus' resurrection body or restrict the impact of the rising Christ to the parochialism of Christian experience. With more liberal theologians, I emphasize the subjective experience of the resurrection as transformative of the lives of Jesus' followers, although I do not limit the power of the resurrection to human subjectivity. The resurrection is much more than an ancient myth about a rising God. Christ's resurrection encompasses in each passing moment the dynamic relationship of our own death and resurrection in God's own everlasting life. Not bound to ancient time or foreign soil, Christ is alive, and the dying still rise—the death-filled are born anew in body, mind, and spirit. In interpreting God's resurrecting touch for our times, I will reflect on four passages from scripture as "windows" through which we can glimpse the past, present, and future presence of the God who constantly gives life to the dying. In the spirit of my interpretation of the healings of Jesus, I believe that our understanding of the resurrection must embrace both the first-century witness and the realities of twenty-first-century pluralism, science, medicine, and spiritual experience.

The earliest written account of the resurrection comes from the pen of the apostle Paul. In light of his own unexpected encounter with the Risen Lord, Paul proclaims the interplay of the metaphysical meaning and personal touch of the resurrection:

> Now I would remind you, brothers and sisters, of the good news that I proclaimed to you, which you in turn received, in which also you stand, through which also you are being saved. . . . that Christ died for our sins in accordance with the scriptures, and that he was buried, and that he was raised on the third day in accordance with the scriptures, and that he appeared to Cephas, then to the twelve. Then he appeared to more than five hundred brothers and sisters at one time, most of whom are still alive, though some have died. Then he appeared to James, then to all the apostles. Last of all, as one untimely born, he also appeared to me. For I am the least of the apostles, unfit to be called an apostle, because I persecuted the church of God. But by the grace of God I am what I am, and his grace toward me has not been in vain. On the contrary, I worked harder than any of them—though it was not I, but the grace of God that is with me (1 Corinthians 15:1–10)

Paul's spiritual journey reveals the startling fact that resurrection happens to the most unexpected persons and at the most unexpected times. "Breathing threats and murder against the disciples of the Lord," Paul journeyed to Damascus to arrest any followers of the Risen One, only to discover that the One he sought to persecute was seeking to save him (Acts 9:1–9). Perhaps Saul of Tarsus (later to become Paul) was struggling, as many scholars believe, with feelings of guilt and imperfection. His animosity toward Jesus' followers may have been motivated by his own spiritual insecurity and the nagging feeling that the Risen One whose reality he denied might, in fact, be the only one who could save him. But, like the prodigal son who deliberately spurned his father's love, Saul discovered that God's love embraced him regardless of his attitudes, behavior, or intentions. Paul's encounter with the

Risen One affirms that there are no prerequisites for God's transformative presence. The message of Paul's encounter with the Risen Lord is that even as we run away from the divine, God is luring us toward the divine center with an unending love. Resurrection may happen in our lives even when we least desire it and are doing everything possible to avoid it.

Although Paul, along with virtually all of the persons in the New Testament healing adventure, must claim his own role in the divine-human synergy, the grace that saves him is ultimately the incarnation of a love that makes no requirements or demands until well after it is welcomed. As Paul proclaims, "By the grace of God I am what I am. . . . It was not I, but the grace of God that is with me" (1 Cor. 15:10). Resurrection comes to those who, like the disciples, have given up all hope; it comes to those, like Saul the persecutor, who deny God entirely; and it comes to those for whom the need for salvation and healing is abstract and meaningless until the dread diagnosis of cancer or ALS or the visit to the graveside reminds us that the logical syllogism "all humans are mortal" applies to us and those we love. The living resurrection gives us a new life, a new center, and new vision of reality in the midst of the darkest valley of grief and hopelessness.

Paul's encounter with the resurrected Christ transforms his life and becomes the center of his vision of reality. From now on, Jesus is not merely the teacher from Nazareth or the object of theological debate; the living Jesus is one with the "cosmic Christ," the reality that "reconciles all things" and lives within each thing as the guiding Spirit who speaks "with sighs too deep for words" (Rom. 8:26). In Christ, the death-filled world is vanquished. Life emerges even in the wreckage of sin, and death can be experienced as an adventure in companionship with God. With words that would astound even a universalist, Paul proclaims that "as all die in Adam, so all will be made alive in Christ" (1 Cor. 15:22), who transforms death in all its physical, emotional, relational, and spiritual manifestations. "Death has been swallowed up in victory. Where, O death, is your victory? Where, O death, is your sting?" (1 Cor. 15:54–55)

As Paul attempts to describe the resurrection body, his mind soars heavenward: his words are those of the mystic and the poet as he seeks to portray a mystery beyond human comprehension:

> So it is with the resurrection of the dead. What is sown is perishable, what is raised is imperishable. It is sown in dishonor, it is raised in glory. It is sown in weakness, it is raised in power. It is sown a physical body, it is raised a spiritual body. . . . Listen, I will tell you a mystery! We will not all die, but we will all be changed. . . . For this perishable body must put on imperishability, and this mortal body must put on immortality. (1 Cor. 15:42–44, 51, 53)

The Greek word *soma,* used by the apostle Paul to describe both the physical and spiritual bodies, encompasses the whole person—body, mind, spirit, and relationships. Far more than the resuscitation of a corpse or the liberation of a disembodied soul, the resurrected spiritual body (*soma pneumatikon*) heals the entire psychosomatic-spiritual-relational self and makes all things new! While Paul does not give us a precise image of survival after death, his image of the body of Christ expresses the profound experience of the unity and dynamic interconnectedness of the spiritual body. The words "we shall be changed" are, for ourselves and the first-century disciples, more than a once-and-for-all event. They embody the surprising transformation from death to life and physical to spiritual within the dynamic and evolving body of Christ that is the deepest reality of the world in which we live.

While all of our images of the afterlife are a matter of "seeing in a mirror, dimly" (1 Cor. 13:12), the twin images of the body of Christ and the communion of saints nevertheless express the lively, dynamic, and relational nature of survival after death. The image of the communion of saints reminds us that the reign of God is a dynamic, evolving process in which there is no absolute boundary between the living and the dead. Indeed, the dead are alive in Christ and intimately connected with one another and ourselves within the evolving body of Christ. In ways we can only imagine, our love and prayers contribute to the ongoing bond we have with those who have died and now live on in God's ever-adventurous and dynamic realm. In the divine holoverse, the power of death to separate us from those we love is overcome. Encounters with deceased loved ones may be intensifications of the holographic nature of reality, in which all the dimensions of existence are united and reconciled within the divine holoverse. In these "thin" places of life the barriers between life and death no longer define us as we glimpse the mystery of the unimaginable, loving adventure that awaits us beyond the grave. Perhaps our loved ones intercede on our behalf; as living, evolving beings they may, within their much broader perspective, also be communicating to us in a "still, small voice" of insight, inspiration, and synchronicity. From time to time, we may hear these voices echoing in dreams and unexpected encounters.

While the process of bereavement involves letting go of the embodied presence of the deceased, it does not mean letting go of the bond of love that unites all things in this life and the next. Just as Christ is alive, those we have loved are also alive in God's resurrection life, shaping us by their continued love. For if personality continues beyond the grave, then our this-worldly loves are also alive, though purified of narrow ego-centrism, in the world to come.

The resurrection of Christ unites the universal and the personal. Holographic in nature, the resurrection is present from the cellular to the intergalactic. Without the universal resurrection, individual healing is an impossibility; and without the personal healing, the universal resurrection is not a lived reality. This interplay is at the heart of Mary Magdalene's encounter with the Risen Lord, described at the beginning of this chapter.

When a loved one has died, the grief process remains incomplete until we have come to terms with the corpse. Despite the opulence of many contemporary funerals, the presence of the body, even when death is masked by cosmetic manipulation, grounds one in the inexorable reality of death. In viewing, touching, and even kissing the body of the deceased loved one, we express our love and we begin to let go of their physical presence into the deep beyond of divine community.

On Easter morning, Mary's confrontation with the empty tomb and the angelic messengers were not enough to heal her spirit. She wanted to see Jesus. Dead or alive, she needed to hold onto him, to touch the body, to give him one last act of love. Her plaintive cry, "They have taken away my Lord, and I do not know where they have laid him" (John 20:13), echoes the cries of all who deeply grieve. Familiar places, the scent of cologne, a favorite song, a favorite pastime, the easy chair or the computer table, remind us of the persons we have loved. At the shadowy edges of experience, we see their faces and hear their voices. We expect them to pick up the phone when we call home. But all these thoughts are like arrows aimed at a target that no longer is present. That morning Mary longed to touch Jesus, not just hear about him. The words of resurrection, even if spoken by an angel, could not satisfy her need for a personal resurrection.

As she walked grief-stricken through the garden, she encountered the Risen Lord. We can only speculate as to why she did not recognize Jesus. Perhaps his spiritual body—vibrating at an energy level far beyond the scope of ordinary sense perception—was beyond her ability to recognize. Perhaps her grief clouded her vision. Perhaps Jesus purposely was masking his identity. To the gardener, once again she cried, "Sir, if you have carried him away, tell me where you have laid him, and I will take him away" (John 20:15).

Mary was lost in her grief until she heard Jesus call her by name: "Mary." The Risen Lord did not give her a doctrinal discourse or unfold the mysteries of Biblical prophesy to her. He simply called her by name—her true name, known only to God!

Resurrection must be personal to be real and transformative. Just as we die our own deaths and struggle with our own demons, we must be resurrected in intimate personal relationship to God. Though the divine call addresses all of us, God's call to each of us is also intimate and personal. The divine circle whose circumference is nowhere is centered everywhere! It centers on us most powerfully when the chaos of life is most destabilizing. God calls our name, speaking the word we need to hear in the voice that we alone recognize. This "still, small voice," speaking in "sighs too deep for words," can come under any guise and in any context. The word we hear does not need to be theologically correct or doctrinally clear. It may come through a sermon, an embrace, a song heard in the distance, or a voice within. The ever-present God speaks in the voice we need to hear through every healing encounter, but seldom do we hear it until that moment when, defenseless and vulnerable, we are awakened by Jesus calling our name. In the image from Revelation, the Risen Christ stands at the door and knocks, penetrating our blindness and grief, reviving what has long been buried in our lives (Rev. 3:20).

Mary's response to Jesus' personal call was the desire to hug and hold onto him. At first glance, Jesus' response, "Do not hold onto me, because I have not yet ascended to the Father" (John 20:17), seems a curious rebuff to her joyful celebration. But like many of the gospel narratives, these words are meant to be existential and spiritual rather than merely literal in meaning. Although the resurrection body might have been purely energetic in nature, the Gospel of John's portrait of Jesus is not that of a ghost or phantasm, but a wholly embodied being who can be touched by Thomas and who can cook a meal beside the Sea of Tiberias. From the spiritual perspective, Jesus challenged Mary to affirm and yet go beyond the personal relationship she had with him. Jesus is the Jewish teacher of Nazareth, the friend of sinners, the one who calls us by name, but he is also the nonlocal, cosmic figure present in every moment of resurrection and transformation. Jesus cannot be possessed even by those who are his closest followers. Jesus is not the property of any creed, church, theological standpoint, or religion. Although his way is recognized most explicitly by those who call themselves Christians, Christ is also the way that excludes no way. Christ's healing and transforming touch can never be localized. The living Christ is constantly rising in new and unexpected ways, shattering the personal, ecclesiastical, and doctrinal limits we place upon him.

As profoundly transformative as the resurrected Christ is in our lives, many persons are unable to affirm this reality in terms of the traditional doctrines, or even of radically reinterpreted doctrines of persons such as Bishop John Shelby Spong and the members of the Jesus Seminar. As one friend of mine confesses, "I can believe that Jesus lived and was a great teacher, but—regardless of how hard I try—I cannot accept the notion of the resurrection and the exclusiveness of Christian truth." Contrary to the judgments of fundamentalists and conservative evangelicals, inability to believe the doctrines of the Christian faith is seldom the result of willful atheism, pride, disobedience, and skepticism. The roots of belief and unbelief are far too complex psychologically, spiritually, emotionally, and relationally to be evaluated in such a simplistic and linear fashion. Historians of the church now note that certain types of current orthodoxy were once viewed suspiciously as heresy and heterodoxy, and that even within the formation of the scriptural canon and first-century theology, there were "many Christs" and "many Christianities." Indeed, many of the most active persons within the church would describe themselves, to use the language of Leslie Weatherhead, as Christian agnostics when it comes to the great articles of faith. As one of the great mysteries of faith, the resurrection cannot be hemmed in by linear and airtight definitions of belief and unbelief. Paul Tillich rightly noted that deeply held faith always courageously embraces the experience of doubt. The tension of faith and doubt, hope and hopelessness, is at the heart of the story of Thomas (John 20:24–28).

While he is often villified as the doubter, Thomas is a model for faithful wrestling with the mysteries of the resurrection life. Absent when the disciples first encountered the Risen Christ, Thomas was appropriately skeptical of their experience. In our world of instant answers and e-mail responses to life's deepest questions and growing outreach by high-pressure cultlike groups, Thomas's response to this great mystery was a reasonable one: "Unless I see the mark of the nails in his hands, and put my finger in the mark of the nails and my hand in his side, I will not believe" (John 20:25). Thomas would not give his heart and mind to the Easter message until he encountered it himself. Few of us can, by force of will, look beyond the darkness that envelopes us or open ourselves to a hopeful future, when death permeates our body, mind, and spirit. For many of us, our only hope is to walk through the darkness one step at a time, without any predetermined destination. Thomas is our guide in the journey through doubt and darkness.

Surrounded by joyful mantras celebrating the Risen Lord, Thomas must have felt profoundly isolated. In light of the cross, Thomas dared not hope for a resurrection. Like the others, he had abandoned Jesus, but unlike the others, he had received no spiritual revelation. Still, Thomas stayed among the faithful, hearing their wild and improbable stories and listening to their growing confidence in the resurrection. Despite the discomfort of his own agnosticism, Thomas waited, hoping against hope for an answer that would also bring him back to life. Eight days he waited in spiritual anguish, doubting his friends and doubting himself, even doubting God. But when the Risen Lord mysteriously entered their locked room, Thomas was transformed as he confessed, "My Lord and my God!" (John 20:28)

In contemporary India, there is group of Christians that traces its origins to the apostle Thomas. Legend has it that only

Thomas, among the disciples of Jesus, ventured forth beyond the boundaries of the Roman Empire to share the good news of Jesus' resurrection with the East. Unique among the disciples, Thomas the agnostic could live patiently with the complex, metaphysical visions of the Hindus and Buddhists. From his own personal experience, he knew that faith is reborn when we walk patiently through the darkness of struggle, doubt, disbelief, and death. Perhaps Thomas discovered the "hidden Christ of India" even as he shared the news of the Risen Christ of Judea. When brokenness of mind, body, or spirit makes belief impossible, we are called—with all our doubts—to place our trust in the mysterious grace of God and the community that believes on our behalf. Even a mustard seed, planted in the soil of doubt, can move the mountains of pain and uncertainty.

In Mark's Gospel, Mary Magdalene is the heroine of a slightly different resurrection account. In this account, the frightened Mary and her companions are comforted by an angelic messenger: "Do not be alarmed; you are looking for Jesus of Nazareth, who was crucified. He has been raised; he is not here. Look, there is the place they laid him. But go, tell his disciples and Peter that *he is going ahead of you* to Galilee; there you will see him, just as he told you" (Mark 16:6–7, italics mine). Once again the angelic message is not merely about geography; it proclaims the ubiquitous presence of the Risen One. "He is going ahead of you." The spirit of the resurrection is embodied by the availability of God's transformative presence in every future that we can imagine. The resurrection is a holographic reality, shaping the whole of our lives by its presence in each moment and each encounter. There are no God-forsaken moments and no God-forsaken places. Each moment is an epiphany, revealing—in greater or lesser degree—the One who rises in and with each of us.

In times of illness, the world shrinks to the dimensions of the death-filled powers that overwhelm us. The future as imagination and possibility is often lost amid the pain of the present and the anticipation that things will only get worse. But before us goes the Christ. He is the one who dies and rises with us in every future. He feels the unremitting anguish of schizophrenia, the unquenchable thirst of substance abuse, the hopelessness of the child with advanced bone cancer, the lostness of the elder at his wife's graveside. He is the future of all who mourn and all who rejoice, giving hope and courage amid the darkness and struggle and the promise of surprise and adventure for those who dwell in the shadows of death. In finding God at the frontiers of life, we discover that the darkness has become the light of the lively adventure ahead. Then even dying can become doxology, and death rebirth. Going to our grave and facing our pain with the Risen Lord, we discover the graceful and everlasting touch of God.

An Experiment in Healing and Wholeness

The Easter proclamation invites us to become participants and partners in God's healing of death and dying. The resurrection describes our lives, as well as the lives of Jesus' first followers. Through imaginative prayer, we discover Christ's healing presence in the death-filled moments of our own lives.

In the first imaginative prayer, I invite you to "come to the garden alone" with Mary Magdalene. Begin your time of prayerful imagination with silence, simply opening yourself to the breath of the Spirit within your life. Visualize yourself entering a beautiful garden at the break of day. Your spirit is broken, and though beauty is all around you, you barely notice it. Something in your life has died. Something has been lost and can never be reclaimed.

What is dead or dying in your life today? What do you mourn? Let the feelings and images of your loss emerge. How do you feel as you walk in the garden?

In the quiet of the morning, your reverie is interrupted by a solitary figure. At first you don't recognize him. But because he seems sensitive and approachable, you begin to share your pain and lostness with him. He listens quietly and nonjudg-mentally until you finish your narrative. How does it feel to have your grief and pain fully experienced by another?

The solitary stranger then looks you right in the eye and calls your name. Do you hear your name being called? How does it feel to be recognized? Suddenly the scales of your eyes are lifted, and you discover that the stranger is Jesus. How do you feel to know you are in Jesus' presence? Share your feelings and thoughts with the Risen One. As you share, you discover that what you presumed to be lost, the source of your grief and hopelessness, is in the hands of Jesus. How does it feel to know that Jesus is caring for the person or event that you presumed lost? Jesus gently tells you that your life will go on, that he will be with you from now on, and that he will hold your loved one and your sense of loss in the palm of his loving hand. As Jesus bids you farewell, he blesses you with the words, "I am with you always."

Quietly return from your imaginative prayer. Take time to thank Jesus for his care for you and those whom you love. Take time to remember that your future is in God's loving arms.

The second imaginative prayer involves the women going to the tomb. As you begin this prayer, simply be still and know that God is with you. Visualize yourself walking along with a number of companions just before sunrise. All of you are shocked, broken-hearted, and bereaved. Your great friend is gone. Your future is uncertain. With the others, you ask, "Who will roll away the stone for us?"

Ponder the image of an enormous stone standing in the way of your future. What stone stands in the way of your quest for abundant life and personal healing? Is there any chance that you can roll away the obstacle that blocks your hopes for future happiness?

As you arrive at the tomb, you are shocked to see that the stone has been rolled away and that the tomb is empty. A bright angelic being stands beside the tomb. What does this angelic messenger look like? What does this angelic presence tell you about Jesus' living presence in the world and your life? How do you feel as the angelic being tells you that Christ has risen and that your future is now open?

Look back at your own life today. What would it be like to have your own stone rolled away? Imagine a divine presence rolling the stone away and beckoning you to enter the promised land that you could not enter before. How does it feel to have an open future ahead of you? What will you do, now that the stone has been rolled away?

With the women, you experience the reality that Christ has risen and that your life has been changed. Together with the women, you run back to the frightened and grieving disciples. Which disciples await your return? What message do you give them? How do they respond to your glad tidings?

Conclude your meditation with a time of thanksgiving for God's rolling away the stone for the women and for yourself. Commit yourself to exploring the future God has opened up to you. Commit yourself in gratitude to becoming a messenger of the Risen Christ.

Chapter Thirteen

The Healing Christ
for a New Millennium

"*C*hrist is alive! I know he touched me. He was with me in the darkest days. He showed me the light and a path to health and healing," exclaims Susan as she looks back over the past year. Plagued by depression and facing exploratory surgery to determine if she had colon cancer, Susan was ready to give up entirely. But as she dragged herself home from work that Wednesday, she felt drawn to attend her church's midweek healing service. When she arrived at the church, she was surprised to see only a handful of parishioners sitting in a circle around the communion table. "I almost walked out. I didn't want to make a spectacle of myself. I didn't want people to know that I had a problem. I wanted to be able to get lost in the crowd," she admits.

The healing service surprised her as well. There was none of the fanfare, bombast, or shouting that she had seen in the healing services on television. Just silence, scripture, and a few words of encouragement from the pastor. As the service was concluding, the pastor asked if any one wanted to be anointed with oil and participate in the service of the laying on of hands. One by one, the congregation of seven moved into the circle to be prayed for, anointed, and touched on the shoulder or back by the rest of the group. As the last person left the circle, Susan nervously stepped forward. "I didn't know what to expect. But I knew that I needed the touch of God more than ever before. As the pastor and the others touched me and as I heard the prayer that I might experience healing and wholeness, nothing dramatic happened. As I left, I felt like the same old person. But something changed as the evening wore on. I felt a peace in my heart and a burden being lifted, gently and quietly, from my shoulders," Susan recalls. Although she does not remember exactly what happened, Susan noticed something odd in the week between the service and her outpatient medical appointment. She no longer had any discomfort, and her bleeding virtually disappeared. She did not feel her accustomed anxiety and fear. When the results of the exploratory surgery returned, Susan rejoiced to find that they were negative—she was cancer-free!

"Could this have been a miracle? Was God working in my life?" Susan asked herself. "If God is at work in my body, maybe God can restore my spirits, too." Although she continued her medication for depression, Susan, with the help of her pastor and a dietician in her church, embarked on an adventure that included daily meditation, biblical affirmations of faith, exercise, and a low-carbohydrate and low-sugar diet. Today Susan still takes a maintenance dose for depression, but she feels vital and alive. She is taking on new responsibilities at work, traveling, and making new friends. "I was changed that evening. God touched me as I reached out to him. It wasn't dramatic. But I was healed in body and soul. Now I meet the day with anticipation rather than dread."

The healing Christ is alive and can touch your life as well. The same healing energy and love that gave sight to the blind, transformed the social and physical condition of lepers, and mediated integrity to the broken spirit is at work in the world today. That same movement of love and transformation is gently moving in your own life. While you may not notice the presence of God, the quiet power of the "sighs too deep for words" is present, just beneath the surface and in every encounter, in your immune and cardiovascular systems, in your emotional life, in your thoughts, and in your spiritual commitments. The touch of God aims at abundant life for all of us, within the unique setting and condition of our lives. Wherever there is healing, God is present, whether that healing is manifest through medication, surgery, meditation, prayer, or touch. The healing Christ is not confined to the pages of scripture, but reaches out to transform your life, regardless of your personal situation. The healing and wholeness, the experience of salvation of body and spirit, that was manifest abundantly and decisively in Jesus of Nazareth is also present today, sometimes quietly growing like a mustard seed, other times dynamically bursting forth like tongues of fire and a mighty wind. However Christ's presence comes to us, it will restore us in mind, body, spirit, and relationships. This omnipresent healing spirit invites us always and everywhere to be partners and cocreators in healing of ourselves, others, our social order, and the planet. Woven into the ecology of life is the deep and subtle ecology of healing that calls us to constant growth and transformation.

While there are countless approaches to the healing presence of God, this book has lifted up five ways that we can participate more fully and consciously as partners in the omnipresent touch of God. We need to embrace a healing theology, a healing spirituality, a healing praxis, a healing community, and a healing hope. The five ways are different aspects of an ecology of healing, each intimately related to and supporting the others. Because the touch of God transcends any compartmentalization, a focus on any of these paths brings changes in all the other aspects of our life.

First of all, we need a transformed mind and vision of reality to facilitate our personal and communal commitment to healing and wholeness. A healing theology is grounded in a number of life-changing affirmations that have been repeated like mantras throughout this book. These are global affirmations, but they are also intimate. Just as all politics is local—to quote former speaker of the House of Representatives "Tip" O'Neill—so all healing and spirituality is local as well. Our theological beliefs must relate to all things, but they must also touch each of our lives. A healing theology is grounded in affirmations of faith such as:

1. God seeks abundant life for all, and God seeks abundant life for us.
2. We are partners in God's healing touch. Neither impotent nor omnipotent, we can make a difference by our thoughts, faith, and actions in the dynamic ecology of life and healing. In the intricate web of body, mind, spirit, and relationships, we are co-creators with God.
3. Our faith, prayers, and attitudes shape our experience and the experience of others. We can change ourselves, and we can change others.
4. God intimately cares for each of us. God embraces our joy and pain and gently works for good in our lives.
5. Regardless of the situation, we can claim enough freedom as co-creators with God to transform our lives in small and large ways.
6. God is always at work, both dramatically and undramatically, in our lives. God is constantly working for good in our lives and the lives of our loved ones.
7. Wherever healing is present, God is its source. God is healing our lives in countless ways.
8. Even when a physical cure is not possible, a healing of spirit, mind, emotions, and relationships may always occur at some level. God is transforming our whole being, regardless of the situation.

In living by these affirmations of faith, we discover that our minds and lives become transformed. We discover that we are not victims of the world, but active companions in God's aim at wholeness for persons and institutions. Wherever we are, we can image an alternative reality and take steps to embody what we imagine. No longer conformed to the world, our lives become adventures in holistic reformation and renewal.

In my own life, I live by simple and yet profound affirmations, some of which I have shared in this book, as a means of transforming my own life and balancing my own feelings of fearful negativity with the abundant possibilities that God is giving me. While I take my morning walk, I regularly repeat affirmations such as "Nothing can separate me from the love of God," "My God shall supply my need," "I can do all things through Christ who strengthens me," "My heart and circulatory system is healthy and clear," "In Christ, I have everything I need to flourish, prosper, and serve others." As you reflect on your own need for a transformed mind, what affirmations are life-enahancing and transformative for you?

Second, the process of spiritual transformation is also grounded in a healing spirituality whose practices embrace the totality of life—mind, body, spirit, relationships, and social responsibility. Historically, spirituality has often neglected the incarnation and embodiment of God's presence in Jesus of Nazareth and in our own lives. The body has been seen as a "prison," to quote Socrates; "an occasion of sin," for certain ascetics; or an "illusion," by ancient and modern gnostics. From this perspective, sexuality, family life, and social involvement have been judged to be impediments or of no value in our spiritual growth. While times of silent and private retreat may be essential for our spiritual growth, ultimately a healing spirituality must include practices that integrate and transform every aspect of our lives, including those aspects often neglected in traditional spiritual formation. A spirituality of healing is grounded in the Hebraic image of "shalom," the wholeness of all things. It involves, to quote Elizabeth O'Connor, both the "journey inward" of quiet meditation, prayer, and personal contemplation, and the "journey outward" of service and social transformation. A healing spirituality also recognizes in its intimacy the uniqueness of each person. No one practice addresses every person or personality type. There is a wealth of spiritual and healing practices available for the seeker after wholeness.

In my own spiritual practices, I have sought to integrate quiet meditation with aerobic walking prayer and spiritual attentiveness to my relationships and social responsibility. In the spirit of Brother Lawrence's *Practice of the Presence of God,* I have discerned God's presence in the hospital room and soup kitchen, as well as in the chapel and meditation room. I regularly visualize God's healing light permeating my knees, intestines, and heart, as well as my mind and spirit.

Third, intimately related to a healing theology and a healing spirituality is a healing praxis. Put simply, a healing praxis involves the commitment to a healthy lifestyle through exercise, diet, stress reduction, and health enhancement techniques. While body, mind, spirit, and relationships are intimately linked, a healing praxis approaches wholeness from the avenue of the body. It might be described loosely as a Christian version of hatha (or body-based) yoga in its emphasis on the role of embodiment in wholeness. In my own life, I try to integrate a number of health enhancing approaches:

1. Regular aerobic walking, often joined with the use of affirmations and prayers of intercession and petition
2. A diet that is reasonable, but low in fat and sugar
3. Regular energy work, usually in the form of self-reiki touch healing (although others might add regular reiki, message, acupuncture treatments along with yoga and Qi Gong exercises)
4. Appropriate medical and dental hygiene, including regular physicals and dental checkups

As the temples of God, our bodies call us to love God in the world of the flesh as we join our physical, spiritual, and ethical disciplines. They call us to treasure our bodies and the bodies of others as shrines of the divine spirit. When I first learned the practice of reiki touch healing, I vowed from that day on to use my hands only to enhance the well-being of myself and others and to refrain from any form of violence, except in the case of defending myself or another.

In the spirit of divine embodiment, it is essential to utilize these practices in times of sickness. The practices that enhance health also serve to nurture the forces of recovery and healing. We can always utilize healing touch, breathing exercises, and energy work to enhance the healing process for ourselves and others. A practical spirituality of embodiment complements any legitimate medical practice.

Fourth, the touch of God can occur anywhere, but it is enhanced by our commitment to being part of a healing community. At the heart of Jesus' healing ministry was the restoration of persons to healthy communal life. Sickness isolates, while wholeness unites. Authentic healing is not just an individual matter, but involves the healing of our communities as well as ourselves.

The power of community is demonstrated by the medical evidence that persons who are active in support groups and in churches have better overall health than those who are not part of supportive communities. Nevertheless, community reaches far beyond the church to include our families and friends, as well as our political involvement. We are meant to touch and be touched, to embrace and be held, in times of sickness and health. Healthy communities keep us in touch with the well springs of healing all around us. Within your community, commit yourself to creative and welcomed healing touch through affirmative hugs and pats on the back.

Healing community calls us to transform our society. As members of an intricately joined body of Christ, we shape one another's health and well-being. Researchers have found that a primary indicator of lifetime health is the education and economics of a child's parents. Healing is a political issue, whether it involves the welcoming of lepers or advocacy for universal health care and economic justice. Without a healthy ecosystem, our own efforts at personal well-being are ultimately of little value.

In everyday life, a commitment to healing community is embodied in healthy give-and-take with friends, family, and religious organizations. It involves an ongoing commitment to affirm and forgive persons intimately related to you, as well as the willingness to ask for health. In a society that promotes individualism, we must commit ourselves to healthy interdependence, grounded in the recognition that we are all members of an evolving, dynamic body of Christ.

In my own life, I regularly use the affirmation "I give Christ to, and receive Christ from, everyone I meet" as a reminder that I am on holy ground. Similar to the Hindu greeting "Namaste," this affirmation enables me to catch a glimpse of Christ in all of Christ's varied disguises. In my daily intercessions, I surround my loved ones and enemies with healing light. I also commit myself to be aware of political issues that affect the health and well-being of persons in America and across the globe. As a tangible sign of the intricate web of life that encompasses body and soul, I encourage my political representatives to support programs that encourage health, education, hunger relief, and peace. In times of international conflict, I surround even our nation's enemies (persons such as Fidel Castro and Saddam Hussein and their peoples) with healing light and the prayer that God will work for peace in their lives and the lives of their people. During the Gulf War, I found that surrounding the Desert Storm forces and the Iraqi people with the light of God enabled me to escape most of the inner turmoil and external projection of hatred that characterized both sides. While I supported our troops, I sought the peace of God and the well-being of persons on both sides. Throughout the Gulf War and the recent military activity in the republics of the former Yugoslavia, my prayers for the respective leaders challenged me to live by Abraham Lincoln's affirmation that it is more important that we are on God's side than that God is on our side!

Finally, we need a healing hope. In all things, God is present, urging us toward abundant life. Hope is the gift of an open future and a sense that change is possible in every moment of life. We are free to make significant changes, regardless of what is going on within or around our lives.

Even at the moment of death, God is working for the transformation of the dying person and her or his family. A healing hope reminds us that even when a cure is not possible, God is at work gently guiding us toward the healing that we need. Ultimately, a healing hope finds its source in the belief that God has prepared a creative adventure for us beyond the grave. Our hope is in the love of God, which joins the eternal and temporal in each moment's experience. This hope is holistic insofar as it encourages us to transform this world, the world of our bodies, governments, and relationships, so that it may take the shape of God's ultimate shalom. Our lives matter infinitely to God. God experiences our tears and struggles and uses the material of our lives—our joys and struggles—as the foundation for life everlasting.

I claim a healing hope in my own life by my daily gratitude for those who are part of that greater communion of saints. I am thankful for their gifts to my own life and for the eternal impact of their actions. In gratitude, I make a commitment to contribute creatively to the lives of persons in this world by acts of love, reconciliation, and healing. Joined with this vast communion of saints, I experience the eternal impact of actions that perish and yet live evermore in the lives of succeeding generations and the eternal mind of God. In hopeful freedom, I recognize that even in situations where I have little external power, I can still choose to make my life a gift of worship to the eternal God to whom all hearts are open and all desires known.

The healing Christ is alive! The God who loved the world and who sent Christ to become flesh for our salvation and wholeness still seeks the healing of persons and nations. Within our intricate holoverse, we are contemporaries with those who gathered on the shores of Galilee or in Nazareth in search of new hope and surprising transformation. We stand beside those ancient people who reached out to Jesus in their vulnerablity and discovered that God had already reached out to them. In their outstretched hands, we also reach out to the healing Christ. Although we are called to reframe these healing stories in light of modern science, psychology, medical care, and global medicine, the healing power of these gospel stories is as powerful and contemporary as it was two thousand years ago. As twenty-first-century partners of the healing Christ, we still reach out to the God whose love encircles us, touching us from the inside and the outside, to give us and the world—in all its pain, wonder, and mystery—abundant life.

Index of Subjects

Index of Names